D1434180

Searching For Daddy

Christine Joanna Hart has worked for several intelligence agencies where she was trained as an undercover operative. Her in-depth investigative journalism and writing on terrorism has appeared extensively in the *Sunday Times* and *Daily Mail*. Christine has found personal happiness through motherhood and lives with her son, Arthur, in Chiswick.

Searching For Daddy

Desperate for love, driven to the edge of hell

Christine Joanna Hart

HODDER

Publishers Note

Names and identifying details have been changed throughout to
protect individuals' privacy.

First published in Great Britain in 2008 by Hodder & Stoughton
An Hachette UK company

First published in paperback in 2009

3

Copyright © Christine Joanna Hart, 2008

The right of Christine Joanna Hart to be identified
as the Author of the Work has been asserted by her in
accordance with the Copyright, Designs and Patents Act 1988.

All rights reserved. No part of this publication may be reproduced, stored
in a retrieval system, or transmitted, in any form or by any means without
the prior written permission of the publisher, nor be otherwise circulated in
any form of binding or cover other than that in which it is published and
without a similar condition being imposed on the subsequent purchaser.

A CIP catalogue record for this title is available from the British Library

ISBN 978 0 340 91924 8

Typeset in Sabon by Hewer Text UK Ltd, Edinburgh
Printed and bound by Clays Ltd, St Ives plc

Hodder & Stoughton policy is to use papers that are natural, renewable
and recyclable products and made from wood grown in sustainable
forests. The logging and manufacturing processes are expected to
conform to the environmental regulations of the country of origin.

Hodder & Stoughton Ltd
338 Euston Road
London NW1 3BH

www.hodder.co.uk

To Ron Dreyer,
from my heart

Contents

I

The Orphan

'Come along, you silly creatures, line up, quick as you can. Face the front, that's it, smile for the nice mothers and fathers who've come to see you.' Sister Agatha's voice was sharp, and despite the smile on her face, her eyes bored into us. The smile was for the visitors. Sister Agatha never smiled at us. When she looked at us it was with disapproval and distaste, as though we were an unpleasant smell under her nose. Obediently we lined up, fifteen or so children ranging in age from two to thirteen. Some smiled hopefully, others looked anxious. We'd all been here before. The couples who'd been invited to come and see us, with a view to choosing a child to foster, stood around in the large dining room, talking quietly to one another or looking over at us. Some of them were clearly curious; others looked slightly embarrassed. All the couples were members of the Church, carefully selected for their spotless religious credentials. Some of them had children with them. These were the ones who'd already fostered or adopted a child and had come back for another child or, as many did, simply to join in with the special occasion.

It was a three-times-yearly ritual in the children's home. They called it a party, although the jelly and ice-cream laid out on the long tables and the balloons hanging from the ceiling were the only things which were remotely party-like. For us children it was a humiliating ordeal in which we were paraded like pets, in the hope that someone might choose us. I was three years old and I'd been to the party several times before.

No one had ever picked me and I didn't expect them to. Only a few children got chosen by a new mother and father and the youngest ones usually went first. The rest of us stood in line, dutifully ate our wobbly green jelly and runny vanilla ice-cream and then returned to the dark grey walls of our dormitories, to be hustled unceremoniously into bed by the nuns. I had lived in the Sacred Heart Children's Rescue Home since I was a couple of months old. It was run by the Catholic Church and staffed almost entirely by nuns. The exception was the woman who ran the place, a bespectacled former nun called Valerie. To the nuns, the prospective parents and the tall, stern-looking priests who flapped in and out of the place in their long, crow-like robes, Valerie was a saint: a noble and tireless woman who did all she could for the unfortunate orphans in her care. But to us she was anything but saintly.

Valerie called us her children, but we felt no affection from her, only brisk efficiency and a cool and remote manner. We found her intimidating and a little scary. It was only much later that I learned Valerie actually referred to the children in her care as 'devil-spawn', but it didn't surprise me. That's exactly how she made us feel. Like the nuns, Valerie viewed us as sinful simply because we were born of sinners. For us, abandoned by our unmarried and in some cases underage parents, there was no redemption.

Even as a very small child I felt desperately lonely. Everything in my world was cold and grey – the building, the food, and the nun's vinegary faces.

I don't remember how old I was when I realised that not all children lived the way we did, and that some had mothers and fathers who loved them and cared for them. Perhaps the nuns told us. I certainly learned from them that we children in the rescue home were different, that we had been abandoned and that if anyone should ever want us we would be very lucky indeed.

We prayed every day, beside our beds, in chapel, before meals. And my prayer was always the same. Please send me a mummy and daddy who want me. Not that I held out a lot of hope. I had watched other children crying, staring with puppy-dog eyes and even clinging on to prospective foster parents. Mostly it didn't do them any good: only a very few children were chosen to go to a new home with the visitors. So as we stood in line I stood apart, quiet, lost in my own little world.

Suddenly Valerie swooped down on me, picked me up and turned to a tall blond man who was sitting nearby. 'Look at this little girl, isn't she pretty?' she said to him. 'I can't think why she hasn't been picked yet. Wouldn't she be perfect to complete your family?'

The man looked at me, smiled and held out his arms. Valerie handed me to him and he sat me on his knee. 'She's beautiful,' he said.

Next to the man sat a pretty, dark-haired woman with a doll-like face, who didn't look as though she thought I was beautiful at all. She stared at me with cold grey eyes. Beside her, a little blond boy, a bit bigger than me, held on to her arm.

'What do you think, Georgina?' the man asked. 'Wouldn't we love a little girl like this?'

As the woman hesitated Valerie lifted me from the man's lap. 'I'll leave you two to talk,' she said, and turned to me. 'Come along, let's get you some ice-cream, shall we?'

Just an hour later, with the formalities presumably rushed through behind the scenes, I was led from the building between the tall blond man and the doll-faced woman. The man, who carried my small bag of clothes, held my hand and looked down at me and winked. But the woman refused to take my other hand. On her other side, the blond boy trotted, still clinging to her.

It was August and the sun was shining, but as we walked through the Rescue Home's gates I felt scared. I wasn't sorry to leave behind my old life of cold baths, cold cabbage and cold nuns, but what would happen to me now? These people were strangers, and though the man seemed to like me, I could see the woman was angry. Was she really to be my new mummy?

The couple drove me to a large Victorian house fifty-five miles away in a picturesque village next to the Surrey hills. The house made a big impression on me; it was so very different to the orphanage and I had never been to an ordinary home before. Inside it was cool and rather dark. Off the long, dark hallway was a living room with wing-backed floral chairs and floor-length floral curtains drawn against French windows. There was a tall Gothic stone fireplace with a thick layer of dust and on the mantel were large curved vases and a small painting of a man in a boat. Beyond that was an old-fashioned kitchen with green striped blinds at the window and a large white Aga.

This was where my new parents, Liam and Georgina, lived with their son Nicky, who was five and had been adopted from the children's home a few years earlier. They had come back to the parties ever since. I don't think they had planned to adopt a second child at all, and if they had done my new mother would have preferred another boy. She made it clear, once she got me home, that she had taken me only because she didn't like to say no to Valerie.

The family lived with Georgina's parents and it was they who owned the house. Her father was bedridden and dying of cancer. One of the ground-floor front rooms had been made into a bedroom for him, and his wife, whom I was told to call Nanna, looked after him there.

I was to share a bedroom with Nanna and that first day I was taken to an upstairs room with twin beds and large red roses and hollyhocks all over the wallpaper. There was a fireplace, a chest of drawers, a dressing table and rose-print curtains with golden tassels on them. It was all very old-fashioned and smelled musty, but it was far grander than any room in the Rescue Home and I was very impressed that I would be sleeping there. There was also a picture of Jesus on the wall and a large Virgin Mary statue.

That first evening everything seemed so strange and different. And while my daddy and Nanna seemed kind, my new mummy was very cold and I felt sure she didn't really want me. And my new brother, Nicky, didn't seem very warm either. Looking back, it must have been difficult for him when his parents came home with another child, but at the time I couldn't understand why he wasn't friendlier.

After we had all had supper in the big kitchen, I was taken up to bed by Nanna, and after I'd been changed into my nightdress I discovered that the big Virgin Mary statue was hollow. It contained holy water and before I got into bed Nanna sprinkled me with it, only she rather overdid it and I was drenched by the time she'd finished. This was to become a nightly ritual and I regularly got into bed with my nightdress and hair damp after her ministrations.

When Nanna had said goodnight and left the room I lay in darkness, curled into a small ball under the covers, feeling scared and anxious. Would my new mummy start to like me soon? Perhaps if I was very good she would. Eventually, exhausted by all that had happened, I fell asleep, only to be woken later by Nanna's snores from the next bed. I wasn't used to snoring, but in time I got used to it, and even found it comforting.

The next day, as we all sat at breakfast, I was told that I was to have a new name. From then on I would no longer be Lucy, the name my birth mother had given me, I was to be Christine Joanna. This was very confusing. I was afraid I would forget my new name and wondered why they didn't like my old one, but I didn't dare say anything.

My new father, Liam, was tall and good-looking, with thick wavy blond hair, a Roman nose and sea blue eyes. He was one of twelve children of an Irish family, but he was ashamed of his humble background and put on an accent which made him sound like Prince Charles, though he some-how managed to pull it off without sounding ludicrous. In an effort to create the English background he'd never had, he bought junk in antique shops or auction houses and passed it off as family heirlooms.

Georgina, who was ten years younger than Liam, had married the good-looking Irishman when she was twenty.

Early on she had suffered an ectopic pregnancy which left her unable to have children. I have no idea what their relationship was like in the early days, but this must have put a huge strain on it. Certainly by the time I came to live with them they never kissed or touched and they slept in separate beds. A lot of the time Liam ignored her, and the rest of the time he called her Mother and treated her as if she was there to clean and cook for him. However, it wasn't a case of him being the 'child' and her the adult. Both of them were very child-like. Georgina called him Daddy, and seemed to long for attention from him. She would say 'Oh, Daddy, can we go for a walk?', or 'Oh, Daddy, I'd like an ice-cream,' though more often than not he wouldn't appear to even notice.

Georgina grew very overweight, but she was pretty and took trouble over her appearance, wearing nice clothes and doing her hair. She had a dark wood dressing table, covered with such delights as rose body lotion and freesia bath oil, which I adored sniffing. She had two antique silver-backed brushes and would sit for hours in front of the glass, brushing her long dark hair. I used to pull the brushes through my own hair, to feel close to my new mother.

However, her efforts paled by comparison with Liam's. He was obsessed with the way he looked. He liked to mimic matinee idols of the forties and fifties, brushing his hair back with Brylcreem, wearing dark glasses and dressing flamboyantly. He would stand in front of the mirror for hours on end, trimming his tiny moustache and the hairs in his nostrils and then arranging his silk cravat.

Liam didn't just try to look like a matinee idol, he also tried to sing like one. His favourite star of all was Bing Crosby. He would go around the house crooning Bing's songs, wearing a dark red silk dressing-gown with black tassel ties, a cigarette hanging from the corner of his mouth, puffing thick plumes of acrid blue smoke that made me cough and narrow my eyes.

He was very good at being Bing. He had a honeyed voice and sometimes sang in the evenings in local pubs and clubs, dreaming of being discovered and whisked off to stardom. Oblivious to the fact that his Bing act was old-fashioned and out of step with the swinging sixties, he was convinced that his moment was about to arrive.

From the start I adored him and thought of him as my Daddy. I was his biggest fan and would gaze up at him and think he was as magical as the stars he emulated. I was a very pretty little girl and, with my big blue eyes and long blonde hair, I looked like him. I was thrilled when people commented on it. He bought me dolls and clothes and I stuck to him like glue, clinging to his hand as he went around the house, terrified of losing him. I would watch him as he sang to himself in the large gilt hall mirror, both he and I convinced that he really was Bing. Then later he would sit me on his lap and I would finish off the food scraps he left on his plate; a half chewed pork chop, his over-sugared weak tea.

While my new daddy crooned and preened, my new mummy looked unhappy most of the time, and was often in tears. She was also eating compulsively and putting on more and more weight, gorging herself on home-made curries, cream cakes and her mother's home-made coconut ice.

And as my new daddy won all my devotion and became my world, my new mummy bitterly resented my attachment to him and turned her anger and bitterness on me.

While Daddy was around she would simply ignore me. But he was out of the house a great deal, an engineer at Heathrow airport, often working night shifts and sleeping for most of the day. When he wasn't around she would push me into an old broom cupboard in the kitchen, locking me inside. It wasn't tiny, I could stand inside it, but it was very dark, with only a chink of light coming through. I would sit inside it, frightened of the dark and terrified that I was going to run out of air. I could hear my mother on the other side of the cupboard door, in the kitchen, sobbing uncontrollably and gorging herself with food between sobs.

After a few hours she would let me out. Often she was still weeping, and she would say to me, 'I can't bear to think about how you were made and the lowlifes who made you. It disgusts me. And now I have to take care of you.'

I was too young to understand what she meant. What were 'lowlifes'? And what did 'how you were made' mean? I didn't know, and couldn't ask, but I knew it couldn't be good. I swallowed my fears in an effort to keep intact the vision of my new mother as loving and caring. Despite the way she treated me I often felt sorry for my mother because she cried so much. I would try to imagine being her, sobbing and stuffing herself with food, and think that she must feel very bad inside.

On one occasion, about a year after I was adopted, when I was four, she hit me so hard that she broke my nose. She stood like a boxer in the ring, panting from the effort, and watched me as I choked on my own blood. She said nothing as I crawled up the stairs to my bed and curled into a ball, unable to think of anything but the pain. When my father got home from work he saw my nose and shouted at her, 'If you do that again I'll report you to the police.' He took me into the front room and sat me on his knee, while Mummy went upstairs to her room and cried.

This incident only served to reinforce my love of my father and fear of my mother. I tip-toed around her, constantly nervous, and ran to Daddy as soon as he came through the front door.

Sometimes I was able to escape from Mummy to be with Nanna, who would sit beside Grandpa all day, with the television or radio on. Nanna had a grey bun, twinkly eyes and skinning frame, and wasn't a cuddly person at all. In fact she could be rather strict and was quite offhand with most of the family. I had heard her shouting at Daddy that it was her house and he was just the lodger, and she sometimes shouted at my mother too, but she was always nice to me and I would creep off to her side whenever I could. I often ate my lunch and tea in the front room with her as we sat side by side, watching endless TV together. We liked dramas like *Crown Court*, which was very popular back then. But most of all we loved watching old Elvis films. When Nanna said Elvis would be too old for me to marry him when I grew up, I cried my eyes out.

Nanna and Grandad had lived most of their lives in British colonial India, where he had been an officer in the army, and where their daughter had been born. Nanna used to tell stories of life in India and I loved to listen. But a tale she came out with one day, while Mummy sat across the room from us, really upset me. Nanna was telling us how she had been a dressmaker and she remarked, 'If my sewing went wrong I would grab Georgina's head and bash it against the table again and again.' She banged her fist hard on the table to illustrate the severe blows. 'If it bled it made me worse,' she continued, in a matter-of-fact voice. 'I would see her blood and get angrier and beat her head harder.

'One day I found her down at the bottom of the road

playing with the local darkies. I ran a cold bath, put her in it and shaved her head, in case she had got dirty nits off those dirty little darkies.'

I was just four, and too young to recognise her racism. But I did understand what she had done to Mummy and I listened with horror, unable to believe that Nanna had been so cruel. I looked over at Mummy, who sat looking vacant, or glanced at me, a pained look on her face, as her mother recounted these tales.

'Poor Mummy,' I said softly.

Later that day Mummy laid me across my bed face down and beat me with a garden cane, using hard, deliberate strokes, venting all her pain onto my small body. Afterwards I couldn't walk and the backs of my legs were covered with bright red lumpy weals that were excruciatingly painful to touch. I don't know if the rest of the family saw them, but no one said anything, and from then on Mummy beat me with the cane at least once a week. Mostly she made me cover my legs with my skirt, or long socks, so that my father and grandparents wouldn't see, and I never said a word, knowing she would punish me for it.

It's hard to know whether the rest of the family had any idea of what she was doing. With her old lady's hearing and the TV blaring Nanna may have been oblivious to sounds of her daughter shouting, beating me and locking me in the cupboard. On the other hand, given the way she had treated her own daughter, she may have known and simply thought it acceptable. But I like to think my beloved Nanna loved me dearly.

Mummy only hurt me when Daddy was out, so he never saw it. When he came in from work he would often come to my room and find me in bed, sobbing as if my heart would break. He would hold my hand for a long time and I would tell him I was scared of him dying and cling on to his hand and pull it under the covers with me. He always asked me what was wrong and I used to say nothing or that one of my dollies had died.

As much as Mummy seemed to dislike me, she adored Nicky. She lavished attention on him and spoiled him. Nicky was a clever, good-looking boy but, perhaps not surprisingly, given how spoiled he was, he had temper tantrums and would throw himself around, sometimes smashing ornaments and dishes.

While Nicky could do little wrong in our mother's eyes, it was clear that he annoyed our father, who would snap at him and argue with him. There wasn't much affection between them and on more than one occasion Daddy hit Nicky on the nose and sprayed his blood up the white living room wall. I cleaned it off afterwards for Mummy with a bucket of cold water and a cloth, scrubbing the spattered wall and the bloody carpet until all evidence of my brother's pain had been eradicated.

Although he was usually loving towards me, Daddy could be moody and changeable. He liked to drink whisky and would often drink so much that he had to take the next day off work. When he'd had a few drinks he would become petulant and call me and Nicky 'our two bastards'. Sometimes he would sit in his red silk dressing gown, legs crossed in the big wing-backed armchair, sipping his whisky from a crystal cut sherry glass, and say, 'Why did we get you two little gob shits? It was the biggest mistake we ever made.' The way he said it was almost camp, as if he was mocking us. Dry, but cruel humour. Sometimes he would lean over and cuff whichever one of us was nearest, using his hand or a rolled up copy of the *Daily Mail*, in case we weren't listening, or his words had failed to panic us.

Nicky became very upset when he did this, but somehow it went over my head and I didn't care. Perhaps it was because Mummy's hate-filled face, screaming insults and violence was so much worse. Or perhaps because, in order to survive, I needed to hang on to the belief that Daddy loved me.

In truth I think he was so ambitious about his singing career that for him I was simply an adoring fan, there to worship him and look pretty on his lap, but at times an irritation too. Nicky had little value to him at all, and as for Mummy, it's hard to know what kept them together. Inevitably it was impossible for my brother and me to become close. Our parents' favouritism affected us both deeply and made us rivals rather than friends.

Nicky took on our mother's dislike of me. He would whisper to me, 'I'm going to make your life a misery,' and he frequently did, hitting me and bullying me relentlessly. If I was playing music he would come in and wrench the plug off the record player and throw it at my leg, leaving it cut and bruised. And he would punch me, hard, for any reason, or no reason at all, so that I soon became afraid of him, and avoided him whenever I could. Sometimes I felt he was like a demon, haunting my already dark world, ready to add suffering and misery to push me over the top.

Mealtimes were almost always stressful. If I said I was hungry Mummy would give me a tiny portion, but if I said I wasn't she would give me a huge amount and sit over me until I'd eaten it all. And both parents would remind us, frequently, how much it cost them to feed us.

We seldom went out anywhere, although occasionally there were family trips to the zoo. There were very few family friends who visited and other children were banned from the house in case they made a mess. However once a year we always went to France or Wales or somewhere nice for a holiday and when we did my brother and I would agree an unspoken holiday truce and enjoy exploring our surroundings together.

The whole family were devout Catholics and every Sunday we went to mass. Mummy used to sing loudly and piously, as if revelling in the suffering of Jesus. She loved putting up pictures of the Pope and carrying her pale blue rosary beads around.

I hated the self-pitying way she sang; it made me cringe inside. But I loved the church, with all its painted statues, its strongly scented flowers and the good-looking young priest, Father Michael, who was kind to me. I believed passionately in God and prayed every day. I felt that no matter what people did to me, God would never fail me.

By the time I was five, my only escape from the misery of life with my new family was in the large, sunny back garden, where I went out to play whenever I could. Down at the end of the garden, hidden from the house by the long wet weeds and safe from my mother's rage, I lost myself in an imaginary world. The flowers that grew there, the pink and purple sweet william and the tall white parrot tulips, were my best friends and I talked to them for hours. The huge lime tree was my magic home and I lay underneath its cool protective shade on long summer days, looking up through the knobbly branches. Sometimes I played on an invisible stage, bowing to my audience or becoming a princess waiting for a white knight to rescue me. If Mummy came and found me there she would look at me, puzzled rather than angry, because she could see I had found something she could not take away from me.

Most of the time I loved being in the garden but often Mummy would lock me out of the house and in winter it would be bitterly cold. Even then I didn't really mind. I played with my bike, pretending it was a magic horse called Mungo that could sprout wings and fly me away somewhere where the people liked me.

The house was never much warmer than the garden in winter. My parents both thought that heating was a waste of money so we woke to the ice that had formed on the inside of the windows. I used to write my name with my fingernail in the frost, as I shivered in my night clothes. I dreaded getting up and hated washing in cold water at the sink in the bathroom that always smelled of mint toothpaste and pink and white Lifebuoy soap.

I had dreamed of a real home, with a Mummy and Daddy who would love me. But life in my new home was far worse than life in the rescue home. I was desperate for Mummy to love me, or even for a kind word from her, and would look at her with begging eyes, but that only irritated her more. Every day I watched her being kind to my brother and to friends and neighbours and longed for a little of that kindness. Yet when her eyes fell on me her face showed only contempt and disgust. She criticised everything I did and said. She told me every day that I was bad and wicked and that evil ran through me like writing on a stick of Brighton rock, and I believed her.

Within months of my arrival I had developed the nervous habit of picking at my scalp. I did it so much that it bled, then scabs would form and I'd pick them off and it would bleed even more. I did it in bed at night and used to wake to find the pillow and my nightie covered in blood. It infuriated my mother, who would shout at me and hit me when she saw it. On one occasion she was so angry she put me straight into a cold bath, in my nightie. I sat there shivering, the water going redder and redder with blood, until I vomited. At that point Mummy exploded with rage and dragged me out of the bath.

I was in a state of deep distress, so much so that despite being only four, I began to wish I could die. I had seen someone on TV kill themselves, with a razor blade. There was one in the mirrored cabinet in the bathroom and I knew I could cut my arms with it and sit in the bath and go to sleep. I used to imagine this over and over again, sitting in the cupboard, or lying in bed at night. A nice warm bath that would turn dark with blood and lull me into a deep and peaceful sleep forever.

But the truth was that I was trapped in a loveless world. No matter what my fantasies, there was no escape, and though I couldn't imagine life being any harder, over the next couple of years I was to discover that things could, and would, get much worse than my darkest imaginings.

2

My New Daddy

It was my adoptive mother who told me the story of how I came to be in the rescue home. She would recount it as a bedtime story, as I lay in my cold bed next to Nanna, who was fast asleep. 'You were found on the steps, one icy January morning,' she said. 'Wrapped in an old blanket. Left out with the milk bottles.'

She used to tell me this story over and over again, taking a sadistic pleasure in letting me know that I had been abandoned. She told me there had been a note tucked into the blanket. It said my name was Lucy and asked the nuns to look after me. Later I learned that the police had managed to track down my mother, who turned out to be a fourteen-year-old schoolgirl. Her family had kept me for two months, before leaving me outside the rescue home. After the police contacted her she had visited me from time to time, for a couple of years. She had refused permission for me to be adopted, perhaps still hoping to take me back, and this was why I had not been offered to prospective adoptive parents when I was a baby. But eventually she had decided, or been persuaded, to give me up for adoption, or so I was told.

All this I had learned when I was older, and able to understand what had happened, but as a very small girl, to hear that my real mummy had not wanted me and had left me on a doorstep made me feel very sad. I was sure there must be something wrong with me for that to happen, especially as my new mummy didn't seem to want me either.

At five I started at the small local primary school where Nicky was already a pupil. I was relieved to be out of the house – and Mummy's clutches – for the bulk of the day. And at home things improved a little. Mummy stopped locking me in the cupboard and beat me less often, presumably because I was underfoot for less of the day. However, she would still lay into me verbally, telling me how worthless I was. Sometimes I seemed to make her angry simply by existing.

The more fuss my father made of me, the more incensed she would become. He loved Turkish Delight and bought boxes and boxes of the fleshy pink sweets for himself. He would offer it to me and although I hated it I ate it until it was coming out of my ears, because it was a way of being close to him. I sat on his knee forcing the thick powdery stuff down my throat, plastering his face with sloppy, sticky kisses and telling him that I wanted to marry him when I was a big girl.

Some days Mummy would sit at the kitchen table, her head in her hands, and say, 'Oh, how I'd love to be a mother. I really would so love to have had a child. What did I do wrong for God to punish me so by not having a child?'

She would talk as though Nicky and I were not there, and we would stand stock still, frozen by her words. I used to feel invisible and wonder why we didn't count. I always concluded it was because we were adopted and therefore inferior to other, decent children. Mummy would often use the word 'illegitimate'. It followed me throughout my childhood, in a sly whisper to any adult who ever looked in my direction.

'She's illegitimate.' Then a long pause of satisfaction from my mother, as if by saying it she was venting something. Then the response, 'Poor thing – such a shame.'

I remember wondering whether it meant that I was good at drawing, but then thinking how could it be if it was, 'such a shame'.

I never knew how Nicky felt; we didn't talk about it. But I have no doubt that his anger was, at least in part, the result of our mother rejecting us.

I liked school, though I made few friends and was one of the quieter children. I found schoolwork easy, and my teachers were encouraging, though Mummy and Daddy didn't seem very interested in how I did.

One day representatives of the charity that ran our rescue home came and canvassed the school for money. Two missionary types dressed in a kind of Salvation Army uniform told the whole school about the little unwanted orphans that they rescued. They gave out little yellow booklets with jokes in them, to raise money for the orphanage. I kept mum, but my brother told a friend that we were rescued orphans and within a couple of hours word seemed to have got round the entire school. That playtime a crowd of children gathered round me asking, 'What's it like to be a bastard?'

After that I felt like an outcast. Most of the children forgot about it, but a hardcore few taunted me day in day out. School had become almost as bad as home. Nowhere was safe.

One night I heard Mummy and Daddy rowing.

'OK, we'll take her back,' he shouted.

'No,' she screamed. 'You like her. I know you do.'

'I couldn't give a toss, if you want to know,' he shouted back.

So now I knew. Not even Daddy loved me. Overhearing that exchange simply confirmed in my own mind that I was worthless. And that at any moment I would be cast out into the street to fend for myself, like the Little Match Girl I had watched on telly over Christmas.

I tried to numb my feelings to avoid the fact that I was a monster that no one cared about. If I could stop feeling, then it wouldn't hurt so badly. I wouldn't be so frightened. But I couldn't stop myself from longing for Mummy and Daddy to love me.

By this time my grandfather had died, and Nanna now dressed permanently in black. His death made little impression on me, as I had never felt close to him, but Mummy and Nicky were very upset. Later my mother told me he used to like me to sit on his sick bed, and called me his little angel, but I didn't remember it. After he died Nicky cried and said to me, 'Grandad's dead'. I stroked his tear-stained face and said, 'It doesn't matter,' which wasn't meant to be as heartless as it sounded – his death simply didn't mean much to me. When Nicky told Mummy what I had said, I was terrified I would get a beating but surprisingly I didn't. I think Mummy was too upset to care. She loved her father, although I later learned that she had been rejected by him when she was a child. Ironically he had wanted a boy, and had refused to use her name, calling her 'Freddy Boy' all her life.

Some of the local children said Nanna looked like a witch in her black clothes, but she was still the same to me, and when we watched TV together I felt safe. We loved ballets, especially *Coppélia*. On my sixth birthday Nanna gave me her old musical box. It was a small green marble box with a gold rim, an antique. It was so old that the dress on the ballerina was torn off. But she still spun round and it played a lovely Rachmaninoff tune. I used to play it over and over again, watching the little ballerina dance.

Three times a year we would be taken back to the rescue home for the jelly and ice-cream parties, to see Valerie and the nuns and give thanks for the loving family who'd taken us in. These visits terrified me, because of my mother's frequently uttered threat to send me back there if I wasn't good. I was so frightened that I would be swapped for another child and left behind in the Home, that when we arrived I would often start vomiting into the buckets of red and orange jelly. I was hauled off to the bathroom like a stroppy kid who couldn't control herself.

Going back was a constant reminder of where I had come from. It was as though I could never escape, never really stop being an orphan. I felt haunted by those grey walls and the nuns' angry faces. We were made to watch the other children line up and look at our parents with puppy-dog eyes. They would stand there in their second-hand clothes, trying to smile, while we visiting children listened to Valerie telling us that 'but for the grace of God' we would still be there with them.

There was always a party at Christmas, and we had to bring our old toys to give to the children in the Home. One year a little dark-haired girl in a rosebud pink dressing gown climbed onto my father's lap and he began to fuss over her. I stood, consumed by jealousy, watching as he stroked her hair and said how pretty she was. I thought she looked prettier than me and it scared me. I was so terrified that he would decide to take her home and leave me that the memory of it haunted me for years.

We got presents at Christmas – I'd have a doll and my brother a train set, or something similar. But we were told that Santa was rubbish, and ungodly, and over Christmas dinner both parents would go on about how much we cost them. We would be told how much each potato or bite of ham cost as we ate it and how lucky we were.

While Mummy would berate us, Daddy would sip his sherry and say, 'It was the worst thing, wasn't it, Mother, the day we went and got these two little bastards from that place.'

I would ignore it, but I could see it hurt Nicky and he would crumble and cry at this merging of Mummy and Daddy into one monster to unite against us lowborn cuckoos in their dark and crazy nest.

By the age of six I was growing prettier. My blonde hair was almost waist length and my eyes were a stormy dark blue, almond shaped and striking. My father started to fuss over me more and more, calling me his princess and coming to collect me from school in the gold Bentley that he treasured. My mother responded by ignoring me more pointedly and putting me down more spitefully. Although she was less physically violent after I began school, her coldness towards me hurt me more than the beatings. One afternoon I was playing in the back garden with my hair flying loose when suddenly she stormed outside. 'Tie that bloody hair back,' she hissed. That night, she hacked my hair off with nail scissors, so crookedly and so short that it looked monstrous. I lay in bed sobbing for a long time.

The next day at school my teacher, Miss Leach, said, 'What have you done to your hair?' I told her that Mummy had done it, and she said, 'Don't be ridiculous; go and stand in the corner. First you do that to your hair, then you lie about it.'

Soon afterwards my teacher called my mother in and told her, 'I'm concerned about Christine. She doesn't ever smile or laugh. Doesn't she smile at home?'

On her way out Mother gritted her teeth, smiled coldly and dragged me across the playground. I knew I was for it. Anything that drew attention to me was a crime in her eyes. She remained cold all evening – yet like a volcano I knew it was dangerous to live close to – something inside me tasted pure cold fear as I waited to be obliterated.

After that I tried very hard to smile at school. I felt the loss of Miss Leach, because when I turned myself into the cardboard cut-out of a smiling child I could no longer be real with her. Until then I had found solace at school from the horrors of home, but now that I was forced to smile constantly, which was a huge strain, I felt that inside I was giving up and turning away from the world.

The greatest pleasure in my life, and my only means of escape apart from the garden, was books. I loved to read, especially books in which children could do what they pleased and lived in amazing magical worlds without grown-ups. *Half Magic* and *Seven Day Magic* by Edward Eager were among my favourites, as was *Holiday House* by Enid Blyton and the Mallory Towers series, the stories of a schoolgirl called Darrell Rivers.

I was allowed to take eight books a week out of the library and I always got through them all. The librarian was so pleased she gave me a special ticket to take out another three a week from the adult section. I would take a book and hide in any quiet corner of the house or garden where I thought Mummy might not discover me. Underneath my red silk eiderdown with a torch after lights out, I grew to love the world of books, which gave me a sense that there was more to life than my sad world; something out there worth reaching for.

Mummy hated me reading, calling me 'the bookworm', and sneering that there was a worm inside my brain which was hungry for the paper. She and Nicky would laugh and laugh at this, but the books were my lifeline. I worshipped them, and dreamed that one day I would be one of the people who wrote them.

One of the people I loved best was my Aunt Cecilia. She was my father's sister, a tall blonde Irish girl with dark blue eyes, who had become a nun with the Daughters of St Paul, in Rome. It was a rich order and she used to travel from their base in Rome to another in Boston and to England, where they had a large convent in Langley, not far from where we lived.

Cecilia used to come and visit us for tea whenever she was in England. She wore a long black habit with a veil and a thick silver cross and chain and I used to float around after her and feel very special because she liked me and gave me a lot of attention. After she had left I would pull a dark towel over my head as if it were a veil, and pose in front of my mother's dressing-table mirror, pretending to be a nun.

Sometimes Cecilia used to take me to mass at the convent, and afterwards we would go into the priest's house. My very favourite priest, a good-looking young one called Father Michael would be sitting in his private room wearing his gold or red satin robes and the pungent smell of the incense and the glow from the silver chalices and tall white candles would entrance me. I would sit and stare at him like an adoring fan, marvelling at his deep voice and wise blue eyes. He and my Aunt would sit for hours discussing the Bible and calling each other Brother and Sister, and I loved listening to both of these beautiful people.

It was Aunt Cecilia who explained to me how to pray. She would take me into the church when no one else was there and read a passage from the Bible. She'd tell me to picture it in my mind and meditate on it. I used to tell her about the pictures that appeared in my mind and she was very pleased and told me I would make a very good Sister.

On Sundays we would sometimes go to the convent for lunch. The nuns were wonderful cooks and the roasts were out of this world. Then we would go for walks in the lovely grounds. In the summer we would have our dessert outside in the sprawling gardens – usually Eton Mess or Tarte Tatin. The tall pine trees had large wind chimes tied to them by the nuns and we would sit in their cool shade, listening to them chime melodically while we read from the Bible and said prayers. At these times I felt deeply drawn to life in the convent and thought about how I would one day like to join the Sisters. They had a life pure, clean and brimful of good-ness. I felt it within myself no matter what my Mother said – goodness – and I liked feeling it.

Aunt Cecilia was quite strict, but she was kind too, and despite her holy status she had a good sense of humour and would often make my father laugh. She taught me that God was very kind and my real Father, and she bought me rolled gold Rosary beads and little presents: books about Theresa of Avila and St John of the Cross, or dolls. I always looked forward to her visits, not only because I adored her, but because when she was there Mummy was nice to me, and that made it like Christmas and summer all wrapped into one.

Around this time, when I was six, my father decided he wanted to take me to Ireland with him. He had always travelled back to his family home in Dublin to see his elderly mother once a fortnight. Because he worked for an airline he got free flights, so it was easy for him to finish work and then jump on a plane on Friday evening, coming back two days later.

The rest of the family had only ever gone with him for big occasions like weddings and funerals. But he announced that now he was going to take me.

Neither Mummy not Nicky minded; I don't think either of them liked visiting Daddy's family. But I was thrilled. I loved flying in aeroplanes, and I loved the idea of staying in Dublin and taking in the different accents and the smells and sights of a foreign city.

Daddy's elderly mother lived in the family home with her daughter, my Auntie Ruth, who had spent her life caring for her parents and so had never married. They lived in the tiny Victorian terrace where Daddy had grown up. It was called Red Fort and was built like a fortress – small dingy houses around a rough area of grassland, on hilly slopes with black spiky iron railings. The thick, yeasty smell of the nearby Guinness factory filled the air and that always excited me, as it meant that I was really there and no longer in England where my mother managed to spoil everything.

The neighbourhood fascinated me. Next door, there lived a wild family called the Dunnings, who had three boys. When Nicky had been over he was terrified of the Dunnings, particularly the oldest boy Val, with his blond hair and his habit of shinning up lampposts and doing wheelies on his bike down the hill. The Dunnings boys would hand out jellies to all the local children, who would run to their door and grab them greedily. I would stand stock-still, unable to reach out for one of the brightly coloured sweets because I was so in awe of Val. He was so free and alive, while I felt so dead and flat and numb.

One time he spoke to me. 'What about you? Here, take one – take the red one – they're the best,' he said. I opened my mouth to speak but couldn't. I looked at him in horror and then ran inside our house, sobbing as if my heart would break. My hero had spoken to me and I couldn't make a sound come out of my mouth to reply to him. I felt I wasn't a girl – I was a freakish dumb idiot.

Daddy's family house had a pristine front parlour, full of plastic flowers, that nobody ever went into. There was an icy cold outside toilet with no loo roll, overlooking a small square back yard and smelling of yellow carbolic soap. At night there were huge black spiders in the toilet. I was scared a monster would burst in from the pitch-dark back garden, so I would go to the toilet as quick as I could, drips still running down my leg in my rush to get back inside in the warm house.

Daddy's mother, who was blind and very old, would sit wrapped in a woolly shawl in a chair by the fire, saying nothing at all and listening to the Angelus on the radio, while mumbling prayers and Hail Marys, eating milk chocolate digestive biscuits and sipping endless cups of weak tea.

As soon as we arrived Aunt Ruth would pull on her white mac and run over to the nearby chip shop, to get us chips. This was a delight for me. I loved to go with her and pour white vinegar all over my chips and stare at the girl behind the till with her strange Irish accent.

Within a few hours of our arrival my father would relax in a way he never did back at home, dropping his posh English accent and reverting to his natural Dublin accent. We would sit around the dining table, where a shiny silver teapot sat on the clean white cloth, and eat thick slabs of fresh cut bread covered in creamy Irish butter, or make chip butties, both Daddy and I happily contented.

Some of my father's eleven brothers and sister were still around. As well as Ruth, and of course Cecilia, there was Aunt Helen, who lived in nearby Dalkey down a wide friendly road called Clarence Street. I loved visiting her house because she had four daughters and two sons who had all married and had children, so the place was swarming with cousins for me to play with. Three of the boys, Mark, Stephen and William and one of the girls, Elizabeth, were my favourites.

We would all sit in Helen and her husband Charles's front room and Daddy would play the piano and sing Bing Crosby songs loudly, and his face would grow red with pleasure and drink, and he'd laugh and laugh in a way he never did in England. My cousin Elizabeth, who was twenty-one and beautiful, would show me her perfumes and make-up. She had a curvy figure I would stare at her, mesmerised. I was fascinated by her Chanel No 5 and the candy pink lipstick called Lush Kisses. Elizabeth let me pat her cocoa-coloured blusher on my pale cheeks, she then sprayed me generously with her precious Chanel. I was shy, but thrilled by her attention and her kindness. She must have known I wasn't really her cousin but it appeared not to bother her. I could hardly believe my luck.

Sometimes we would go to Howth to visit my Uncle Joe who lived by the sea. I loved Uncle Joe, he was my favourite of them all. He was a real sea dog and would take us out on his boat. He always wore a black peaked captain's hat and he looked like my father, though his eyes were a more intense blue. I often thought he was very like my father in personality too, except that he was stronger, with all the bad bits taken out. All these lovely people all accepted me completely as Daddy's daughter. With them I was no longer an orphan, nobody's child. I was one of them and it was a wonderful feeling.

On Sundays, we would take my Grandma to see Uncle Edward. He lived in St Brendan's, a large mental hospital just outside Dublin. On the long hot walk from Mass to the mental hospital, my father would push his blind mother up the road in a wheelchair, as it was too wide to fit on the pavement. Daddy's face would be all red and wet with sweat and effort as he pushed her along. Cars would beep and honk at us and he would get more and more angry. I felt afraid of his rage as I followed behind, my feet aching and brow wet with perspiration.

He would periodically turn and shout at me in his new thick Dublin brogue. 'Pick those feet UP. Get a bloody move on.'

The busy road became a country lane that led to the hospital. When we got there we would sit with Uncle Edward for an hour or two. His parents had put him in the hospital after he jumped out of his bedroom window as a boy and then set fire to himself, and he had spent his life there. He was a little odd, and talked to himself, but he looked remarkably like Daddy, so I wasn't afraid of him. He looked so sad and he often sobbed, so I used to climb up onto his knee to try to make him happy. He would sit and tap his endless cigarette ash into the open can of Pepsi Cola that we had brought him, not realising what he was doing. Then he'd drink it, complete with the fag ash. I found this mesmerising and would watch him intently. Daddy would smoke a lot too, and look upset for his big brother, and I felt sorry for both of them.

On one occasion I needed to use the toilet, so I wandered off once into the massive grounds of the sanatorium, looking for it. I found a room with a man in a white coat and asked him to take me to the toilet. He showed me where it was and told me that he was a psychiatrist and when I asked what that was he said that he helped to cure people. The man said to hold my nose and go quickly – so I did. I sat on the toilet and looked all around me and saw that the walls were thick with excrement that the inmates had smeared on it. It was brown and runny and even though I was holding my nose the smell was horrifying. I thought to myself, this is where poor Uncle Edward has to live all the time, with the smell of poo every time he goes to the toilet and the long, dark corridors and the patients in dressing gowns, sitting in their rooms sobbing.

When I came back to my father, a woman who was clucking loudly like a chicken was demanding cigarettes from him. She scared me and I was worried she would hit him or hurt him and went over and clung on to his hand protectively.

Dad went to the toilet later and came back looking pale and sad. As he hugged his brother goodbye, both of them were crying.

When we got home Aunt Ruth would get us fish and chips and we'd eat them in front of the fire. I was allowed to stay up a bit later in Ireland, and Aunt Ruth always put Daddy and me together in a bedroom with a big oak double bed. I felt safe and warm with him close by, and he snored a lot less than Nanna.

One night we came home after a visit to Helen and Charles's and Daddy got into bed with me as always. But this time it was different. In the darkness he began to do things I didn't like. He said 'Kiss Daddy' and I kissed him on the cheek, but then he lifted my nightdress and put his fingers inside my private place. As his fingers pushed he watched me intently, his face expressionless. It was as if he was trying to burrow deep into my soul.

As he raped me with his fingers he said, 'I'm putting my finger in your little honeypot. You're not dirty, are you, like women are. Women are all filthy, dirty whores. No, you're clean. No one's touched you, have they? You're mine, all mine. My clean, pure little Princess.'

I didn't like what he did, it hurt and it frightened me, but I didn't say a word. I couldn't. And after he finished he cuddled me and we went to sleep.

The next day I woke and looked around me at the room lit by a harsh morning sunlight. Everything seemed the same and yet different. I could not make sense of what it was. It was almost as if some part of me would not wake up. A part that had died in the night. I felt that the girl who rose from the bed was a pale ghost, a twin who began to live my life instead of me.

The next night it happened again. Then it always happened.

I didn't like what Daddy did and I knew it was secret and forbidden, yet I liked being warm and close to him and it made me feel special. He was my father and I loved him very deeply. With no mother love, I clung to him for dear life. So when he did those things, it was confusing. And I was scared that Mummy would somehow find out. I knew she would be angry and I was scared she would kill me.

From then on my father did bad things to me in the bed every time we went to Ireland, though never at home in England. I loved Ireland, and all the family there, with their loving acceptance. But Daddy started to do more and more things that scared and hurt me and I learned to split off while he was doing it. I would feel I was somewhere up on the ceiling, floating about. It created a dark cloud that never left me, like a black rain cloud. I cut off something inside of me. And I developed a hate of myself so strong it was tangible. I knew that my mother had been right to hate me. I was evil. I had made my father do evil things.

Over the next few months my mother seemed angrier than ever. When my hair grew long again and a neighbour remarked on how pretty it was, she had it all cut off again, though this time by a hairdresser. She compared me to my friends and said that they were beautiful and I was ugly. And that I would never be kissed, never marry, never have a baby of my own.

On one visit to Ireland, Daddy took me in a black cab, with two other men. Both had cloth caps on and were young and nice looking, like Daddy. He sat between them and his Irish accent came thickly out of his mouth. It sounded so alien to me, and I started to feel a sense of dread and foreboding. Whatever it was that normally made me feel secure with my father was not there in the back of the noisy cab. The two men were singing and being loud and fear welled up in me as I sat meekly on the spare seat. I started to cry and one of the men noticed and said, 'Ah, your little girl's crying. Hey there don't cry, hinny.' He poked me under the chin, but it seemed to make the fear worse and I cried harder. Daddy got angry and shot me a look that said, 'Shut up.'

We all got out of the cab down a busy street in the city centre and the two men said goodbye to my father and walked away.

There was a growing twilight and a mist was gathering around the orange lampposts. It was cold and I was glad I had my coat on. We walked for a long time, and the busy streets got quieter and quieter as we tailed off into lanes. We walked on, Daddy silent, lost in his own little world, me quiet and clinging on tightly to his hand to try to feel safe.

He took me down the dark streets of Dublin, along winding lanes, to a Portakabin. Inside was a nice man with blond hair that looked dyed. My father left me there with the man, who said I was going to be in a film. 'Are you pleased about that?' he asked me.

I was an obedient child, so I said, 'Yes I am.'

He said, 'Go over there, then, and take your clothes off.'

I pulled off my clothes – a little dress, knickers, socks – till I stood bare. Then he took me into the other room, where four men were lined up. I had to do to them what my Daddy made me do with him. Each one of them put his pee-pee in my mouth. It tasted awful. I didn't feel afraid, I just felt numb. Afterwards the man asked me to open my legs and stand with them apart. I did the splits like I had seen ballerinas on the telly do. I imagined myself dressed in pink, like on telly. He took photos of me.

Eventually he said I could put on my clothes and gave me a small red lolly from a drawer. 'It'll take the taste away,' he said. 'Ooh nasty taste, hey.'

I nodded. 'Am I going to be a ballerina in the film?' I asked him. He looked at me oddly.

My father came to the cabin and the blond man gave him money and didn't look at him. He said, 'Don't bring her back.'

I stood there and felt I must have done something bad.

Daddy said, 'Why? Wasn't she any good?' The man said, 'Oh, she was good. Don't bring her back.'

We walked to a café, where Daddy ordered chips and I was allowed to have a few off of his plate. He counted the money over and over and seemed very angry. He said, 'Don't talk if you know what's good for you.' I sat silently watching him. He was wrapped up in his own world and even though he'd been angry I wanted to comfort him.

Later on we went to a house. Daddy got on the bed with a woman and made grunting noises while I was made to sit in a chair and turn away. My father didn't know the woman, but as we left he gave her some money.

Afterwards we wandered the dark streets to find a night bus to take us home. I shivered in the icy cold, held his big warm hand and looked up at his handsome face. He was miles away. I saw my Uncle Edward's sadness in his face for the very first time and imagined my father sobbing, and walled up in a mental hospital like his brother. Then I realised something very important about Daddy. Something that helped to explain what he did. The man in the mental hospital who was stark, raving mad was his brother. That had to mean Daddy was mad too. I squeezed his hand tighter and moved closer to him. I knew I must try to help him. For the very first time I knew with a passion what I wanted to be when I grew up. I wanted to be a psychiatrist, like the man I met in the hospital, and wear a long white coat. I wanted to cure my father.

3

The Novice Nun

Back in England things reverted to normal, and I didn't let myself think about what Daddy did to me in the big bed in Ireland. Somehow when we were back home it was easier to feel it wasn't real, and that he was still my lovely Daddy.

And by the time I was seven my mother had begun to soften a little towards me. She was a lonely woman with few friends, and she began to treat me as a companion. She needed someone to talk to, and I was there, and so filled the void.

I was very happy when she was nice to me. At those moments, when she seemed to be almost fond of me and was kind, albeit in a careless, almost indifferent way, I held my breath, hoping I could find a way to make it last.

She got a part-time sewing job and in the school holidays I would take my bike and cycle up the road to meet her after work. She would come out of the factory entrance and smile when she saw me and I would hold her hand all the way home. We sometimes stopped off at the shops and she would buy me a *Bunty* or *Judy* comic and some salt'n'shake crisps. Then we would go to the butcher's to get the family dinner, and I'd stand kicking at the sawdust, hating the smell of the meat.

And finally we went to the off-licence to get a few bottles of brown beer for my father.

When we got in we'd make fish finger sandwiches in white bread with butter and tomato sauce and eat them with Nanna, followed by chocolate biscuits dipped into milky coffee and eaten in front of our favourite programmes like *The Tomorrow People*, *Follyfoot Farm* and *Sapphire and Steel*. Mummy would throw me and Nicky small bars of Curly Wurly and packets of Refreshers and Spangles in the evening as we lay on the floor watching television.

These happier times were marred only by my fear that Mummy would somehow have an accident at work and die. This fear grew more intense: it stalked me and spoiled what seemed to be the beginning of a warmer connection between us. Mummy had even started to lose weight, and she seemed happier.

Sometimes she would start talking to me – and to Nicky too, if he was around. She would come out with a story about her childhood, almost blurting it out, as though she wasn't sure if she should be telling it or not.

She told us that she'd been very lonely as an only child, and that she'd had a dog called Harry who was her only companion. Harry died when she was eleven and she said she never really recovered. He had been a lovely pedigree collie, with a light gold coat and a little white face like Lassie, and while her parents had been distant, Harry had always been there for her.

Another of the stories she told us was about the chickens they'd kept when she was a child. She fed them and gave them all names, growing very attached to each of them. Then one day her father said he wanted chicken for dinner, so he went out into the back garden with an axe and ran after a chicken she had named Jenny. Her father chased Jenny around the garden and hacked her head off with an axe. She hadn't known about the reflex that makes headless chickens run around for several minutes, and she'd screamed in horror as Jenny ran in circles, blood pouring from her neck.

Mummy used to cry deeply while telling this story but, while I did feel sorry for her, its impact was lost because my father found it funny and would be trying not to laugh. I'd try to avoid meeting his eye, in case I laughed too.

We still went to France a lot, on family holidays. One of our Irish cousins, Carmel, had settled in Provence and we'd stay in her large house. I loved French food: the runny cream cheese that you mixed with sugar, the fat red tomatoes that grew in Carmel's garden. We would sprinkle them with garlic salt and eat them with our mud covered fingers straight from the stalk. My brother and I always got on better when we were away, and would play in the barn with some of the local children. We always went to Paris en route to or from the south of France and I loved going up the Eiffel Tower in the hot summer months and then eating snails in outdoor restaurants. But Mummy often managed to be in some kind of sulk, or to be tight-lipped with disapproval over something, which meant the pleasure of the holiday was diluted. I would be aware of how much I longed to please her and, despite our new closeness, how often I failed.

Back at home my brother would revert to bullying me. He carried on until I was eight, when I became so angry that I squared up to him one day and said, 'OK, let's fight – come on.' He looked frightened, and from then on stopped bullying me and simply ignored me.

Soon afterwards, when some local boys who were very rough and used to throw stones at old ladies bullied my brother, it was I who went and faced them down and told them to leave him alone, fists clenched and voice fierce.

Daddy still took me with him to Ireland every other week or so. He called Ireland 'home'. He'd say 'I'm going home this weekend,' and I'm sure that for him it represented a means of escape from the rather stifling world he inhabited with my mother's clingy, childlike neediness.

In the dark of the night, in the large oak bed, he continued to do things to me that hurt and made me feel frightened. But I told no one. He often said that if I did, lots of men would make me do bad things and he would not be able to stop them. And he said I was bad and that I was a girl who bad things would always happen to. So I made myself forget what happened at night. And during the day I still loved being in Ireland, where everything was so much more relaxed and Auntie Ruth would give me ten pence to run up the road and spend on liquorice AllSorts and Sherbet Dip Dabs.

One of the boys playing outside was usually Val Dunning. With his long, dirty blond hair, his too-big second-hand clothes and dirty face, he fascinated me. He was the same age as my brother, and yet so very different. My brother cried easily and showed no interest in getting dirty or climbing up trees. He seemed to fear other boys and rough play, while Val was bold and fearless. He rode his bike fast and often went flying off the small muddy mounds beside the road, crashing onto the pavement with a bang and getting a bloody knee that he would dismiss with a wipe of a dirty hand. In Val I saw the phantom brother of my dreams. One who would have protected me.

I used to look at Daddy sometimes as he sat watching telly, wearing one of his grubby white string vests, cigarette in one hand, blond stubble evident on his face. With his blind mother nearby, he seemed contented in a way he never was in England. I used to watch him closely and try not to think of the night. Of a hand placed where it should not be, a smell I should not smell, an intrusive finger and something large and private that he made me caress. He'd catch my look, and his look would say he had all the power. And I had best forget if I knew what was good for me. His look told me he was quite capable of killing me if he had to. So I would squash the memories of the night and the little girl inside who knew the truth – squash her until she didn't exist any more. So tight that I'd be barely breathing. And I'd think to myself, 'If the little girl never lives, I can make Daddy better, I know I can.'

Back in England, at school I told my teacher that I wanted to be a psychiatrist. I could barely pronounce the word, but I knew it was a person who helped mad people to get better and that if I did that I could help Daddy. All the other children were saying they wanted to be nurses, or train drivers, so when I said what I wanted to be the teacher looked surprised and then laughed.

I did well in primary school, despite the lack of interest from my parents. They seldom helped me with homework or praised anything, but I was a natural straight A student and I loved reading, writing stories and learning new things.

My teachers recommended that I try for a prestigious grammar school some miles away – and when I got in, at the age of eleven, my parents were stunned. My father was proud but my mother said nothing to me, although she did tell the neighbours.

The softening which had drawn her and me a little closer over the past few years seemed to evaporate. Once again she seemed to see me as a threat, not just to her, but to my brother. He had always been given the role of the little professor of the family and greatly encouraged. He wanted to be a pilot or an astronaut and when our parents were told that he needed glasses they were very upset that both these dreams were now impossible. In truth, although Nicky was bright, he suffered from Mummy's constant pushing. And at the same time she couldn't accept that I might be bright too – possibly even brighter – and my achievements simply made her angry.

Because the school was so far away I had to make a two-hour journey each way, on two different buses. If the buses were late my journey could be even longer. In winter we would all wait at the bus stop in the freezing cold as bus after bus went by full to the brim with the nearby comprehensive school kids. We were often still outside school at six o'clock. So most days I left home soon after six in the morning and often got home at eight in the evening, sick with the cold and so exhausted that I struggled to do my compulsory two hours of homework.

My new school was very posh. We wore straw boaters and played lacrosse and most of the girls came from incredibly rich homes and lived in mansions near the school. A lot of them had limousines to pick them up and mothers who looked like beauty queens. I was too shy to make any friends, although I excelled at my studies and was consistently top of the class. I hid this from my mother after she recoiled in horror when I showed her an A I had been given for an English essay. My father didn't recoil, but he showed very little interest in my schoolwork. I found his disinterest hard to take, and longed for encouragement from him.

Despite my parents' indifference I loved my studies. My favourite subjects were Latin and Greek, and I loved physics and English too. I read T. S. Eliot and Shakespeare and books and poetry became even more important to me. My English teacher, who was very trendy and wore long skirts with – we were convinced – no knickers, often read my essays to the class and praised me, and I blossomed.

Much as I enjoyed lessons, though, I found break time hard, because I was painfully shy and had no confidence. The courage I'd had at eight, to square up to my brother and then the bullies, seemed to have deserted me in this new environment. I didn't dare go up and talk to other girls, and often sat alone, praying for the bell to ring so that I could go back into class. If anyone did talk to me I blushed scarlet and couldn't think of anything to say.

One day a very popular and lovely looking girl called Nicola Dickenson, who had long blonde hair, stopped and said, 'Hello Christine.' I gaped at her, unable to speak and blushing deep crimson, until she carried on up the school steps, probably vowing never to pass the time of day with me ever again.

It didn't help that my mother made it clear I wasn't to bring any friends home. Most of the girls went to one another's homes at weekends and after school, and knowing that I couldn't ask anyone back simply dented my confidence even more.

On the rare occasions when I did have permission to bring a friend home my mother would ridicule me, saying to them, 'Look at Christine – she acts big but she's got teddy bears in the cupboards and she's hidden them because you were coming.' Then she would pull them out of the cupboards as my friends stood, not knowing where to look. She would round it off by asking them. 'Are you lovely girls short of friends? You must be or why would you bother with Christine? She's so dull and boring and always has her head stuck in some rubbishy book.'

I thought of my Mother's Danielle Steele novels underneath her bed and wanted to retort about trashy novels but remembered that I enjoyed reading them too and liked to let her see me reading them as a kind of tie between us and a common bond.

By this time I was approaching puberty and my blossoming body seemed to have a profound effect on both my parents. Abruptly, my father stopped taking me with him to Ireland. This meant that he stopped interfering with me, which was a huge relief. But at the same time I felt rejected by him. I was no longer his special girl, no longer his princess and we no longer made our weekend trips together. I also lost all of the Irish family I had come to love. I grieved for them and I missed the lush green, fresh smelling Irish countryside and the taste of the wild grey salty sea when we went to Uncle Jim's.

During the week I was so exhausted from the long hours of school and travelling that I was barely able to think of anything but crawling into bed. But at weekends I was now left at home with my mother when Daddy made his trips. I took to spending most of the weekend in my room, curled up in bed reading, in order to stay out of her way.

Mummy often compared me unfavourably to other girls in the street or Rosemary, who lived next door to us. 'Look at Rosemary with her lovely dark hair,' she would say. 'She's pretty, really pretty – not like all this blonde hair.' Or 'Rosemary's doing so well at school in art – not like all this maths and writing that's for boys.' Mummy had always hit me, but now she took to regularly slapping me around the head. I was terrified of her and crept around the house hardly daring to speak.

Meanwhile, although my father no longer took me to Ireland or touched me, as I developed he began staring at me in a way that made me feel he could see me naked. He would look at me and go into a dreamy state and I felt somehow dirty and exposed. My growing sexuality seemed to me to be dangerous and I hated it. So I dressed like a tomboy and tried to look frumpy around the house, in a long baggy, pink cardigan. I was mortified when my father announced, in front of my mother, that I looked sweet in it. My mother glowered as though she had just heard something horrendous.

Despite this, there seemed to be no escape from either of them. My mother would peer though the crack in the door curiously as I undressed in the bathroom – I could see her eyes peering at my body and I felt as grubby as when my father watched me.

At twelve I started my periods. My mother had told me about them, so I knew what to expect. But what I couldn't have anticipated was her reaction. One day she found a used sanitary towel I had left in the bathroom and attacked me with it, rubbing it into my face and calling the menstrual blood 'disgusting' . I was horrified, filled with shame and so frightened that I attempted to hide all signs of my period from her after that.

The long journeys to and from school were making me increasingly tired. I felt drained by it and inevitably my work began to suffer. Because I had so little time at home I tried to get some of my homework done on the bus. This meant it looked scruffy, and a couple of the teachers laid into me about it. My maths teacher, Mrs Terrar, would mimic me and say, 'I can't do my homework, I don't have enough time, I'm on the bus all night.' I loved maths and it spoiled the lessons for me. Gradually I began to stop working, or caring how I did. I began sitting at the back of the class in lessons, doodling and not listening to the teachers. I felt overwhelmed by life, the demands on me and the lack of love and support at home and I think I came close to a breakdown. I was so desperately lonely.

At home I spent most of the time in my room, and when I did venture out it was to watch telly with Nanna in her room. I found refuge in sitting side by side with her, too close to the television set, watching Bette Davis and Dirk Bogarde in old black and white films. But sadly, Nanna wasn't the companion she had once been. She was going blind and losing her hearing and she seemed to be shrinking back into herself. I felt my only real friend was beginning to leave me.

Two of the girls from school who took the same bus home would tease me relentlessly about being posh and always having my nose stuck in books. Philippa Cunningham and Ellen Jones were loud and pretty and wore high heels and lipstick and boys always gaped at them. I knew they thought I was dull and a swot and I used to wish I could be more like them.

But one day, perhaps bored with the teasing, Philippa began talking to me. Eventually we got to know one another and became friends, which gave me confidence. Philippa was loud and played the fool and I tried to be like her. I became friends with Ellen too. She was extremely pretty and came from a very rich family and I was so in awe of her I couldn't believe that I was able to call her my friend.

With my new-found confidence I made another friend at school, Penny Watson. She was the well-spoken, pretty daughter of a doctor. She was clever and had strong political views, which fascinated me. Although I couldn't ask her home, Penny began asking me to her house at weekends and I leaped at the chance. Suddenly I didn't have to sit in my room on Saturday afternoons: I could go to her house, where her family welcomed me.

Penny soon became my best friend, all the more precious because I'd never had a best friend before. We used to go out to the shops and try on make-up together in Boots. We would borrow her mother's perfume, which was called Wind Song, when she was out, and we used to raid her parents' drinks cabinet, getting woozy on Cointreau, Crême de Menthe and other brightly coloured liqueurs.

My new friendships helped me to open up and I found I was good at making others laugh. At school I began playing the clown. I used to write stories and read them out to a crowd of girls at playtime. But as I gradually became more confident and popular, my schoolwork started to decline.

My mother seemed glad that I was failing. So I failed even more, to please her. And it did – she softened a little towards me and we got on better.

One parents' evening my parents set off for the school, locking the downstairs front and back rooms, as they always did, so that my brother and I only had access to the kitchen. The previous year I'd had glowing reports and neither parent had said anything to me about it. But this time my teachers told them that I had stopped trying and asked what was going on.

I spent the evening in the room I still shared with Nanna, and decided to wash my hair. I was drying my hair in my room when they returned, and because of the noise of the hairdryer and the Carpenters music I was playing, I didn't hear the car draw up. So I was startled when my father burst into my room, and embarrassed because I was in my bra and knickers.

He grabbed for my hand, but only managed to get hold of my right forefinger. Suddenly he wrenched it back as hard as he could, so that I fell to my knees, screaming in agony. He let go and I crawled onto the bed, sobbing with the pain. I was hysterical and screamed, 'He's going to kill me.' He had stormed off, but he was raging and I was terrified he would come back and hurt me even more. I lay sobbing until, hours later, my mother came up and gave me some painkillers. She said nothing and went straight downstairs again.

The next day my finger was swollen and terribly painful. We had art and I had to tell the teacher, Miss Murray, that I couldn't paint. I was good at art and she liked me, so she was very upset because it meant I couldn't take my upcoming art exam. She thought I'd injured it mucking around and I couldn't bear to have her think that, so I broke my habit of silence and told her that my Dad had done it, over my school report. Clearly shocked and upset, she sent me to the nurse who put a splint on it and then called in the head-mistress. After that I was told there was a notice up on the staffroom wall saying my father had broken my finger and that teachers were forbidden to talk to him about me. No further action was taken – they didn't call social services or, to my knowledge, contact my father. But it had meant a lot to me to tell the truth and to be believed.

When I got home my father was upset to see that I was wearing the splint, realising that this must mean I had drawn attention to my broken finger at school. We were in the kitchen, and I went to make a cup of tea, reaching over to the kettle to fill it. As I did so I realised Dad had got there first and the kettle was about to boil. I began to pull away, but he grabbed hold of my arm and held it over the steam from the boiling kettle.

I squealed like a scalded cat and looked up at my father, begging him to stop. The look on his face shocked me. It was almost merry. He was enjoying himself, revelling in the power he had over me. I was left with a bright red scald on my arm. But I told no one, I just covered it with my sleeve and rubbed antiseptic into it to stop the throbbing. The antiseptic had a strong smell and at school the next day Penny asked what the stink was. I told her I'd leaned up against the cooker and had to rub Germolene cream into my arm. She kept saying, 'Ooh, that stuff is stinking the class out,' and I wanted to cry and tell her the truth, but I didn't. The memory of the look in my father's eyes was enough to keep me silent.

My father had a side to him which could be devastatingly cruel, as well as physically violent. But he was also a charismatic, charming man and I loved him, so I forgave him whatever he did that hurt me – including this. A day or two after any cruelty he would be making jokes and singing his Bing songs and I would love him again.

Over the next few months I continued to neglect my schoolwork. Although being clever and doing well at school had given me a little of the self-esteem I so badly needed, it had also separated me from my peers at school and stopped my mother from loving me. I desperately wanted to leave all that behind, and the easiest way was to fail at school. Instead I put my energies into my friendships, especially with Penny. I went over to her house whenever I could and at home I tried to keep a low profile, while my mother continued to belittle and criticise me.

The summer after I turned thirteen my parents arranged for the family to go to America, where we were to stay in a small villa in the grounds of my Aunt Cecilia's convent in Boston, for a month, and then fly on to Miami for a two-week holiday.

I was very excited about visiting the convent. I adored my Aunt Cecilia and I had told my parents several times that I would be happy to follow her example and become a nun. I used to read the Bible a lot and one of my favourite people was still Father Michael Fewell, the young priest at our church. I used to have long discussions with him about what happened to you when you died and whether God really forgave people who did bad things. He gave great sermons and very spiritual masses. The idea of spending my time talking to deep thinkers like Father Michael and Aunt Cecilia and becoming a person that others sought out for spiritual advice really appealed to me.

The convent was magnificent. A huge and very grand old gothic house of sand-coloured stone, it was surrounded by fountains and sweeping grounds, which included a large grey shimmering lake surrounded by leonine weeping willows and tall, juicy larch trees.

The nuns ran a boarding school there for girls who wanted to train to become nuns, and soon after we arrived Aunt Cecilia drew me to one side and asked me whether I would like to stay at the convent, with a view to becoming a nun. No doubt she had spoken to my parents about it beforehand, but it came as a complete surprise to me. She explained that if I said yes I would remain there full-time, studying in the convent school with the other girls my age, and becoming a novice nun. I would see my parents only on holidays, when they came to visit, or I went back to England. I didn't hesitate to say yes. I was in love with the idea of becoming a nun, in this beautiful fairytale place.

My parents were, of course, more than happy to let me stay. They would stay to settle me in, they said, and then go on to Miami, leaving me at the convent. I was warmly welcomed by the nuns, and even though I was a little scared about being parted from my family, the thrill of becoming a Daughter of St Paul was so great that I had no doubts about staying.

So I began my religious life, wearing a little blue novice's veil of which I was deeply proud, and praying for up to three hours, morning and evening. I liked to pray and I didn't mind the long hours, I threw myself wholeheartedly into what I felt was now my vocation.

I slept in the long dark dormitories with the other girls my age, and we would all sing hymns together before bed. I would listen to the high young voices echoing around the vast room in the pitch black darkness, and the crickets chirping outside the windows in the almost tropical heat of the American summer and think how beautiful it all was.

But my attempt to dedicate myself to God was abruptly halted the day I showed one of the nuns my book on the Beatles and told her how much I loved George Harrison. She complained to the Mother Superior about the evil of the Beatles' songs and my despicable carnal lust for George Harrison. That was it – I was deemed not fit to be a Daughter of St Paul as I was far too worldly.

I was deeply upset when I was told I must leave and had to remove my blue veil. Taking it off, I felt once again worthless and despoiled.

My mother was also very upset, though not so much over the loss of my religious future as being forced to take me with the family to Miami and then back home to England. She remained livid for most of the holiday.

We stayed at a motel called Ocean View situated right on the beach and, despite my mother's grim mood, I enjoyed swimming and sunbathing. I soon turned golden brown, but my father walked up and down the beach all the first day and was confined to the hotel for the rest of the holiday with bad sunburn.

It was in Miami that I met a handsome American boy called John who was playing mock skiing on the beach. He was much older than me and had silky dark brown hair. He looked like George Brent, an actor I was mad about. He took me for a drive in his big American van, pulled over into a leafy lay-by, leaned over me and kissed me. I was both startled and thrilled when he pushed his tongue into my mouth. He tasted of peppermints. I started to cry with happiness, as for a long time I had been afraid that I was never going to be kissed. All my friends had, but I was so shy I never managed it.

I told John that he was the first boy I had ever kissed. He clearly didn't realise how young I was and he looked at me in horror and promptly drove me back to the beach. But his kiss had made me feel that I might not be as ugly and unlovable as I thought I was and I decided that I was glad I had been thrown out of the convent and that I wanted to marry and have a family after all.

I got back to my Motel room where an Afro-Caribbean maid was polishing. 'I just had my first kiss,' I blurted out, excitedly.

'Oh, you is joking, oh, that's great,' she said, beaming.

I was elated at her response. How I wished I had a mother who would greet the news in the same way.

When we came home from Miami I went back to school and was delighted to see Penny again. It was the punk era and Penny and I would buy crazy coloured hair dye and make-up and go back to her house to try it all out. I didn't dare dye my hair, I would have got into terrible trouble, but I helped Penny dye hers.

I was mad about make-up. Just the smell of a little gold pot of glittery blue eye shadow was enough to send me into raptures, and I'd happily plaster it on at Penny's, even though I had to wash it all off before I went home.

One afternoon, when my mother and I were both in the garden, our next-door neighbour Aurora leaned over the fence and asked me if I'd like some spare make-up samples she had. Aurora was an Avon lady who sold cosmetics to people in their homes. I took the samples she handed me and rushed up to the bathroom to try them out. Mum had been in a good mood that day so I didn't think she'd mind, especially as she'd seen Aurora give them to me and I wasn't going to wear the make-up out anywhere, just try it on.

For the next hour or so I stood in front of the bathroom mirror and carefully applied a parrot blue eye shadow, black eyeliner, thick black mascara and some glossy scarlet Marilyn Monroe-style lipstick. I was delighted with the result. I felt I looked like a gorgeous starlet. I heard my mother come into the bathroom behind me and turned, eager to show her how I looked. But as she saw the make-up her whole face seemed to crumble in on itself with a look of horror and fury.

Shocked, I reached a hand up and touched my face. What had I done? My mother grabbed a flannel, her hands shaking, and leapt on me like a cat, scrubbing at my face with it and calling me a little whore. It hurt so much that, in that moment, I felt she wanted to kill me. I had never seen her so angry. Terrified, I pushed her away and ran. Her shrieks followed me out of the house as I slammed the door behind me.

I ran all the way to Penny's, where she and her parents were startled, but very kind. Her mother called my mother to say where I was and even though I was very tearful and frightened and my face was covered with bruises, I assumed that after a couple of hours I would go home. But my mother told Penny's parents that she didn't want me to come back. They offered to let me stay with them while it was all sorted out, assuring me that my mother would calm down by the next day, and that night I shared Penny's room.

The next day, however, my mother had not changed her mind. She told Penny's parents that she and my father had rung social services to tell them that the adoption had broken down and they were not willing to have me back. They wanted the adoption revoked.

When Penny's father told me this, as kindly as he could, I went into shock. Surely Mummy wouldn't send me back because I'd put make-up on? How could my parents simply give me back? I had been their daughter for ten years. I didn't have any other parents, or any other home.

I stayed at Penny's for a week, during which I remained numb and disbelieving. A social worker named Adrian Walker called to see me and ask me about what had happened. I asked him where I would be going, but he couldn't, or wouldn't tell me.

One morning my father arrived. I was so glad to see him, I threw myself into his arms. 'Daddy, Daddy,' I cried. 'Have you come to take me home?' It had all been a horrible mistake, I was going home. He looked at me sadly, and told me to get my things and get into the car. As we drove away he said, 'I asked her could I leave instead and she said no – you.' He began to cry. 'My little princess will have to go back where she came from,' he wept.

Panic twisted my insides.

'She wants you to change your name. Back to your real name, Lucy.'

I looked at him. I had no memory of my real name. Lucy. I hated it.

I sat in silence, paralysed by the enormity of what was happening to me, as my father drove me to a children's home I had never seen before. I was too old to go back to the rescue home, so I was to stay in this new place until somewhere could be found for me.

My father took me in, before turning and walking away. He didn't even kiss me goodbye. I stood watching him go. He was sobbing like a child, in the same way I had seen Uncle Edward sob in the hospital. Mummy, Daddy, Nicky and Nanna were my family. How could they simply get rid of me? I had always believed that, no matter what happened, they would be my family for the rest of my life.

I felt that the world was still spinning round without me, and that I had been made to get off and was floating in space, lost, and utterly alone.

4

The Wolf Boy

The next day I was handed a couple of supermarket carrier bags containing my things. They had been delivered that morning. I pulled the contents out on my bed: clothes, toiletries, school books, a few toys. But some of my most precious possessions were missing. My Beatles album collection, given to me by a neighbour, a gold bracelet engraved with my initials, given to me by my cousin Carmel in Provence. And the musical box that Nanna had given me, with the dancing ballerina and the Rachmaninoff tune that I prized.

I felt my past had simply been taken away. I was no longer Christine, but I knew I wasn't Lucy either. All my feelings, the hurt and pain and fear and desperation, were pushed deep inside and I felt completely numb. I was beyond pain, and probably becoming quite ill. All I could do was function, like a robot. I appeared to be coping but inside I felt I was dying. I wanted to run to someone who cared and fling myself onto them, sobbing, yet there was no one.

I told myself that it was all my fault. I had failed at school, I had failed at being a nun, I was a bad girl who wanted to wear mascara. I was a failure as a normal person, and my family were right to get me out of their nice family home.

I heard later, from the mother of a friend of mine, that my mother had said, 'We really tried with Christine, but I always feared she'd turn out like her mother. She's got bad blood from her real parents. I can't have it in the home. The adoption hasn't worked out and she's better off trying to find her real family.'

The words went through me like a burning lance. I thought *she* was my mother. I thought *they* were my family. Now they didn't want me. Even Penny, my friend, planned a night out with her friend, Frances, as I left. I found it so hard that for her, for all of them, life just went on without me when it felt as though mine had ended. I was no longer Christine, the nice, normal girl with a proper name and a good family. I was Lucy, an unwanted orphan. Perhaps I had always been Lucy to them.

I was scared. I had no one. Absolutely no one. I had failed at being normal and it was my fault.

I took in very little of the place I'd been taken to. I spent most of the time in my room, and crept around the edges when I had to come out for meals, or to use the bathroom. After the first few days I befriended three of the little children there. They had all been dumped by their mothers and I felt so sorry for them. One little boy would come and sit on my knee and wind his arms around my neck. I would cuddle him and the other two and put them to bed and tuck them in. It broke my heart to see such young children with no one.

I was only there for a couple of weeks. I made friends with another new kid, Craig, and one night, when both of us were freezing cold, we got into bed to cuddle. It was innocent, we had our clothes on and weren't even kissing, but we got caught and I was immediately moved on to a large home for teenagers, Greengage House. A social worker drove me there in a metallic blue Rover, while I sat in the front seat with my two carrier bags perched on my knees, gripping on to them tightly, my gut contorted with fear. After about half an hour we arrived in front of a large red brick house. It was only ten miles or so from the rescue home where I had lived as a small girl, but it felt like another country. Everything looked strange and foreign.

The social worker who delivered me drove off, leaving me standing alone in the brightly decorated reception area. I had been there for half an hour when a tall dark-haired man appeared.

He smiled. 'You must be Christine. I'll take you to your room and let you settle in.' He told me his name was Dave Lord and that he was in charge of the home. He had kind brown eyes, floppy dark hair and he looked a bit like Paul McCartney. The room allocated to me was one of five leading off a long stark white corridor. Halfway along it was a burgundy-coloured reinforced door, which led to the boys' end of the corridor, which also had five rooms. The boys' and girls' sections each had a large bathroom and a small toilet.

'See you later,' Dave Lord said. 'I'll get one of the others to show you around in a bit.'

I looked at the single bed, with its folded blue nylon sheets and mustard yellow blankets, and perched on the edge of it, not knowing what to do next. It was twilight outside before someone knocked at the door, a blond boy with a body like a weight lifter. I thought he was one of the staff, but I found out later that he was sixteen and one of the older kids. His name was Edward Goodman.

'You're new, aren't you?' he said. 'They told me to tell you dinner's ready. You have to be quick if you're hungry.'

I followed him to the dining room, where I soon realised what he'd meant by being quick. The kids were grabbing the food and shovelling it into their mouths. Anyone who was too slow had the food taken from their plate by someone else. I had always been a slow eater, chewing every mouthful. But I soon learned to gobble like the others, if I didn't want to go hungry.

Over the next few weeks I became used to life in Greengage House. It wasn't easy being back in an institution, with its impersonal corridors and endless rules. I found life there very dull, and spent as much time as I could alone in my freezing cold room, where I consoled myself with books like Emily Bronte's *Wuthering Heights* and Daphne Du Maurier's *Rebecca*. Reading was my comfort and my means of escape.

I missed home. Even though my parents had often treated me very badly, they were still my family and having a family, however imperfect they were, was a million times better than being in an institution, unwanted and uncared for. I missed all of the family. I missed the warm familiarity of my room. I missed being called down for dinner. I missed that Tuesday was stew day and Wednesday was chicken pie day and Saturday was cheese on toast day. I missed watching telly with Nanna. I missed going to Ireland and playing in the garden or sitting in a deckchair on hot days and talking to my lime tree. I missed meeting Mum from work in the school holidays and her buying me my *Jackie* comic.

There was a large television room and a table tennis room for the kids, but I seldom used them. Instead I would go down in the large spotless kitchen to talk to Peggy, the grey-haired woman who came to cook the dinners, or the various prickly cleaning ladies who came in the morning to vacuum the rooms and corridors.

The staff worked on a rota system, changing over at two in the afternoon and at night. None of them lived on the premises except for Dave Lord, who lived in a small house at the side of the main building. While Dave was popular with the kids, his plump, blonde wife wasn't because she nagged us all the time.

I remained at the same school. No doubt they felt it would give me some kind of continuity, but for me it was very hard. The journey, which was now by train, was a little shorter, but I missed the other bus girls like Philippa and Ellen.

I would turn up in my smart uniform and straw boater as always, but painfully aware that I was no longer like the other girls.

The school dealt with it by putting another notice up in the staffroom, announcing that I was now in care. Mrs Terrar, the maths teacher who had bullied me, used to hide her face when she saw me in the corridor, presumably because she thought I was going to act all tough and jump on her. A few girls I didn't know asked me about the home. I didn't feel embarrassed, but I felt disconnected; everything felt a bit unreal.

I did my best to be cheerful and friendly at school, and my friends still invited me to their homes. I sometimes went to Penny's for tea, where her family were always nice to me. When I left her father would give me a pound to get myself some toothpaste and soap. I'd use it to take the bus to the street where my family lived, where I'd stand on the corner underneath the orange lamplight and look over at what had until recently been my home. I'd stand there for hours, wondering what they were doing, and longing to walk over and knock on the door and say, 'Mum, it's me,' and have her hug me and say, 'Tea's ready,' in that dry way she had. Then I'd run upstairs and cuddle down with a book under my red silk eiderdown, with my Beatles posters on the wall beside me, my books on the bookshelf and my old teddy bears at the end of the bed.

After a while I gave up going to Penny's. The smell of chips, eggs and sausages cooking as I came through their door after school and the sight of the kitchen windows steamed up with the heat from the cooker, reminded me achingly of my own lost family life. It was easier simply to go back to the home for my tea.

One afternoon my brother came cycling up to the home on a brand new red Raleigh bicycle. He handed me a five-pound note and said, 'They told me not to come, but I thought, well, you were my sister once, weren't you.'

I was pleased that he had come, even if his manner was a little offhand. This was Nicky trying to make a kind gesture. But then he ruined it, when I asked him tentatively, 'How are they?'

'Oh, they're happier now you're not there,' he said, matter-of-factly, childishly not realising the effect of his unconsidered words. Then he jumped on his bike and cycled off.

I gave the fiver to another girl, Jess. What Nicky had said made it all worse. They were happy, and so was he on his brand new bike, and I was a thing of the past.

The other kids in the home didn't know what to make of me. Despite my attempts at a cockney accent, I sounded more like Margo from *The Good Life*, one of the programmes everyone loved at the time. Penelope Keith played Margo, and her hoity-toity accent was just like mine. I also went to a posh grammar school and spent most of my time in my room, so to the other kids I must have seemed very stuck-up.

One day one of them grabbed my straw boater and started playing piggy in the middle with it, with me as the piggy grabbing at it as it flew over my head. Another time one of the girls grabbed my flute and started blowing smoke rings through it. It was a silver Yamaha but after that it smelled so bad that I tasted smoke every time I played it and in the end I gave up playing.

Despite these incidents, I got to know the other kids and to be friends with some of them. I had a crush on a dishy skinhead called Oliver who had come from borstal. I was scared of him, so I watched from a distance as he paraded around. He had been thoroughly rejected by both of his parents and when upset he would get all the food out of the cupboards and pour it all over the floor in the large kitchen. Then he would skate around in it doing pirouettes and saying he was Robin Cousins.

In the room next door to me was a girl called Beth who used to slash her wrists weekly. Along the corridor was Jess, an Afro-Caribbean girl a bit younger than me. The head of the girls' section was Cora, a skinhead, who had her pale red hair shaved close to her head and wore scuffed red Doc Martin boots. She'd been in care all her life.

Cora wasn't around much. She had a gun-toting gangster boyfriend called Kevin who was much older than her and who looked like a gypsy. He came to pick her up in various battered old cars. Some of the kids said that he was using her for sex, but she said that he was going to marry her and she proudly wore an emerald-green glass engagement ring he'd stolen for her. Kevin had a reputation in the local pubs and most of us were scared of him because we'd heard that he'd shot someone in a fight over a girl.

Cora's parents had put her into temporary care, as they couldn't cope with her as well as their three older daughters. But they never came back for her. She knew where they lived, and she kept a framed photo of them hidden in a drawer. Cora acted the hard nut, and most of the others were frightened of her and avoided her. But her room was next to mine, and I often heard her sobbing pitifully through the night.

Although they still weren't quite sure what to make of me, the other kids could see that because I hadn't had the same sort of lives as them, in care, I'd learned things about the world that they hadn't. Some of them began to look to me for advice and in responding I found a strength that I'd never known. I used to type out their Saturday job applications and advise them on how to save their pocket money.

Life in the home was hard. There were very few pleasures and most of the care workers who watched over us had no interest in us. The highlight of our week was at the weekend, when two of the kids would be given ten pounds to go and get what was known as the 'supper stuff'. We would go into town on the bus and buy crisps, ice-cream and biscuits from the supermarket. Then we'd come back and put it all in the cupboard.

The idea was that it would last for the week, but that never happened. We'd grab the stuff and eat it on the day it was bought, in one massive binge. A sad posse of unloved kids with ice-cream round our mouths, who'd follow the feast by chain-smoking Rothmans and swigging from a large bottle of cold double strength cider smuggled in by Oliver. I used to take a swig and feel sick, then watch in fascination as Oliver downed most of the bottle.

One day I was sitting at Sunday dinner when I heard all the others talking about a child called the Wolf Boy. Someone had found out that he had attacked a little girl and been sent to borstal. It seems they'd found this out at his previous home and the kids had made it difficult for him to stay there, so he was being moved to ours.

Most of the kids were fuming as we sat around the large dinner table discussing it, after all the dinner plates had been cleared away. The table was still messy, with watery tomato soup splashes, and I sat at the end watching Cora admiringly as she nonchalantly smoked a Benson and Hedges while spooning yoghurt into her mouth in between puffs. Apparently the Wolf Boy had been given his nickname because of his unkempt appearance. His real name was Joe, but he was already the Wolf Boy to us. When he arrived we were all curious, but he spent his first week in bed, and no one really saw him. He had a sparsely decorated box room at the end of the boys' corridor, with no curtains and yellow-stained walls. The first thing you noticed when you went anywhere near his room was the smell. It was as if a real live wolf had nestled down and made its own home inside the room.

Cora and I tiptoed down there and peered in through the keyhole. All we could see was masses of dark brown on the pillowcase and a thin frame outlined beneath dirty grey sheets. Cora said, 'Boo,' and we both collapsed in giggles as we ran down the corridors.

A few days later I saw him sitting in the laundry-room wrapped in a towel, watching a lone red tracksuit spin round and round in the washing machine. He was short and sallow-skinned and there was a sad, despairing look about his owl-like brown eyes and down-turned mouth. I thought he was about the same age as me – fourteen.

I found out Joe's history by accident one day, when I overheard a conversation in the staffroom. Before he was born, his mother had had an affair with a married man. Joe was the result of that affair and her husband, who became Joe's father, had resented him deeply. Then his mother died and his father married again and had twin girls, both blonde angels.

Joe was not blood-related to either parent and they treated him like an outcast. He was told that he was dirty and to stay away from his two sisters, and when he came in from school he was made to do most of the housework.

Most evenings his father would beat him with a leather belt with a pointed silver buckle on the end of it and Joe's back was badly scarred because of this. In the end, at twelve Joe had taken an overdose of paracetamol and drunk some toilet bleach in an effort to kill himself. His father found him and after his stomach had been pumped out, they put him into care.

Joe had been bullied a lot because he was small and, as his parents had never taught him personal hygiene and had made him sleep in the barn like an animal, he smelled bad. He was also very shy, and didn't know how to mix with others. Hurt and angry at the bullying, and his family's rejection of him, he had attacked a girl five years younger. Perhaps in his wounded mind he was punishing one of the little sisters who had been loved while he had not.

He had been sentenced to two years in borstal and after he came out he had gone to several children's homes and assessment centres, where he had also been bullied, until finally he arrived with us. I used to watch him and think that we weren't so different. Both of us were outsiders, unwanted and unloved.

After he had been around a while, I tried to talk to him. At first he wouldn't reply, so I'd catch him as he came out of the bathroom, with his hair soaking wet and wrapped in an old bath towel. I'd haul him by the arm along the girls' corridor and into my room and make him sit in front of the old record player I had rescued from downstairs and I'd comb his hair and blow it dry for him. He would mostly sit in silence during these sessions, though sometimes he would put on Bob Marley's 'Could You Be Loved'. He always chose the same record.

Eventually he began to talk to me. He told me that he had been raped by a social worker at his last home. I was horrified, and wanted to organise some of the boys to go over and beat up the social worker, but Joe told me not to. 'No one will believe me if we tell,' he said. So I said nothing, and in time a kind of trust was established between us. I identified with Joe, I knew what it was like to suffer and keep silent.

The other boys would beat him up on an almost daily basis or, if there was an observant social worker on duty to stop them, they would go up to his room, urinate on his bed and pour tomato sauce between the sheets and up the walls.

One day they jumped on him and shaved off his hair with the aid of a Bic razor. With a bald head, he cut a strange figure around the place, always alone, not even attempting to talk to anyone.

Then one day Joe's father came to the home. His wife had gone into hospital, and he had been left looking after the twins. He told the staff he had decided he wanted to have Joe back to live with him again, but it was obvious to everyone that his father just wanted him to help with the housework. But Joe wanted to go. He worshipped his father and he thought that this was his father saying, after all these years, that he loved him and wanted him after all.

Sadly, as we all expected, when his wife left hospital three weeks later, Joe's father gave him the beating of his life with the studded belt and returned him to the home, where Joe was sent back to his empty room at the end of the corridor. Two weeks later the police came and took him away, and we heard he had been sent to borstal. We never knew why.

The day I heard he had gone I went upstairs to his room and stood looking at his sad little bed with its piss-stained sheets. Out of curiosity I opened one of the drawers. There was a note pad in there, and inside he'd written in pencil, 'Christine is my real mummy and I love her.' I was so surprised I stared at it for a minute. Then, unable to express how deeply it touched me and how much I felt for him, I said aloud, 'Oh, how stupid, that's childish'. But I couldn't hold back the tears. I leaned my head against the wall and wept.

In November I turned fourteen and I began to think a lot about my birth father and my roots. I wasn't interested in my mother. At least that's what I told myself. It was probably a defence because I couldn't get it out of my mind that she had been the one who had given me away and I couldn't face a second rejection by her if I found her again. I didn't think then about the fact that she'd been fourteen, my own age, and a child herself. I just felt hurt and angry and decided I didn't want to know her. But I was curious about my father. Perhaps he was out there and cared about me, but didn't know where I was or how to find me.

I began to dream about him every day. I imagined he was wise and handsome – a bit like Roger Moore, who starred in my favourite programme, *The Persuaders*. My longing to find out something about him grew stronger. I knew the information was likely to be in my file, but that was kept in the locked filing cabinet in the staff office.

I was determined to find a way to see my file, and a few weeks later my chance came, when one of the social workers was called to the residents' phone in the hallway. She'd been looking through the files, and she left the filing cabinet open. I slipped in and flicked through until I found my file, stuffed it up under my jumper and ran upstairs to the privacy of my room. It was a large, buff-coloured file and as I began to read the notes inside the first thing that caught my eye was the phrase 'emotionally deprived'. It made me feel like a freak, some kind of exhibit they were all talking about. I read that my real mother's name was Olivia Matheson. Then I found my birth certificate with my real name on it – Lucy Matheson. But where it said 'name of father', there was just a line.

I figured it must have been some sort of mistake. I managed to slip the file back without getting into trouble, but I wanted to know more. I knew that all the birth, marriage and death certificates were kept in Somerset House in London and that you could see them. So I decided to go and find mine, and see for myself.

I was used to going into London. I sometimes went with one of the boys from the home, Christopher. We'd use our pocket money to get the bus in and hang around central London, in places like Piccadilly Circus and Trafalgar Square.

So a few days later I slipped out of school early and went up to Somerset House. I looked at my mother's birth certificate and saw that she had lived in Hull and moved to London when she found she was pregnant. Then I checked my birth certificate, but it was the same as the one they had in my file. Where it said 'name of father' there was just a line.

I was shocked. Surely everyone had a dad? Why wouldn't his name be there? I didn't know then that a father had to accompany the mother to register a birth in order for his name to be included. When that doesn't happen, for whatever reason, mothers can't simply add the name, as they could choose anyone. But, unaware of this, I once again blamed my mother, convinced that she had simply left him off for some reason.

Why did she do it, I wondered? My imagination began to work overtime. Maybe it had to be a secret? Maybe he was someone famous, a pop star or a film star whose identity had to be hidden. I was desperate to know. I began to feel like an alien that had been hatched, or landed by the side of the road in a pod.

Back at the home I asked the staff question after question, and badgered the friendlier ones into trying to find out for me. One of them, Michael Briggs, a tall man with long, dark brown rocker's hair and Doc Martin boots, listened to me and seemed to take an interest. He was fairly new to the home and had singled me out for attention a few times. So when I told him I wanted to know who my father was, he told me he would try to find out.

Two days later, he knocked and came into my room. There was a worried look on his face as he sat next to me and took my hand.

'Christine, I know you've been imagining that your dad was a famous film star or royalty, but I'm afraid he wasn't. The truth is he was a criminal and after you were born he went to prison to serve a long sentence. Your mother didn't want anything to do with him because of his crimes, which I believe were quite serious.'

Michael told me that I could find out more from the principal of the rescue home where I had been left as a baby and he helped me compose a letter to her, telling her I wanted to know about my father. I had to wait three months for an answer, but eventually I was told that I would be given a counselling session and then I could go to see the principal for the information.

The counselling session was fine. I told the counsellor I felt I could handle whatever information I was given, and that I really needed to know. But the next step, my interview with the principal, was a disaster. As I was shown in she was sitting behind her desk holding a blue file. I knew that it contained the information I so desperately wanted and that she had the power to decide whether to give it to me or not. I resented that bitterly. I felt I had a right to know, and after half an hour of being grilled by her about why I wanted to know, I lost my temper and shouted at her, 'Are you going to bloody tell me or not?'

That was the end of our interview. I was ushered out and later told that the principal had said I was 'too emotionally immature to handle the information'.

I was devastated. I deserved to know who my father was, and if she wouldn't tell me, I thought bitterly, then I would find out by myself.

5

The Man in the Picture

My father was a criminal. It was hard to take in. My image of a debonair Roger Moore type was replaced by a dark, shadowy figure. What had he done? I wondered. What could be so bad that my mother didn't want to know him?

I built it all up in my mind. Whatever he had done must have been terrible. Maybe he had actually murdered people. That was the worst crime there was. If he was a murderer, then that would explain why no one would tell me about him. And he must have been famous, or there would have been no need for my mother to keep his name a secret.

Awful as the truth might be, I wanted to know. One afternoon, I spent three hours in the true crime section of the local library. I was looking through books like the *Murderer's Who's Who*, and *The Encyclopaedia of Crime*. The crimes I read about were horrible; some of them made me feel sick. And the pictures of the murderers were so ugly – they all looked old, with staring eyes and pale faces.

Then I came across a picture that immediately caught my attention, of a man who was so young he seemed almost like a boy. He looked so out of place amongst the corrupt faces of the murderers, not just younger but less evil. I stared at his picture. It was almost as if he was trying to tell me something.

I looked at the description under the photo. His name was Ian Brady, and he had murdered three children, with his girlfriend, Myra Hindley. The two of them were suspected of murdering two other children. He had been just twenty-six at the time of his crimes. And it said that he had been in borstal in Hull when he was seventeen.

I was shocked – and fascinated. Although his crimes had been over ten years earlier, I had never heard of him. Could it have been him? Could this man have been my father? He looked like me, I was convinced of it. And he had been in Hull, where my mother had lived. A crime like that would explain so much: why he had been kept a secret, and perhaps even why my mother gave me up. Who would want the child of such a man? I stood behind one of the shelves in the library and ripped the page out of the book, coughing to cover up the tearing noise. Then I stuffed it into my pocket and hurried out.

When I got back to the home I folded it into a drawer and later, when Michael came on duty, I showed it to him. He looked at me, puzzled.

'Why are you pulling pictures of Ian Brady out of books? I thought you went to the library to try and find out something about your father? But if you're interested in Brady I've got a book about him you can read if you like.'

'Yes please,' I said, and he promised to bring it in when he was next on duty.

The book he handed me was called *Beyond Belief*, by Emlyn Williams. I quickly turned to the part on Ian Brady's life and what I read there fascinated me. Just like me, Brady had been given up as a baby by his mother. He had been a lonely child, whose four foster brothers and sisters took little interest in him. As I read on I began to feel that we had a great deal in common. We both knew what it was to be rejected and unloved.

At seventeen Brady got into trouble for petty crimes and was sent back to live with his real mother and a stepfather he didn't get on with. Although the police had told him he had to return to his mother or face borstal, I saw it as a rejection by his foster family. He must have felt they were his real family, his real parents – they were all he had ever known. Yet just like me, he was dumped.

My imagination worked overtime, putting all the pieces together and convincing myself that I had indeed found my father and that we had similar life stories. And I was happy, because I was sure it meant that I wasn't unwanted after all. It was his awful crimes that had changed everything. For a moment I stopped hating my mother for dumping me. She had loved me, I was sure of it. She just hadn't been able to keep me. It was such a relief to stop hating her. I felt as if a weight had been lifted from my shoulders.

It all seemed to fit. Brady had committed terrible crimes, but I felt sure that he hadn't always been bad. And although the book didn't spell it out, I became certain that he must have been abused as a child. How could he have done such terrible things if he hadn't suffered himself? He had turned bad because he had been so hurt by what had happened to him. By rejection from two mothers.

He did become evil, I knew that. But I was evil too, my adoptive mum had told me that so many times. And that was why no one wanted me, and no one could love me. Did being rejected by two mothers make you evil?

When I returned the book to Michael he asked me what I'd thought of it. Enthusiastically I poured out my thoughts. 'He didn't mean what he did, Michael – I know it. Something strange must have happened to Him. They say that he had bad blood. That he was a monster. But they say that about me too, and it's not true, I'm not a monster, I'm not really evil. Perhaps he wasn't a monster either.'

'Of course you're not a monster,' Michael said. 'But what Brady did was terrible. You can't be sure he's your father, Chris, unless you can check it out somehow.'

But I did feel sure. I was certain that I understood Ian Brady in a way that no one else did, that there was some kind of bond between us, and that I could help him.

I never finished reading *Beyond Belief* once I got past Brady's childhood, so it didn't occur to me that he might still be alive. I assumed that he had been hanged. No one who had done something so evil could still be alive. I was so sure that I didn't even think to check, or ask Michael. And believing that he was dead, it felt safe to think that he was my father, and that had he known me, he might have loved me. He was a ghost, a man in a picture who helped me cope with life. I kept his picture in my drawer and whenever I felt sad and lonely I took it out and stared at it, looking for a resemblance to the face I saw in the mirror and feeling a sense of comfort because there was someone I was linked to.

I clung even more desperately to this fantasy after bumping into my adoptive father in the street one day. I was on my way to an interview for a Saturday job in a bakery when I saw him coming in the opposite direction, carrying a bag of potatoes.

My heart pounded. I hadn't seen him for a couple of months and I had missed him so much. I went towards him, smiling nervously, to say hello. He looked up and saw me, and frowned. Then he spat at me, called me a whore and walked away.

I ran after him. 'What do you mean, Dad?' I called.

He turned, and said coldly, 'I hope you're not using our name – I want you to change your second name back to whore.'

I watched him walk away, dumbfounded by his outburst. What had I done to make him hate me so?

I didn't go to the job interview. I got the bus back to the home, went inside, got an unopened bottle of milk from the fridge and poured it all over the floor. I stood watching the milky white rivulets flow over the red carpet in the living room, while the duty social worker, Janice, said in a tired voice, 'Christine, don't do that.' She didn't bother to ask me what was wrong. I went outside and screamed till I was hoarse. And I threw the empty milk bottle with all my might against the path, smashing it into a million pieces

I was made to stay in my room all evening as a punishment. I didn't care, nothing could have touched me after my father's words. They burned into me, as I sat in my room, in the dark. Why did people who should have loved me, hate me? Was it me? Or something in me – something so dark and ugly that, even though I couldn't see it, it made my own family turn away from me. I came to the conclusion that it was badness. I was bad – evil. A monster outcast.

I took out my picture of Ian Brady. Would he have loved me? I wondered. Would he have understood what it feels like to be rejected and hated when all you long for is love? It comforted me in the darkness to think that perhaps he might.

From time to time, prospective foster parents came to the home to meet us. Although we were all teenagers, most of us hadn't given up on the idea of finding a family. And although most foster parents wanted small children, a few were prepared to take in teenagers.

I was already beginning to worry about what would happen to me when I left Greengage House. Kids had to leave as soon as they turned seventeen and then, if they had no family to go to, they all ended up in dingy bedsits and dead-end jobs – if they were lucky. The unlucky ones went into bed and breakfast accommodation and scraped by on benefits or ended up in Ladybird House, where you went if you couldn't cope with life.

One of the girls, Beth Mitchell, was always at the front of the queue for foster parents. A dark-haired girl who had been in care all her life, she used to smash cups and slash her forearms with the sharp edges until they bled. Beth would always be waiting at the door expectantly, if she knew foster parents were coming. She would run around making trays of tea, dressed up in her frilly-white second-hand best.

By this time I had become good friends with Jess, the young Afro-Caribbean girl, and we would hide up in our rooms if we knew prospective parents were coming. We didn't want to join in the circus, and we'd cringe at Beth's efforts to appear sweet and girly, especially as she'd swear like a trooper about the foster parents after they'd left, calling them 'cunts' for turning her down because of the ugly scar tissue on her arms.

Though I laughed at her, I wasn't really any different to Beth. I longed for a family that would genuinely want me – I think we all did. But I kept it a secret from Jess that I had filled in a form which was shown, with my photo, to all the prospective mothers and fathers.

One evening I was called down from my room and introduced to a couple from Slough, Mr and Mrs Walker. I shook hands and beamed at them gratefully and it was arranged that the following Sunday I would go to their home for tea and meet their daughter, Jennifer.

The following Sunday saw me dressed in my best clothes and waiting just as eagerly as Beth did for them to come and collect me. They were taking longer than I expected and my stomach was sick with nerves, so I went into Jess's room, sat on the edge of her bed, and told her how terrified I felt.

As I was talking, I felt the bed shuddering under me. I couldn't see her small face, because she was lying on her stomach and it was buried beneath the sheets. I wrenched back the covers angrily.

'Jess, for God's sake, what's so funny?'

I stopped. Great sobs were shuddering through her body.

'I don't want you to go to a family and leave me all on my own in this place.'

I didn't want to hurt her. But I had to go. I couldn't face a future in an anonymous, rundown bed and breakfast hotel. I wanted a family, and this was probably my last chance.

I left Jess's room and went downstairs. The Walkers had just arrived.

They drove me out to their house in Slough, chatting cheerfully all the way.

When we arrived at their pleasant semi they showed me the bedroom I would be having and then we sat down over some tea. Jennifer was not around after all, she'd been invited to a friend's house. But Mr and Mrs Walker said there would be plenty of time to meet her later, and they asked me about my interests and what job I hoped to get in the future. I liked them; they were easy to talk to and seemed kind and interested. We had a nice meal and they took me back to the home and said they'd see me soon. I felt it had gone well, although I tried to hide my excitement and relief from Jess, who stared at me with puffy eyes on my return.

Dave King told me the next day that the Walkers definitely wanted to take me. I told him I was happy to go to them. The paperwork would be done, he said, and they'd be back in a week's time for the handover meeting, after which I could go home with them.

I was so happy. They had seemed like genuinely nice people. Mrs Walker had been warm and sympathetic, and Mr Walker was jolly and friendly. Was this really going to be a new start for me? A last chance at real family life? I hoped Jennifer was as nice as her parents, and that she would accept me. My only worry was that I would have to face my adoptive parents at the handover meeting. As they were officially my parents still, they had to agree to me being fostered.

On the day of the meeting I once again dressed as nicely as I could. I had already packed all my belongings into carrier bags, and stripped my bed, ready for the next kid to use the room. I went into the meeting with Michael, glad that I had a new family to go to, but very nervous about seeing my adoptive parents. I hadn't set eyes on my Mum since she had attacked me in the bathroom. Both sets of parents were waiting, with the Head of Social Services, a man called Ian Milne.

My adoptive parents didn't look at me. They stared straight ahead. It hurt, but I thought, 'At least this will show them that someone else wants me, even if they never did.'

I looked over to the Walkers. They weren't looking at me either, which was strange. In fact they looked very uncomfortable. Almost immediately Mr Walker cleared his throat and stood up.

'Look, I think I should get this clear straight away,' he began nervously. 'We've been thinking this over, my wife and I, and we think, well, she's been in an institution for the past couple of years and she's picked up some very anti-social habits. We're worried that she may pass them on to our daughter. Over tea last weekend, she used the f-word five or six times. We have to think of her corrupting influence on our daughter, who will be going to university.'

I cringed inside. If you didn't say 'fuck' as every third word in Greengage House, the others would ostracise you. It was bad enough that I had a posh speaking voice. I'd soon learned to swear my head off if I wanted to fit in, but I'd tried to mind my fuck-yous when I went to the Walkers. A few must have slipped out without me realising. But it didn't mean anything. I would stop saying it in a nice home. I didn't even like saying it.

I opened my mouth to say all this, but Mrs Walker stood up and spoke in the soft voice that had sounded so maternal and had prompted so many daughter fantasies since I knew she had accepted me.

'We would like to go now,' she said.

They didn't look at me as they left. Ian Milne and Michael both looked ashen. Ian shot me a sympathetic glance, but I looked away. I was burning with shame. How had they found out about my criminal blood so quickly? That had to be it. They couldn't really have decided against taking me because of a few swear words. They had to have found out about my father.

Michael leaned forward to squeeze my hand and I pulled away. My adoptive father, Liam, stood up.

'We're too old for any responsibility and we can't have her,' he said coldly. 'And I want to make a point. She's using my name. She's not my blood daughter, and I don't want her using my name. We were decent enough to take her out of the orphanage. But I don't want, sorry to use this word, a "bastard" using my name.'

How could he be so cruel? Why had he turned on me like this? I wanted to stand up and say that it was my name too. They had given it to me, when they adopted me as their daughter. They couldn't just take it back. I had been so young when they took me, I had always thought of them as my real family. It hit me then like a huge lump of rock crashing down on my stomach, that they had never loved me, never accepted me. I had tried so very hard to make them love me, I had done everything I could. But I had failed.

I got up and walked slowly to the door, my legs wobbling underneath me and I walked up the stairs to my room as if I was somehow disconnected from my body. A few minutes later Michael came up and sat on the bed beside me. He reached for my hand, but I pulled away and sat silently looking out of the window. My packed carrier bags were on the floor at my feet. I felt Michael's hand on my back and dug my nails into the palms of my hands to try to block out the pain of his concern. He was sorry for me, but I knew it was what I deserved, because I was bad. They were respectable people and I was the one with bad blood who everyone wanted out of their homes. Maybe it was that evil was toxic, I wondered.

Eventually Michael got up and left me. I took out my photograph of Ian Brady.

'I wish you were alive,' I whispered. 'You wouldn't mind me because you're an evil monster and an outcast too. We could be each other's family. I won't mind you – if you don't mind me.'

I stared for hours at the photograph, believing I saw acceptance in the cold grey eyes that stared back at me.

Later Jess came and tapped on my door. 'I'm sorry it didn't work out for you, Chrissy,' she said as she fiddled with my favourite perfume, Eau Jeune, and sprayed it all over her neck and under her arms. 'But I'm glad you didn't go.' I managed a smile as I lay, rigid, on top of my bed, but inside I felt dead.

The next few weeks were bleak. Ian Milne came to see me and told me that he was appalled by the way the Walkers and my adoptive parents had behaved. He said the Walkers could have phoned to pull out, rather than doing it in front of me. He had no idea why they'd put me through that, and they certainly wouldn't be offered another chance to foster. He reassured me that the problem was theirs, not mine, but nothing and no one could lift the gloom that encased me. I no longer hoped for a family to come along and save me. I knew that I faced the same grim prospect as all the other loveless kids turfed out into the world from the care system.

When Christmas came that year, there was only me and one other kid, a boy called Christopher, left in the home. All the others had gone to relatives or temporary foster homes. We got no treats or special Christmas dinner; all we did was eat crisps. By Christmas Eve we were bored and restless as we sat with the social worker in charge, Don Partridge, in the staff-room. He was reading the paper and ignoring us, until he glanced at me over the top of his paper.

'Your friend's won the prison chess championship,' he said.

'What friend?' I said.

'The one you've got that old photograph of.'

Everyone in the Home knew, by this time, that I had a photo of Ian Brady pinned up in my room. Nothing could ever stay secret. I looked at Don in amazement.

'He's dead, he was hanged back in the sixties, wasn't he?'

'The death penalty had just been abolished, unfortunately,' he said. 'Brady just missed it. He was sent down for life. And in his case, life means life. He's quite infamous, you know. The Moors Killer, they call him. He's only in his late thirties now.'

My stomach lurched. I had become emotionally dependent on the photograph. It was safe to need Brady because I believed he was a ghost. A dead man can't reject you. Now here he was, not dead at all.

I went back upstairs to my room, re-reading the article in the paper on the way. Christopher followed me.

'It says here he's in solitary confinement,' I said as I sat down on my bed. 'How weird.'

'Why is it weird?' snorted Christopher.

'It's weird that he's alive,' I said. 'Because all this time I've been talking to the photo of a ghost. Now suddenly he's alive. And what's more, he's not far from here, in Wormwood Scrubs.'

'You're just mad,' Christopher said. 'Anyway, I'm probably going to prison myself, I'm in court next week for burglary and I don't suppose my mum will even bother showing up.'

'Well, don't worry, silly, I'll come,' I said. 'And I'll write to you if you do go down. I'd better write to him as well.'

'To say what?'

'I should thank him, shouldn't I? I would have slashed my wrists, like Beth, after the Walkers, if it hadn't been for him. He saved my life Christopher. I owe him everything.'

'He's insane anyway,' said Christopher. 'Locked into a room all on his own waiting to die. And serve him right. He'll just think you're a nutter.'

Christopher went off to his own room and I sat down to write a letter to the man I had believed was dead. I told him I had been rejected by two mothers, just as he had. I said, 'Have you thought about what made you commit your crimes? And that you may not be truly evil? Was it a mistake?'

After Christmas I put my letter in the post tray. Would he reply? I wasn't even sure whether I wanted him to or not.

It was only years later that I discovered that my letter had never been sent. The secretary had spotted the address and had informed Dave King. The staff had agreed that it would be unthinkable for them to allow me to write to a serial killer. They had quietly thrown my letter away, and hoped I would forget about it. In fact I thought of little else. Had he got my letter? Why hadn't he replied? Or had he known about me already?

I decided to go and see Wormwood Scrubs, the prison where he was held in the highest security wing. I knew the staff wouldn't agree to me going, so I planned to sneak out at night, when no one would notice. The following evening, when everyone had gone to bed, I tiptoed to the end of the girls' corridor. The window there was quite heavy and made a creaking noise as you opened it. I pushed it open slowly, so as not to wake anyone, then heaved myself up through it, onto the outside windowsill, and along the sloping roof where I jumped to the ground. As I landed I hurt my ankles and smacked forward onto my hands, cutting one of them on some jagged glass from a broken bottle of cider in the grass. I ran up the lane until I was a safe distance from the building and then checked my hand. Blood was pouring from an inch-long cut in the palm of my hand and I started to feel faint at the sight of it. I pressed the cut against my jeans as I ran along the dark tree-lined lane and to the main road. When I got to the main road, I started walking, and stuck my thumb out. It was not long before a white Volvo stopped.

'You shouldn't be hitching lifts, especially not at half-past one in the morning,' the driver said.

I got into the front seat beside him. He said he was going to Shepherds Bush and that it was near enough. I could walk the rest of the way. The driver introduced himself as Tony, a bookie, and said he had just finished work. I told him I lived up in White City and was late home because I had stayed at my friend's house too long. When we got to Shepherds Bush, he decided to take me all the way to White City.

'Du Cane Road,' I told him. 'That's where I live.'

'Oh, right near Wormwood Scrubs. Handy if you're a naughty girl,' he joked. He pulled over and began leering at me. I saw he had undone his flies.

'I'll pay you if you suck it,' he said.

I jumped out of the car and ran.

Wormwood Scrubs turned out to be a huge building, like a castle, with white-painted turrets, a twenty-foot high wall around it and a vast wooden gate at the front. On top of the wall there was barbed wire.

I walked up to the gate. There was a bell on the side. I pushed it and a uniformed guard suddenly appeared from a side door.

'Which wing is Ian Brady in?' I asked.

He looked taken aback. 'How old are you?' he asked.

'It's a school project,' I said. 'I know it's late, but my Dad's round there in the car, waiting. I was passing, so I thought I'd ask.'

'D-Wing,' he snapped then he went back through the door and closed it behind him.

I pressed the buzzer again. He appeared, looking extremely annoyed.

'Which wing is D-Wing?' I asked.

'The furthest on the right. Now go home.'

He disappeared and I walked round the wall to the right, looking up at the furthest wing. So that's where he was, D-Wing, all alone, locked up, way up in one of those turrets like the man in the mask.

I made my way around to the side of the prison, and stood right underneath the wing, on a piece of wasteland. I must have stood there for hours. Here was a person who would never leave me as everyone else had done. He was locked up, so he could not run and I would never meet him. And that made him safe. In my unhappy, desperately lonely, fourteen-year-old mind this man who had wrecked the lives of so many people was, to me, a safe haven.

6

James

A few weeks later a new helper arrived at the home. His name was James Stratford-Barret and he was a student at Oxford who was doing a summer attachment as part of his studies. I first set eyes on him standing in reception, his dark gold hair illuminated by a sudden shaft of summer sun coming from the open office door.

He was impossibly suave and elegant, the way I imagined an oil millionaire might look. He had a Roman nose, haughty blue eyes and a pale, thin-lipped mouth. He was so genteel in his bearing that he was almost feminine. Later I learned he had been abandoned by his mother aged five and sent to boarding school. So, he was left by his mother, I remember thinking excitedly – we have exactly the same scars.

James came from a world I had only read about – a world of privilege and money. But he wasn't in the least stuck-up, he was funny and kind and I soon developed a huge crush on him. He made me feel that for the first time someone was genuinely interested in me and liked me. He saw that I was bright and gave me books to read, classics like Jean Genet and Proust which I'd read avidly, looking forward to discussing them with him afterwards.

I was still only fifteen, but James made it clear he was keen on me, and I was flattered and excited. One day he kissed me, in a poppy field in Abinger Hammer on a hot summer day. The attention and affection James gave me was like water in a desert. Later he took me to his family home, which was nearby in Shere and was called Coverdale.

His father was very senior in the army and they lived in a mansion, with oil paintings in the hallway and family silver everywhere. I wandered around his home and the grounds in raptures. The grounds were extensive and tree filled. I dreamed of marrying him and living with him in that lovely country pile.

Inevitably James had to leave the home, as he was only on a short-term work placement. I knew he would have to go, but I hoped we could still find a way to be together. I imagined a tender parting, with James promising to come back for me. But one day I looked out of an upstairs window to see James loading his things into his blue Spider sports car. He was going, without warning and without saying goodbye. He looked up at me and waved, but I couldn't move. The sky was grey and it looked as if it was about to rain, and my heart was breaking. Even though I knew he had to go back to university I was convinced he was leaving me as he had found out about my father and it had put him off me. Once again I felt abandoned, and desperately alone, and blamed myself. I knew it was my fault James had left me. I was a bad and unlovable girl.

Back in my room I lay on my bed and sobbed, then took out my picture of Ian Brady. 'You won't leave me, will you,' I whispered. 'You can't go anywhere, and neither can I. Both of us are trapped.' Somehow, believing that we were in the same situation brought me a shred of comfort. I didn't know whether I would ever hear from James again, but a couple of weeks after he left the house phone went and it was him, asking to speak to me. He said he was sorry that he had left so suddenly, but that he hated saying goodbyes. He chatted about what he was doing at university, and asked me how I was. I missed him terribly and longed for him to come back. But I couldn't say so. I knew that he had moved on. He was wrapped up in his university life, and I was left behind.

After he had said a breezy goodbye, with a vague promise to see me soon, I felt so low that I didn't want to live any more. No one cared about me, or where I might end up. A few days after James's call, I took some paracetamol from the medicine box in the kitchen while everyone else was watching TV. The medicine box wasn't locked; it was always just left for us kids to help ourselves to what we needed. So, pills in hand, I got myself a bowl of ice-cream from the big tub in the fridge and went up to my room, where I swallowed about fifteen of them, with the ice-cream.

I wanted to die, but when I'd taken them I felt shocked by what I'd done, and frightened of dying painfully. I ran out of my room and found Oliver in the corridor. He didn't seem too worried when I said I'd taken an overdose, but he went and got Cora, and together they took me to the local hospital, which fortunately happened to be across the road.

The hospital staff were kind and efficient. I was by no means the first Greengage House resident to be taken in after a suicide attempt; they were used to the sad kids who lived over the road and they swung into action. I was put on a trolley while my stomach was pumped. It was a foul business. My head was put in a clamp and three nurses held me down while a thick rubber hose was passed down my throat to my stomach. Water was poured through it, so that the contents of my stomach – my dinner of spaghetti bolognese as well as the pills – was forced back up.

After this frightening and painful procedure I was kept in for a few hours and then sent back across the road. No one asked me why I'd done it, or suggested any counselling or psychiatric help. Dave King came to talk to me after I got back, but there was very little he could do. I still felt suicidal; my only regret was that I hadn't succeeded.

Suicide attempts were so common in Greengage House that no one behaved as though it was a big deal. Each time someone tried, Jess would cry. Beth, who self-harmed on a daily basis, would say, 'You should slash your arms with a razor like I do,' and Oliver would look philosophical and discuss the ins and outs of dying and the possible reality of a better afterlife than this unimpressive dimension.

There were blood stains all over the dirty beige carpets in the hallway, left by the kids who favoured wrist slashing, though the most popular method was still overdosing. At the time 'Suicide is Painless', the theme tune from Mash, was all over the place and every time we heard it on the radio we'd all go quiet – though none of us ever said it, we all knew it was our song.

At school my mock O levels were looming, but I didn't really care. I had passed my English and maths O levels early, without much effort, and if I'd worked hard I could have done very well. But I had long since given up trying to study when all the other kids around me weren't even bothering to go to school.

Despite doing little work, I managed to pass my mocks, and even to get some good grades, the February after I turned sixteen. But it didn't seem to matter. Who was there to care whether I did well or not? There was certainly no adult concerned with my welfare or future. And while I had become closer to the other kids in the home, most of them had no interest in education. It was a big enough challenge just getting through the next week without attempting to top themselves.

The other kids were the nearest I had to a family. We did have some fun times. We used to wake up in the night and sneak out for midnight walks. We would climb over the roof, which wasn't very high, jump down and head for the local graveyard, where we'd sit and chat amongst the graves. Oliver would terrify everybody by pretending to be a dead body coming out of one of the graves and we'd take turns to tell each other scary stories. Oliver said jokingly one night that we were like the Famous Five, and we all laughed. After that we'd call ourselves the Famous Five, or the Secret Seven, depending on how many of us there were. There was something both sad and funny about the idea of us tough-nut care kids identifying with Enid Blyton's jolly, old-fashioned characters.

There was a great sense of freedom and adventure about these midnight rambles. We felt in charge, no one was telling us what to do and we often stayed out for most of the night, laughing and playing around. I still liked Oliver, but I was in love with James and didn't want to go out with anyone else. So when Oliver asked me I said no – though we did share a kiss one night. It was nice, slow and sensual, like the first sliver of strawberry ice cream on a hot summer day. I loved him dearly, but I knew I couldn't go out with him or marry him because I wanted stability and he was in as much of a hole as I was.

One night my old friend Penny and I went to a concert by a group called the Satellites and met a boy called Barney. He was very good-looking, with dark hair and piercing blue eyes, and he asked me out. Barney was tough yet very protective of me, which I loved, and he took me home to meet his Mum, Claire. She was very kind and warm towards me, and going to his house became one of the main attractions of going out with Barney.

When Oliver realised I liked someone else he announced that he was going to fight him over me. And when Barney heard that Oliver was after him, he came round one after-noon to confront him. Instead of squaring up to Barney, Oliver suddenly grabbed me and dived into his room, where he barricaded all the furniture in front of the door. I started crying, I didn't want anyone fighting over me, but I didn't want to be a hostage either. I was scared of Oliver's smelly pet hamster, which was running wild around the room. He picked it up and kept thrusting it into my face, which made me scream. But I was even more scared when he produced a knife.

Dave King stood outside the door and said, 'Christine, you don't have to let them fight over you. You don't have to agree to this.'

Somehow I managed to pull myself together. It hadn't occurred to me until then that I might be able to stop it. I started talking to Oliver, telling him that he didn't have to fight, that I cared about him and was his friend. Oliver said, 'I know if I fight him I'll lose, 'cos he's better than me. Then you'll go off with him and I'll lose you and I can't take that, Chris. I'd rather we died together now. You're all I've got in the world. All I've ever had.'

It was terrifying. We were there for four hours and for most of that time I thought that Oliver might use the knife to kill me at any moment. All I could do was to keep talking, reasoning with Oliver and telling him not to do it. Oliver paced up and down, the knife in his hand the whole time, while Dave King sat on the floor outside the room and never left us.

Eventually, cold, hungry and fed-up, Oliver agreed to let me go. I came out, crying with relief, and Dave hugged me, before taking Oliver off to his office.

The incident shook me badly. I had trusted Oliver, but he had turned on me and really frightened me. I wasn't really in love with Barney, in fact I cared more for Oliver, but I went on seeing Barney for a while. It was almost as if I felt I had to, after causing such a commotion. But Barney was so gorgeous that every girl who met him wanted him and I wasn't secure enough to handle that, so I broke it off, though I stayed friends with him, and with his mum, who remains a friend to this day.

Though the Oliver-Barney fight was averted, there were often fights between the boys. One of the worst happened when Edward Goodman split with his girlfriend. He was distraught and I could see he was about to lose it. It was a Sunday and my turn to cook, and I'd I made roast chicken dinner for everyone. Edward walked over to the oven and pulled the chickens out, saying I'd cooked them all wrong. He threw the hot pan, with the chickens on it, at me, scaring me so much that I screamed and ran out into the street, where I wandered around crying and afraid to go back.

When I did return and go up to the girls' corridor I found Dave King with blood pouring from his nose, and Edward standing behind him, panting.

It seemed Edward had attacked Oliver, and then turned on Dave, who was trying to calm things down. I was terrified I'd be next. I started talking to Edward, saying, 'Come on, let's get some tea and see what's on telly.' I was very scared, but I tried to sound as though it was just a normal evening. We were still standing in the girls' corridor when the police arrived, sirens blaring. One of the other members of staff had called them. Three burly officers came up and led Edward out, and as he passed me he said, 'I'm out of here. I'm going to prison now. I was going that way anyway'.

That night, in bed, I cried for Edward. He was a nice boy, kind and always ready for a laugh. He had been seventeen and due to leave Greengage House soon. He faced the same grim future as all the kids – a dingy bedsit and a meaningless job, or benefits. Maybe he couldn't face that, I thought. Maybe he felt he'd rather go out in his own way than wait until he had to leave, and feel chucked out of the only place he'd ever belonged.

Another temporary helper arrived at the home, a blonde student named Jan, who studied at the local university. She seemed to take an interest in me and would sit and chat. I was never sure whether she genuinely liked me, but I wanted her to, and tried to please her. So when she told me that education didn't really matter, and not to bother to go in and take my O levels if I didn't fancy it, I believed her. She made dropping out sound glamorous, so instead of going to school and taking my exams I stayed in bed all day long, sleeping and feeling as if doing that would somehow make me beautiful and sophisticated, like Jan, and bring James back to me.

It was an odd thing for someone who was studying to discourage me from doing the same, but looking back I think

Jan had double standards. She thought of us as 'care kids' who didn't matter and wouldn't really amount to anything.

Later I was to deeply regret not taking my exams, but at the time I was so easily influenced by anyone who took even the slightest interest in me, that I lost any ability to make decisions of my own. If I'd thought about it I'd have seen that, while preaching to me about the benefits of ignoring education, Jan was busy getting her Masters degree.

At sixteen and with only the two 'O' levels I'd taken a year early, when I was still working hard, to my name, I left school and was expected to find a job. Most of the other girls I'd been at school with were taking A levels and going on to university, but I had blown my chances and was sent down to the local job centre. No one was remotely interested in what I liked or wanted, or what my talents were. They just wanted to shove me into the first available job. So when the owner of a computer-repair business came to the Job Centre to look for recruits, I was sent in for an interview. He wanted someone with nine O levels, but I impressed him with my knowledge of physics – a subject I had been good at – and he gave me the job of trainee computer repairer.

I hated it. I had to spend from nine to five each day in a classroom full of men, poring over computers and manuals or studying complex diagrams on the blackboard. I wasn't even interested in computers; I still wanted to be a psychiatrist. And I felt so lonely, sitting in the room with a lot of computer nerds, learning how to build a computer from scratch. The others, mostly very brainy young Asian men, were nice to me, but it just wasn't a situation I could be happy in.

It was Jan who told me to jack the job in, and this time I knew she was right. I just couldn't do it. So after a few weeks I walked out and Jan got me a job in McDonalds, frying donuts. Within a couple of weeks I was feeling desperate. The future stretched ahead of me like a great black hole of pain. Not only was I in a dead-end job, but I was soon going to have to leave Greengage House. My seventeenth birthday was approaching and I would be offered the same grim bed and breakfast option as all those who'd gone before me. The thought was unbearable. I would have to leave the few friends I had and go out into the world with nothing and no one, and with no prospect of making something of my life.

Already Cora had disappeared, only to reappear months later with her wrists bandaged, and disappear again the same day. Later I heard she had become a prostitute. Oliver had already gone into a bed and breakfast hostel in a grim part of London – dispatched early after the incident with the knife. I went to see him a few times and found him sad and lonely. I lay in his single bed with him and cuddled him for a while and felt at a loss as to what to do for him. He seemed lost and said he was going to rob a bank and buy himself a house opposite Greengage House. Like many of the others who had left, he was missing the place that had become our home.

Years later I read about him in the paper. Just as he planned, he had robbed a bank, but instead of a house he'd got a long prison sentence.

Others in Greengage House fared no better. All struggled against poverty, some went to prison, others ended up as prostitutes. Seeing what happened to my friends I felt life wasn't worth living. Why struggle on?

I took another overdose, this time a bigger one. Thirty paracetamol and ten sleeping pills I had nicked from the bedside cabinet in the room where the duty care workers slept overnight. I was found when I was unconscious and taken to hospital, where once again my stomach was pumped. This time I was kept in overnight, and when I got back to the home, Dave King called me into his office for a chat.

He told me he wanted to approach my adoptive parents to see whether they would have me back for a while. 'I know things have gone wrong in the past,' he said. 'But you're older now, a bit of time has gone by and I think they might agree to give you a home while you find your feet. I know how much pain you're in and I think you need to be back with them, for your own sake.'

He was right. Although I had been so angry and hurt after the meeting with the Walkers, when my adoptive parents disowned me, three years had passed and now I didn't feel angry, I just missed them. And I felt terrified of going out into the world with no one and nothing. Even a rough time with them would be better than being on my own. But I didn't think they would accept me.

Dave said he'd talk to them and let me know, and a few days later he told me that they had agreed to have me back. Perhaps hearing that I had been suicidal had stirred their consciences. I was stunned, and pleased too. I wasn't sure what kind of reception I'd get, but at least I had somewhere to go that wasn't full of down and outs.

So it was that one day, soon after my seventeenth birthday in November, I packed my possessions into plastic bags and said goodbye to my closest remaining friends – Jess, Beth and Christopher. Jess had got into Black Power by this time and liked going round saying all white people were devils, but we were still friends.

Dave King took me on the half-hour drive back to my adoptive parents' house. As the car drew up I felt sick with nerves. I had missed them, and wanted to see them, but I was so afraid of rejection.

My mother opened the door. She said hello, and told me to take my things in and up to my old room, while she talked to Dave. I said goodbye to him and climbed the stairs to the room I had once shared with Nanna.

Very little in the house had changed. It was still dark and all the heavy old furniture was still there. Nicky was at work – something in computers – and my father was out, so there was no one else in the house. It felt so strange to be back. Everything was familiar, and yet I didn't feel it was my home any more.

After Dave had left I went down to see Mum in the kitchen. 'How are you?' I asked. 'Can I do anything to help?' She looked at me. 'No, you can't,' she said. 'Just stay out of our way'.

My heart sank. Nothing had changed. She still didn't want me. I was just here because Dave had persuaded them, not because they cared about me. I went back up to my room, sat on the bed and wept. After I dried my eyes I pulled a gold box out of my carrier bag. Inside was my black and white photo of Brady. I stared at it. I could cope, I told myself. I was not alone. He was with me.

Later in the day my mother called me down to the kitchen, where she sat me at the table and produced an exercise book and a pen.

'If you're going to live here there are going to have to be rules,' she said. 'If you break them, you will go – do you understand?'

I nodded.

She went on to dictate a list of rules for me to write out in the book. These included no make up, no improper clothing –

such as short skirts – and no friends coming to the house. She ordered me to the bathroom to wipe off the dark eye make-up I had been wearing for the past year, and which I felt was part of who I was. Then she showed me the outfits she had bought which she felt were suitable for me. There were four of them, all dresses, all in dark colours like navy and green and all with high necks and falling below the knee.

I was also told to keep my hair tied back or cut it, so soon after I arrived I went and had it styled into a short bob, like Purdey, the glamorous character in the Avengers. I hoped it would please my mother, but nothing I did ever really pleased her. My father, when he came home, seemed uninterested in me. He didn't seem to care whether I was there or not. He was quieter than he had been, he seldom sang and he spent less time in front of the mirrors. He seemed to have aged, and I felt that I just wasn't part of his life any more.

Soon after I arrived I got a job as a trainee book-keeper for a small local firm. It was a dull job in a dull firm, but I took it to make my mother happy. She made it clear that I was never going to amount to anything and should be grateful for any job, however menial.

For the next few months I lived through the same monotonous daily routine. I got up and put on one of my prim dresses, went to work on the bus and did my dull job without speaking to anyone. I felt so inferior to everyone else that when anyone spoke to me I would blush and stammer and in the end they all avoided me. At the end of the day I would get the bus home and spend the evening alone in my room, ignored by the rest of the family. They would pass me on the stairs in silence and my parents still locked the downstairs doors when they went out, so that the only room I could go into was the kitchen.

Although I handed over forty pounds a week for my keep – which was most of my wage – I was now expected to shop and cook for myself. I hadn't learned to cook much in Greengage House apart from the Sunday roast, so I lived off pre-packed pies, and microwave boxed dinners, and I ate my meals alone, before going back upstairs. My parents ate theirs in front of the television in the front room and made it clear that they didn't want me around. Nicky was out a lot, so I barely saw him.

Occasionally I managed to sneak out and see Penny. On one of these visits, I confided in her that I thought Ian Brady might be my father. We'd been at her mother's Cointreau again, and bolstered by the alcohol Penny rang up Wormwood Scrubs and said she was a relative of Brady's and wanted to know how he was. The man who answered was very nice, and said he had just given Brady his tea. Penny put the phone down and fell about laughing and I did too, both of us tipsy and giggly. I felt very strange. Until then Brady had been an almost fictional character, but Penny's call had confirmed that he was a real person.

Visits like this one to Penny's were rare. Mostly I crept around the house like a mouse, seeing and speaking to no one. Lodging with a family of strangers might have been less lonely. At least someone might have spoken to me.

In my lonely bedroom I missed Nanna and wished that I was dead too. I had no hope for the future, no sense of where I might go or what I might do. My one plan for the future was not to be in it. To die. I thought about going and throwing myself off a building, but I was too scared. I often took mini-overdoses, swallowing more paracetamol than I knew was safe, hoping that somehow I would die in my sleep or that the pills would have a cumulative effect and eventually kill me. I regularly swallowed ten or more pills, but all that happened was I slept it off and woke groggy.

It was during this time that I began writing to Ian Brady more regularly. It was a way of being the real me – the one at Greengage House, the one my mother had wanted me to leave behind when I came back to her house. The one she wanted to blot out forever. I would sit in my room and compose letters to him about my life and thoughts, asking him about his life. But the letters were always returned with a note from the prison governor saying, 'I am afraid it is not possible for you to correspond with this inmate, as you did not know him prior to his sentencing.'

I missed Greengage House terribly – the friends, the freedom of our midnight rambles, even the chaos and terrible food. There had been life there, and we had been, in our odd, mixed-up, crazy way, a family. Writing to Brady was a way of connecting to Greengage House, because I had written to him there. It linked me to a life I had left. And it was safe, because I was never going to have an answer. I didn't trust real people, but he wasn't real, he was someone I could make into anything I chose.

This grim existence went on until I was eighteen and it might have gone on for a lot longer, had I not provoked my mother and been thrown out of the house for a second time.

My offence was similar to the one that got me put back into care at thirteen. I was so tired of looking plain and old-fashioned when the other girls at work dressed up and had fun. So I took a chance and put on some mascara. It wasn't a lot – in fact so little that I thought you could barely spot it. Since I didn't see much of my mother I hoped she wouldn't notice. But she did, and she couldn't have been angrier if I had dyed my hair pink and gone to work in a G-string.

She said nothing in the kitchen, when I was having breakfast. But I came home to find the door locked. I had no key, and when I rang the bell she stuck her head out of the upstairs window and shouted, 'You're not *my* daughter.'

I rang Michael Briggs, the care worker from the home, from the phone box on the corner. He was busy, so it was dark and I had to wait several hours for him to fetch me. When he finally arrived it was eleven o'clock at night and I was sitting on the corner, shivering with cold, my scarf pulled up round my mouth. He looked upset as he opened the car door.

'Imagine just chucking someone out in the street knowing they've no money and nowhere to go. And you're a bloody kid. It's not as if you're any trouble – you wouldn't say boo to a goose.'

I wanted to cry at his kindness but I did not. I almost hated him for his love. It hurt me. I was growing used to the ice – it had its own odd comforts.

He took me back to Greengage House, but the next day I was told I couldn't stay, and a couple of days later Michael took me to a bed and breakfast hotel. He had been to collect my things from my mother, who had dumped them in plastic bags again, and he helped me carry them up the dark, smelly staircase to my room.

It was everything I had dreaded and feared. A small, grubby room with damp patches on the faded wallpaper, a filthy patterned carpet and a bed with an ancient counterpane. There was a small table, a chair and a battered wardrobe. Michael gave me a hug, said he'd check on me in a few weeks, wished me luck and left. I sat in the chair and looked out of the dirty window at the street outside. There were people hurrying along the pavement, coats wrapped around them against the cold. I imagined them going home to warm houses and loving families.

That night, after making myself a cup of soup for supper, I took out my small, frayed black and white photo of Ian Brady and wrote to him. I told him I wanted to die, and asked him if he felt the same way.

7

Becoming a Spy

The thing I dreaded most had happened. I was living in a miserable, tatty bed and breakfast hostel alongside drug addicts and down and outs. Most of the people I passed on the stairs terrified me. And at night I lay in bed listening to sobbing, shouting and loud music coming from the other rooms.

Somehow I managed to stay in my job. Awful as it was, at least it gave my day purpose and earned me some money. I threw the ugly dresses my mother had forced me to wear in the bin and bought myself a few pretty clothes. Then I sat and cried, because I had no one to show them to and nowhere to wear them.

It was James Stratford-Barret who helped me escape. Someone at Greengage House had told him where I was and he turned up at the hostel one evening, looked around and said, 'Don't worry, I'm going to help you, Christine.' He took me out for a meal and told me he knew of a job that would suit me, and said he would help me find a nicer place to live. I felt he was my knight in shining armour.

He looked wonderful and smelled of lavender aftershave. Being with him again felt so good. I still dreamed of marrying him and hoped he might want to rekindle our relationship. I wondered if that was why he had come to see me, but it was only much later that I understood the true reason. James told me he was now working for MI6 and that two ex-colleagues of his had started their own security agency and were looking for a recruit to train in surveillance and investigative work. They wanted a graduate and had put an ad in *The Times*, he said, but he promised to put in a word for me and thought I'd be just right for it.

I thought it all sounded very glamorous, and I was excited at the possibility of moving up in the world. Two days later I turned up for my interview with James's friends, Rob and Gary. We chatted for half an hour and they asked me if I felt I could pose as another person. I said I loved the idea. I didn't tell them I'd have preferred to be anyone but myself. They promised to be in touch and the following day Rob rang to say I'd got the job, and beaten fifty other applicants.

At the time I didn't know why they had chosen me, I was just thrilled. But the truth was that I was an ideal candidate for this kind of work. I had no family ties, I was bright and quick, and people were less likely to suspect a pretty girl of being a spy.

Unaware of this, I was thrilled to be joining the world of espionage and undercover operations, though I had no idea what my new job would really involve. I chucked in the book-keeping job, and on the promise of my new improved wages James helped me find a flat in Shepherd Market, close to my new office. It was tiny – just one small bedroom, but I loved it and I spent the first few days there painting it all in fresh, clean colours.

I loved being around James again. I knew he wanted to sleep with me, but I had decided that I wouldn't make love with him until he asked me to live with him. And he didn't. I could see that although he cared about me, he had his own life and I wasn't part of it. Not that it was easy to let go of my dream of marrying him, not for a while, anyway. He came to see me every now and then, and I hoped every time that he would burst in and announce that he couldn't live without me. But he never did.

My new job soon took up most of my time. It wasn't a nine to five job: I had to work all kinds of crazy hours, and I was glad, because it beat being at home on my own. Rob and Gary's company organised investigative and surveillance operations both in Britain and abroad. In other words they were spies, who did a whole range of jobs for both private and government organisations.

Overseas they hired former army intelligence men to work on security operations helping gold fields, diamond mines and oil refineries fight terrorism and piracy. Their contracts included work in 'sensitive' zones such as Sudan, Albania, Angola and South Africa. It was highly dangerous and secretive work.

I wasn't involved in that side of things; I did the so-called domestic work. This could include anything from following someone, to checking out suspected insurance frauds or going undercover. It was Rob who trained me, and he taught me how to follow someone without losing them or being seen, how to carry out due diligence and how to work undercover. He showed me how to think my way into a situation, choosing the most effective approach and getting inside high security buildings.

Over the next couple of years I posed as cleaners, office workers, glamorous, seductive party girls and a host of other characters. I spent long hours looking through documents, tracking down and following all kinds of suspicious characters. I planted bugs, uncovered frauds and cornered spies. But despite the glamorous image, it was a lot more mundane than James Bond. It's not really very exciting, waiting around for hours or even days for someone to turn up, or working as a cleaner in order to plant a listening device in someone's office.

Still, I found I had a real aptitude for the work. I had a kind of sixth sense that often told me what to do to get the result we needed. And I found I could lose myself in it, and I loved being someone else, even when it involved danger, which it often did. That was when I came to worry about why James had picked me out for the job – was it because no one would care, or even notice, if I went missing or was bumped off by someone who didn't like what I was doing? And that was always a very real possibility. It hurt, knowing that James may not care about me. But then he was at risk himself. Feeling close to him, I threw myself into the work.

Given the risks I took and the high level investigations I cracked I was paid peanuts. But the job gave me something more than just money – it made me realise I had ability. I was good at the work, very good, and I was soon being trusted with the most sensitive jobs. At last I had something to feel good about. Sometimes I was loaned out to other agencies for a specific job, and I soon gained a strong reputation in the closed world of ex-army intelligence agencies in London, so that when they came back they would request me for the next job. Inevitably, though, this highly charged and often dangerous work began to take its toll. I was still a teenager – only nineteen, and yet I came very close to being killed several times.

On one occasion we were watching a Russian exile. I didn't even know who for – our side or theirs – but we had been tailing him for days and I was given a night duty, pairing up to follow him with an ex-army guy called Martin, whom I liked. We tailed the Russian, a tall blond man, from his exclusive apartment in Park Lane towards Buckingham Palace. Martin and I were together, but had walkie-talkies to keep in touch if we had to separate. Suddenly the Russian turned off the road and headed across the park near the palace. Martin hailed a black cab to go round the outer ring of the park and catch him on the other side. He called me to go with him, but I was afraid we'd lose him and headed into the park after him. With hindsight it was a crazy thing to do, but I always threw myself into each job. I was naturally brave, but I also put no value on myself or my life.

It was dark in the park and I could see nothing, especially as we were going into a wooded area. I stopped, straining my eyes to spot him, slightly out of breath, when he lunged at me from behind with his long umbrella. I thought he was going to kill me, as umbrellas with poisoned tips are a Russian speciality. He stuck it into my back, hard, and I fell to the ground. Rob had made sure I knew how to handle myself by sending me to a friend of his who was a black belt in Tyger karate. But the Russian was far heavier than me and as I lay groaning he threw himself on top of me and put the umbrella across my throat, nearly choking me. 'Who are you with?' he rasped. I told him I worked for a private security firm and I had no idea who we had been hired by and he whacked me again with his clenched fist and ran off into the dark woodland beside the Palace.

I radioed Martin, who spotted him on the other side of the park, but later lost him after he left a cocktail bar in Piccadilly. Our bosses weren't pleased, but I was just grateful to be alive.

On another occasion I was given the job of setting up a sting on two men who had stolen de-bugging machines from their employer. I was supposed to be a girl who was opening a business and wanted them to supply me with machines. But my bosses made a mistake – the two men hadn't yet advertised their machines and they immediately asked me how I knew about them. They questioned me for some time, and then drove me to waste land and beat me up. I needed fifteen stitches in my nose and face and had black eyes. That was probably when I came closest to giving up the job – I was sorely tempted to walk out. But I didn't know what else I could do, and there were many aspects of the job that I loved, so I carried on, vowing to be more careful in the future.

Sometimes I got to play a glamorous woman and I loved that. I was never comfortable dressing up as myself, but if I could play someone else I loved wearing beautiful evening dresses. I wore designers like Katherine Hamnett and Versace, jewellery by De Beers, glossy high heel Manolos and gold and silver strappy Gina sandals, all paid for by my bosses as necessary expenses of the job. Rob told me to get the best underwear. I chose La Perla, jewel coloured and light as a feather, as it made the beautiful clothes hang right.

Sometimes I felt dirty being a spy. Poking and prying into other people's business wasn't the nicest of professions. But I distanced myself from the grubbier side of my work by using a fake identity. In my work I was called Faith. Faith wore different clothes and makeup to me. I liked to look natural, while Faith wore bold reds, black smoky eyes and chocolate and vanilla scent. As Faith I could flirt and be seductive, something I would never have done as myself. And while I was being Faith I felt I kept the real me clean. It was Faith who was the spy, I told myself – not me.

On one occasion I had to 'befriend' a South African film-maker. He was making a sensitive political film and we were hired by a foreign politician who wanted to know whether his dirty dealings were going to be exposed in the film. My instructions were to get myself invited back to the film-maker's house and see what I could find out.

I wore a short black sequinned Katharine Hamnett dress and burgundy thigh-high leather boots, my blonde hair shiny and hanging loose down my back and went to the club where the film-maker was partying. He soon invited me back to his gorgeous rented mansion, where we laughed and joked as we shared a few ice-cold cocktails, and I told him I'd love to see him again, but never slept with a man on the first date. He was fine with that, he showed me to a spare room and kissed me goodnight.

As soon as he was asleep and I could hear him snoring from the master bedroom across the hallway, I crept downstairs and started to rifle through his drawers, looking for phone bills with lists of the calls he had made, and paperwork relating to the film. Then I turned on his computer and although I didn't have his passwords, I knew enough about hacking to get at his data.

I was slipping back upstairs when I bumped into him, coming downstairs. I gasped: I could barely see his face in the darkness, but could make out what looked like a silver German Luger pistol in his hand. My heart raced and I felt fear shoot through me but he laughed and said, 'I thought you were a burglar'. I told him I had been thirsty and had just been to the kitchen for a drink, and thankfully he believed me. I breathed a sigh of relief and wound my arms around his neck seductively. Later on that night, Faith, in her red lace La Perla underwear and her sexy vanilla and chocolate scent made passionate love to him.

The next morning I went home and he rang me several times, asking me out. I had given him the number of my dummy mobile, so I was able to avoid his calls. I wasn't about to risk going back when I knew he had a gun. In any case, I had got enough information to satisfy our politician client.

The most frightening job of all was when I was investigating an insurance scam. A large family were supposedly faking deaths and claiming on the insurance, and I was sent round to see the wife and try to get her to talk. My brief was to get an idea how they were doing it. From the start I had a bad feeling about the job, so I asked for some of our toughest ex-SAS guys to back me up. They waited outside while I went into the huge mansion where the family lived. After a few minutes of chatting to the wife, I excused myself to go to the loo. I decided to leave – something about this job felt really wrong. But as I went towards the front door several men rushed in, all brandishing machetes. They held me down, screaming, 'Who are you? Are you police?' I was screaming too, but thankfully the ex-SAS guys backing me up kicked the door in and grabbed the ringleader. The others backed off, and we got away. Afterwards our boss, Rob, said they were linked with the Triads and it was a Triad gang that had rushed in to attack me. Rob hadn't felt he needed to share that information with me before I went on the job. After that I suffered from panic attacks for several months. I had come very, very close to being hacked to pieces with machetes.

Once I was back on my feet, with my own little flat, I decided to contact Penny again. I hadn't seen her for a while and missed her. So I called her and we met for a drink. She was at college, studying biochemistry, and when I told her what I was doing she was quite upset. As schoolgirls we had both been into left-wing politics and very anti-establishment, though Penny was far more into it than I was. We'd read Karl Marx and gone to a few left-wing rallies and Ban-the-Bomb meetings. So she couldn't believe I'd taken a job that meant working for government agencies. 'It's like Ronnie Biggs becoming a police officer,' she said.

She asked me whether I had got over the idea that Ian Brady was my father. I said I hadn't; I was still writing to him, every now and then.

'You should hate him,' she said. 'He's not your father.'

She was right on both counts. But I couldn't see it. I knew, deep down, that he probably wasn't my father. But I clung to the idea, unwilling to let it go. I was still full of unresolved grief for my adoptive father and for the 'family' I'd found at Greengage House, and I think a lot of the misguided sympathy I felt for Brady was based on my love for the harried and unloved boys I'd spent my teens with – the surrogate brothers I had been close to and missed so very much.

I felt desperately sad for them, because they'd all been abused, neglected and hurt. But they hadn't killed, and that was the distinction I simply couldn't see then. Even my best friend's disgust wasn't enough to pull the wool from my eyes. I wanted someone to belong to, someone who couldn't leave me, someone who represented my roots. Having Ian Brady was better than a completely blank space. And there was something else that kept me focused on Brady. I felt there was a mystery to be solved: why someone so normal-looking would kill children. I began to believe that I alone could solve it. I still had my dreams of becoming a psychiatrist; I longed to see inside another person's mind and understand why they did what they did. I wanted to understand my adoptive father, and I wanted to understand Brady. I felt that if I could discover the key to his behaviour I could redeem myself for all of my failings.

So it was that I went down a path I should not have taken, writing questioning letters to Brady and reading endless books on psychiatry, crime and good and evil. Books such as Silvano Arieti's *Interpretation of Schizoprenia*, Hervey Cleckley's *The Mask Of Sanity* and Thomas Aquinas' *Summa Theologica*. I decided that all serial killers had committed their crimes because they had troubled childhoods, and that it was my job to announce this to the world. And hopefully become renowned for doing so. I saw a future ahead of me in which I would overtake my peers who had gone to Cambridge and Oxford. I would no longer be an idiot who had screwed up my life and was stuck in a job where I risked my neck to earn a living. I would be envied and respected and redeemed.

I didn't see clearly enough that even an extremely troubled childhood is no excuse for crime, let alone the crime of murder. Or that many people suffer the most terrible time in childhood, but do nothing but good in their adult lives.

I became convinced that I was an expert, and that the views of others were based on ignorance. I was right: I knew the truth about 'evil' people. And of course, behind my passionately held view was the fact that I felt I was evil too, and that if a killer like Brady wasn't really so evil, then I wasn't either. In my effort to find what we had in common I lost sight of what distinguished him from me – his inhumanity.

So I continued to write to Brady, mostly with questions, knowing that I would probably never get the answers. In an effort to contact him I even wrote to Lord Longford to ask whether he could pass on a letter from me. A famous prison reformer, Lord Longford had visited both Brady and Myra Hindley, and was actively campaigning for the release of Hindley. Lord Longford wrote back to me to say 'Dear Miss Hart, I had a visit with Ian Brady a few weeks ago, during that time he was unable to speak and he is so highly disturbed that there is no point in your writing.'

He asked me, instead, to write to Myra Hindley and to lend my support to her bid for parole. But I had no interest in writing to her and didn't support the idea of her being released. It was Brady I wanted to hear from. I wanted to be the woman in the white coat, discovering the secret of what really made him tick.

A couple of years after I had begun my job as a spy I went to a pub in south London with Penny. I was now nineteen, we were seeing quite a bit of each another, and I was enjoying getting out more. We chose this pub because it had a live stage show.

As soon as we got inside the noise coming from the stage was deafening. The tall figure singing was clad in a white leather jump suit, he was tanned and had glossy black hair that flopped down in a quiff.

He was singing an Elvis song, 'Stuck On You' and his voice was so powerful and honeyed it sounded just like Elvis. I watched mesmerised. He even had the leg shake and the uh-huhs.

My jaw dropped as I left Penny and made my way past the throng of adoring women to the front of the stage. Nanna had been wrong, I could marry Elvis, I thought to myself excitedly. I felt like crying as I stood beneath the stage and looked up at his handsome face illuminated by the flashing strobe lights. He leaned down and kissed a couple of the girls in the front row as he sang and I could see beads of sweat standing out on his chiselled face.

The girls at the front let out a squeal of delight as he started on a song called 'The Girl of My Best Friend'.

By the time he had finished singing it I knew that I was in love and my one aim in life was to make this 'God' love me back.

After his performance I caught sight of him standing by the bar. I caught his eye then mouthed from a distance, 'You look like Elvis.'

He mouthed back, 'What?'

I tipped back on my chair to mouth it again, tipped it too far and fell over. I got up, my back in agony, and saw that he was laughing.

His name was Linton York and he was singing as a favour for the landlord, who was a friend. He bought us drinks and sat and chatted. For the rest of the evening he made me laugh and when he asked me out the next night I said yes. I wore a white dress when I met him at a riverside pub in Hammersmith the next evening. I was wearing a flowery new perfume, Mitsouko by Guerlain, and I asked him if he liked it. He said it smelt like his granny's underwear and I laughed so much I nearly fell in the river. For the rest of the evening he came out with joke after joke and I didn't stop laughing. I thought he was very handsome too, and noticed that everywhere we went girls were watching him.

Linton was twenty-one and I was nineteen, and we got on fantastically well, though when I told him what I did for a living he got worried and asked me whether I was investigating him over his VAT. He had a window cleaning business, with an employee who did the actual cleaning, while he found customers and did the paperwork. He said he thought I was very posh, and to be honest, I thought he was a bit common. He ate chips with his mouth open and smoked. But these things soon ceased to matter.

We began dating, and Linton soon introduced me to his friend Jeremy Lennox Thornton, a boy who reminded me of James, blond and very good-looking. Despite his obviously well-to-do background and good looks, Jem, as he was known, was the one who worked for Linton. Jem also cleaned the house. And, strangest of all, he slept on a pile of duvets on the kitchen floor. Linton did all the paperwork and seemed amused by Jem's hero worship of him.

Linton explained this slightly odd set up by saying that Jem had suffered a nervous breakdown while at university and Linton had rescued him. I knew that Jem must have gone through something awful. But he never talked about it, and the relationship seemed to work for both of them, as they were clearly friends, and Jem often came out with us.

With his fine-boned face, lean frame and scruffy clothes – usually Linton's cast-offs – Jem was fascinating. He looked very like the missing peer Lord Lucan. He had ethereal blue-grey eyes that never met mine, or anybody's for that matter, and if he hadn't appeared so timid, he would have been very attractive. Linton, on the other hand, exuded confidence and charisma in his green Armani suit, which always had a wad of fifty-pound notes folded into the top pocket. With his pale tan, dark green eyes and swept-back dark hair he was fantastic looking.

Linton had a 'no rules, no worry' view of life. He was laid back and laconic, in total contrast to my nervous jumpiness, and I soon came to feel that I needed him like a drug. With Linton I felt as if I could escape from the world of fear and worries that I inhabited, into a safe and easy-going world I longed for.

He spoiled me, buying me all kinds of presents and taking me to smart restaurants. We loved going to Peppermint Park, next door to Stringfellows nightclub. We'd go into the cock-tail bar there and down White Russian cocktails, one after another.

A few weeks into our relationship Linton invited me to go with him to Devon. He had a red two-seater TR7 sports car, so Jem, who came with us, squeezed himself into the back seat for the whole of the five-hour journey. We had a wonderful time, and when the weekend was over we drove back to London in the early hours. It was summer, we had the windows open and as the sun came up we were all singing a spiritual:

> You get up in the morning with the rising sun,
> Working and a toilin' till the day is done,
> One more day, one more day,
> And closer to my Lord – one more day.

I was glad that Linton believed in God. He always liked to sing Elvis gospel songs and he reminded me to pray daily. I did go to church from time to time, but I tended to forget to pray, unless I was being rung by Aunt Cecilia, who still phoned me from time to time to say, 'Have you prayed for your mammy and daddy?' With Linton I felt so happy. He was so free and alive: he didn't care what anyone thought and I had never come across that kind of confidence before.

Linton had a small recording studio in his house, full of expensive equipment. He spent hours in there, but he never sent his recordings to anyone. When I suggested he did, he'd say, 'I'm not ready.' Then he'd add, 'I have to take it easy and time it right, because when I do send it, they won't know what's hit them.' But the time never was right, and the only time Linton ever sang before an audience was when he gave unpaid performances as Elvis Presley. In this respect he was uncannily like my father, and I was afraid that he too would end up bitter because his dreams had come to nothing. He had such an amazing talent and yet did not do the work needed to break into the big time.

After we'd been seeing each other for a few months Linton asked me to move in with him. He had a large Victorian house in Chiswick beside the river, and I loved it there, so I said yes. Although we were a couple and we slept together several nights a week, he gave me my own room, and I loved it. He put Winnie-the- Pooh wallpaper up for me and filled it with cuddly toys. He said I hadn't had a childhood and he wanted to make up for it.

Soon after moving in, I gave up my job. Linton had plenty of money as his business had spawned spin offs and said I didn't need to work, and I was tired of the long hours and the risks. I had learned a lot that would be valuable later in my life, but at that point I was happy to take a break. Jem still lived with us, and these were some of the happiest days of my life. Linton would often cook big fry-ups in the warm homely kitchen – clowning about and throwing eggs and beans at the wall if his cooking went wrong, and bring me breakfast in bed. Jem would be out at work on the windows, or cleaning the house with so much bleach that it smelled like the local swimming baths. And I would spend hours in my room and feel free, at last, to be myself, without fear of reprisal or criticism. There was no doubt that my relationship with Linton was often more parent-child than that between two adults. He wanted to look after me, and it was wonderful.

The three of us were to live together for four years. Us against the world, as Linton said. We felt like the three musketeers. Linton found an old can of bright green paint in the overgrown back yard and painted 'Paradise Lost' above the front door, and insisted that all bills and letters be addressed to that name, or he would send them back unopened. In many ways I think the three of us were outsiders who had found one another. And all we wanted was for everything to stay just as it was in our own, perfect little world.

8

The Psychic

I had told Linton that I sometimes wrote to Ian Brady, and that I thought he might be my real father. I said I knew that he probably wasn't, but somehow I couldn't let go of the idea of having him as my roots. I had become compelled to understand what had driven him to become what he was.

Linton was not impressed. 'Don't you see how insane it is, writing to someone like that?' he said. 'If he were your real father you'd have a lot to worry about, you silly fool. For goodness' sake, give up these crazy ideas.'

Linton and I often quarrelled. He could be very dominant and I could be very stubborn, so we'd shout at each other until I locked myself in my room, or ran out of the house and went for a long walk.

One day we quarrelled so badly that I walked out. I had a few things in a small suitcase and no idea where to go. I walked around for an hour or two and went and sat in a café. With no job and no money of my own I had very few choices. I decided to go back to my adoptive parents' house and ask them to let me stay.

It wasn't an easy decision. After being thrown out and disowned twice, I knew I wasn't likely to get a warm welcome. But like so many children of cruel and rejecting parents, I never let go of the hope that things would be different the next time. I still loved them and longed for them to love me, and I dreamed of my mother welcoming me with open arms and telling me how sorry she was for all the hurts of the past. So I plucked up all my courage and set off.

They didn't live far from Linton's house. I sat on the bus, my bag at my feet, my mouth dry and my stomach in knots. What would I do if they turned me away? I walked up the street to their house – still the closest thing I had ever known to a real home – and stood outside the door for a full ten minutes before pressing the bell. My mother answered, as I knew she would. She stared at me, her expression grim, as I told her I had nowhere else to go and could I please stay for a few days. Then, still without a word, she stood aside and indicated that I should come in.

There was no hug, no 'How are you?' and no smile. But she agreed that I could stay, and at that moment, it meant a lot. Once inside I went and said hello to my father. I hadn't seen either of them for over four years, but little had changed. Nicky had moved out, so there was only Mum and Dad left at home. And Dad was clearly growing older. He sat by the fire, looking grey and tired. His heart was not in good shape, and it showed. When I went in he smiled at me in such a resigned and defeated way that it reminded me of a fly that had been trapped in the web of a spider.

The first thing I needed to do was to get a job. I would have to pay rent and I could no longer lean on Linton. I was still in touch with James Stratford-Barret and knew he had set up a new investigation company in Berkeley Square with an ex-

MI6 friend called David Steele. I called him and he immediately offered me a job as an investigator. He knew I had done well at his friends' agency and said there was plenty of similar work for me. And although I had become disillusioned by the time I left Rob and Gary's agency, after being away from it for a while I found I actually missed the work. The thrills and dangers of surveillance work were quite addictive.

James's agency took on jobs the Special Branch, anti-terrorist or other specialist police and government departments had given up on, many of them top secret. I knew I'd enjoy the challenge and threw myself into the work. And it was good to be working alongside James. Although I had given up my dream of marrying him, I still had a soft spot for him.

Not long after Linton and I split, he got in touch and asked me to come back. He missed me and he told me my room was still there if I wanted it. I was glad to hear from him: I had missed him too, after four years together. But I wasn't sure whether I wanted to move back in. Linton was eccentric, and we had argued a lot, so I decided to stay where I was. In the meantime I often went round to see him, or he'd take me out for a meal. He was my best friend, and he still made me laugh. It was as though we couldn't be together, but we couldn't break up either.

A few weeks into my new job James asked me to do some work with a friend of his called Harry, who'd had his own agency in South Africa and was now operating over here from a glamorous office in Chelsea harbour. Harry took me on a few jobs with him as his 'wife'. He was great company – a highly intelligent man who knew a lot about investigation work. I liked him and learned a lot from him.

One of the jobs we did was tailing a Middle Eastern man who was a security risk and of interest to the government.

One evening he was gambling in Aspinall's, the ritzy Park Lane casino. I was dressed in a scarlet silk dress by Chanel. It had a deep slash in the neckline and a tight waist and showed my slim figure off to perfection. With it I wore silver high heels that made me feel ten feet tall, Chanel's pirate red lipstick, ruby and diamond earrings and a white fake fur coat. My long blonde hair was done up in a perfectly coiffed bun.

I arrived with Harry, who was tall, dark and good-looking, in a false black cab, which we often used on these operations. We swept into the casino while two of our men remained outside on surveillance. I let Harry take over, placing bets on the roulette table and cashing in our chips. We watched our target until he left. We slipped out after him and got into our waiting taxi to follow him.

All of a sudden a team of armed police swooped down on us. I heard later that our two men outside had been seen acting suspiciously and the casino security people had checked on the cab and found that it was a fake. Our agency should have called the police in advance to notify them of our operation, but had clearly not done so, and when the casino called them, believing we were planning a robbery, the police sprang into action.

Within seconds I was spread-eagled on the ground, with a shotgun at my head. I asked to be allowed to get up, but the policeman holding the gun pushed it into the side of my head and said, 'You're going nowhere'.

We were handcuffed, taken to the police station and thrown into cells, where we stayed for several hours, until the police were informed who we were. By the time they released us my gorgeous Chanel dress was ripped in three places and covered in oil. The story appeared in the *Daily Mail* the next morning under the headline 'Bungling Spies'.

I got on really well with Harry and could have fallen for him, but he was married. He was the nearest thing I ever met to James Bond and I sometimes wished I had met him before his South African wife did. After we stopped working together we stayed friends for the next couple of years. One evening I was due to visit him. I was looking forward to catching up with him, but at the last minute I had to cancel because I was working late. The next day I was horrified to hear that he had been murdered that evening, beaten senseless then plunged into a cold bath of water and drowned. The thought that I might have found him – or been with him when his killers called – sent a cold shiver up my spine.

Harry's wife was later found guilty of the murder and sent to prison for life. She had hired two South African security operatives to do the actual killing. Apparently she was bored with him, but why she killed him rather than just leaving him, only she knew. She was a hard, beautiful woman who became known in the media as the Black Widow. It seemed desperately ironic that, after facing danger all his working life, Harry was murdered at home, by his wife. It took me a long while to get over it.

Now that I was an adult my mother no longer told me what time to come and go, or told me what to wear. But I made sure that she never saw me dressed to the nines for a glamorous job. Mostly I dressed demurely and slipped quietly in and out of the house. I barely saw my parents.

One morning that summer of 1985, I opened the newspaper and a headline jumped out at me.

'Ian Brady the Moors Killer moved from prison into Park Lane Top Security Hospital for the Criminally Insane.'

So Lord Longford had been right about Brady being disturbed, I thought. He had been moved. What struck me was that if he was somewhere new, I might have a better chance of getting a letter to him. Perhaps the Park Lane rules were more relaxed than those at Wormwood Scrubs.

I wrote again, asking him about his childhood and how it had affected him. This time there was no letter from the governor telling me I couldn't write to him. But there was nothing from Brady either. I thought that maybe he hadn't wanted to tell me his secrets.

I had been toying with the idea of moving back in with Linton. The two of us were getting on well, and I knew I couldn't stay with my parents for too long. My mind was made up for me when my mother announced that Aunt Briony, one of my Irish aunts, was coming to stay and my room would be needed. Since there was a spare bedroom in the house it was obvious that she felt it was time I left. I took the hint and moved back in with Linton.

For the next year or so I yo-yoed back and forth between my parents' house and Linton's. When things got too volatile with Linton I left and went back to my parents, and they accepted this, as long as I didn't interrupt their very quiet and sedentary lifestyle. Then when my mother began hinting that she needed my room for Aunt Briony, or found some other way to let me know that my time was up, I went back to Linton's. He and I always stayed in touch, even when I was living with my parents. I often felt Linton was the only person who understood me – and who could make me laugh and get me to see life as absurd. I felt he was my family.

One night at my parents' house I had a dream. I was leaning over a tiny little boy. He was so small he was no bigger than a matchbox and he had dark hair and blue eyes and a tiny perfect body. I felt such love for him that it was overwhelming. I said to him, 'I love you. I so love you.'

He replied, 'You will kill me before I get much bigger.'

I said, 'Oh no, why would I kill you? I love you.'

A week later, I started getting sick in the mornings. I got myself a home pregnancy kit. It was positive.

I told Linton and he was delighted. He went and bought some baby books and kept saying, 'A muchacho (this was a Mexican term which Elvis used for babies) for you and me. I can't believe it. It will be good-looking, anyway, Cilla.'

But I was afraid. Although we were close, we were more like friends than lovers, and when I was honest with myself, I knew I didn't really love Linton like a man. Sexually, I could not open up and trust him – so I kept closed. I had always wanted to have a child with a man that I was madly in love with. I longed for that sexually bonded feeling. But I rubbed my stomach and felt such love for the child growing inside me that I decided I would have the baby, and manage alone if I had to.

I told my mother, hoping that she might be pleased, that maybe this would be a chance for her to be loving towards me. But all she said was, 'You can't have it here. I'm not having it in this house. Get yourself a mother and baby hostel.' She told me not to tell my father. I rang my old social worker at Greengage House, Michael Briggs, to see if he could help me with housing. He picked me up in his car and took me to his home, where I met his wife and newborn baby. Then he took me to the pub, where he told me, 'You can't do it, Chris. You have that child and it will end up in care and have the life you've had. I'll make the arrangements to terminate the pregnancy – it'll be easy.'

'But you've just had a baby girl. Don't you love her?'

'I'd do anything to have it undone. Every day I just want to run away. My life is sheer misery. She never stops screaming – on and on and on. On your own you just wouldn't be able to take it. No. You have no choice. It's not alive yet. Terminate it.'

The next day he arranged for me to attend a pregnancy advisory clinic, to have the termination. All my determination to do it on my own had evaporated. With my mother and Michael against me, I just didn't feel strong enough. However, it wasn't easy, as Michael had said it would be. As I lay in the recovery room, I remembered my dream of the matchbox boy. His prophecy had been correct.

I heard someone screaming and crying. It sounded a long way off. Then I half woke and realised that the girl crying so desperately was me.

I went back to my parents' house. My mother was waiting tight-lipped. 'It's gone,' I said numbly. 'The baby's dead. I killed him.'

She didn't miss a beat as she replied, 'You have to get out in the next few days. I need your room for Auntie Briony.' She turned away and went to make dinner for my father.

I met Linton in a café on a cold, rainy morning a few days later. I told him about the fate of our baby as he ate a full English breakfast. He stood up. 'Now you'll have more in common with Brady,' he said, knocking over his teacup as he turned to walk away.

Later I went for a drink with a friend and I cried over my dead son. After a few more drinks, I left the pub and stepped out in front of a speeding car. I saw it coming; I was playing my usual deadly roulette game with life. I just didn't care whether I lived or died.

As it happens, I was very lucky not to have been killed. My face hit the bonnet and the bone in my nose split through the skin. I had ten stitches, four across my brow and six across my nose, but I was left disfigured, with the bone jutting out of my nose. The doctors said they would wait three days for the swelling to go down, and then perform reconstructive surgery.

No one came to see me in hospital. I went to the small hospital library to try to find something to take my mind off my face; my slitty black eyes and bent nose, and the ugliness of my lifeless, loveless life.

In the library I found a book called *Strangers Among Us* by Ruth Montgomery. It had a very serene woman's face on it and I was drawn to it, so I took it back to bed with me.

The book turned out to be all about people who wanted to commit suicide. It said that instead of destroying their bodies to escape life, all they had to do was pray to Higher Beings. If they prayed hard enough then the Higher Beings would help the sufferer die and someone else would take over his or her body and continue living their lives with the original occupant's memories – walk-ins, they were called.

The book explained that the Higher Beings would make people aware of the reality of the spirit level of existence. This would help in the years ahead when, it said, millions of people on earth would transfer to spirit form rapidly, and in shock, due to the worsening weather conditions caused by the shift of the earth's axis which would herald the end of this age with fires and floods. The book said it would help this chaos if people were aware of where they were going and less afraid of dying and moving to the fourth dimension, which had different laws to our three-dimensional reality.

That night I clasped the book to me underneath my white hospital gown and I prayed and prayed, as never before.

'Take me. Pick me. Please, please pick me. Please take me. Take me,' I whispered. Nothing happened, but I continued to pray to be taken for many weeks and months to come.

The surgery on my nose went so well that I had a new and better-looking nose, much smaller than the original. I had wanted to die, but ended up with a new nose that made me look like Christie Brinkley. I posed in a photo booth – it was odd – somehow even my eyes looked prettier and less of a victim somehow than they always had. I would have laughed, if I hadn't still felt so very low – grieving for my lost baby boy and deeply hurt by the rejection from my parents and Linton.

I think that's why I found it so hard to let go of my need for Brady.

I began thinking about how I could get him to respond to my letters. Then an idea struck me: why not visit the area where he had last lived, Hattersley, on the outskirts of Manchester? Brady was Scottish, and had only moved to the Manchester area at seventeen, when he was sent by his foster parents back to his natural mother. But he had lived in the Manchester area for the next eight or nine years, until his arrest. And of course his crimes had been committed there too.

The idea of going to have a look at Brady's last home, and the surrounding area, remained dormant for a few months. I wasn't sure I would ever really do it. Then something happened that shook me badly, and made up my mind.

In the summer of 1986 I was back living with my adoptive parents. By this time I had learned to drive and bought myself a little second-hand pale blue Citroen. I loved zipping around in it. That summer Linton and I went to the Glastonbury rock festival. Despite – or perhaps because of – all that had happened between us, we were still seeing each other. We met most days, often just to chat, and sometimes I stayed over at his house.

At Glastonbury we had a great time and I drank rather a lot, so we left my car there and got the train home. The next day we went down in Linton's car to collect mine. We were driving back along the M4 in our separate cars and I was behind Linton, doing about 70 miles an hour in the middle lane of the motorway. It was a dark and wet night, but there wasn't a lot of traffic about and I was humming along to the radio, when all of a sudden the car started to sway around, backwards and forwards across the motorway. The steering wheel seemed to have worked loose. I had no control of the car and I was terrified. The car swung wildly across three lanes and I knew it was only a matter of time before another car hit me. Panicking, I slammed on the brakes – which is the worst thing you can do if it's wet. The car spun around three times and ended up facing the opposite way on the hard shoulder of the motorway. I had hit my lovely new nose on the steering wheel and it was bleeding all down my T-shirt, but I barely noticed, I was shaking so badly with shock.

Thankfully, Linton had seen what happened. He got the police, who came to get me and told me I was very lucky to be alive. They took me to meet Linton, further along the motorway, who drove me back to my parents' house.

When we got there Linton told them what had happened and my parents asked him if he was all right, while ignoring me. Linton was stunned that they appeared so uninterested in me, despite the state I was in. He had met them before, and knew quite a lot about our relationship, but their apparent callousness in the face of a near-death experience shook him.

Then my father pulled something out from under his armchair. It was obviously some sort of car part.

I said, 'What's that?' and he said, 'It's a bracket for the steering wheel, the car probably needed it.'

I could hardly believe it. My father, it seemed, had taken the bracket that held the steering wheel in place out of my car and hidden it under his chair. I looked at Linton, who was staring open-mouthed.

I said to my father, 'What were you doing with it under your armchair?'

'I was fiddling around with the car the other day and took it out,' he said.

'Took it out!' I repeated numbly. I looked at him, horrified, and his blue eyes glinted smugly as he looked back at me.

But he said no more. No explanation of why it had been taken out in the first place, or why it hadn't been put back. My father had almost killed me. And I had no idea whether he'd done it on purpose or simply been forgetful. He offered no apology and seemed oblivious to the ordeal I'd been through. That night I went home with Linton. I was terribly upset.

Linton asked me whether I thought they wanted to kill me, and made a joke about them being sick of me turning up asking to stay. But I wasn't in the mood for jokes. I sobbed all the way back to his house.

For the following weeks I struggled to make sense of what had happened. I couldn't work out why my father would have done such a dangerous, stupid thing. He wasn't senile or even particularly forgetful. So had he really hoped I would have an accident? I couldn't help wondering, and feeling terribly sad.

I thought about moving permanently back in with Linton, but I didn't want to be with him all the time any more than I wanted to be at my parents' house. So I continued to stay with them, while spending most weekends, and sometimes nights during the week, with Linton.

Once again feeling lost and rejected, I began thinking of Ian Brady, and of the idea of visiting his home. I wanted to make sense of what he had done, in the same way that I had always struggled to make sense of my father. I decided that I really would go. Perhaps I would learn something about Brady – and perhaps it would allow me to forget about him and move on.

As soon as I had a few days off work I packed a small bag and took the tube across London, then headed for the M1 motorway, where I thumbed a lift.

A huge articulated lorry pulled off and stopped. I ran to climb into the cab and thanked the driver. My luck was in, because he was heading my way. For the next couple of hours we chatted. He was called Kenny and was from Newcastle. I told him I was off to visit a friend.

Kenny dropped me off at Manchester Station, nodded at me and winked, then heaved his heavy truck round and went on his way. I went into the station bar and drank a glass of Martini and lemonade straight down. I felt horribly nervous, but now that I was here I was determined to go through with my plan.

I found a policeman and asked him the way to the suburb of Hattersley. He told me to take a local train. By the time we arrived it was snowing and my boots crunched on the snowy ground as I made my way down the station approach road.

The cold wind bit through my bones. I went into a pub and asked for another Martini and lemonade. The pub was full, but I spotted a free corner table.

A few minutes later I finished my drink, pulled my coat back on and headed out into the night. I knew the name of the road I was looking for, but I had no idea which direction to go in to find it. I set off, trusting my instinct, and five minutes later I saw it: Wardle Brook Avenue. I walked down the street to another pub, the New Inn. A group of five young men stood in the doorway, and tried to bar my way. I pushed past them and they followed me inside. I felt scared and shaky, afraid they might turn nasty.

'Are you a model? My mates are all in love with you,' one of them said.

I breathed a sigh of relief.

'Are you German or Swedish?'

I smiled. 'I'm from London.'

I ordered a drink and sat down. I needed time to think about my next move. Two of the young men came and sat either side of me. They were friendly and to be honest I was glad of the company.

They asked me what I was doing there and various excuses went through my head. I said I was a journalist from a newspaper doing a story on the Moors Murderers and I had lost my photographer. One of the two young men asked me had I seen the house. When I said not properly, he offered to take me over the road to see it. I finished my drink, and we made our way there.

Number 16 was just like every other house in the street, small, nondescript, the last in a small, sloping terrace of four, with a white gate and a tiny front garden. Except that this house had padlocked shutters across the windows and the front door. I later learned that local kids had often tried to get in and spend the night there, as a dare, sniffing glue and taking drugs.

This was it: the house where Brady and Hindley had lived from September 1964 until their arrest in October 1965. It had been newly built when they moved there with Hindley's grandmother, their two dogs and their budgie, after their previous home in Gorton, where Myra and her grandmother had lived for many years, was condemned.

In this tiny, ordinary, two-bedroom house they had carried out two of their three terrible murders, one of them while Hindley's grandmother slept upstairs. And there may have been two more. Hindley and Brady were believed to have killed two other children who had disappeared around the same time, but had never confessed.

It seemed so unreal. Surely it couldn't really have happened, I thought. Surely it was just a horror story. The kind people told one another to scare themselves rigid.

There were several children on bicycles in front of the house and they stared at me as I went past them up to the front door.

I turned to look for my companion. He was standing some way up the road. 'I'm not going near it,' he said. 'I don't care what you say, it's full of evil spirits, demons and things like that.'

He had a comfortable white Rover and he offered to take me to find a bed and breakfast. We drove to a pretty village outside Hattersley called Glossop and after I'd booked in to a nice-looking little pub called The Red Lion, that also rented out rooms, we went for a drink in the downstairs bar.

We sat sipping cold pints of brown ale, as he talked to me about the effect the murders had had on the whole area.

'It's all anyone ever talks about,' he told me. 'It's the biggest thing that's ever happened round here. All that ever happened before it and since was everyday life. It is a mystery, you see. People want to know why they did it.'

'David Smith,' he went on, 'the one who was married to Hindley's sister, he's the one who went to the police after they made him watch the last of the murders and tried to get him to join them. He was just a teenager at the time, about seventeen. He still goes into the local pub. But his life has probably been ruined because of it. How do you ever recover from something like that?'

Listening to him I wondered why I was trying to involve myself in all the shame and horror and grief associated with Brady.

My companion got up. 'I have to go now. I'm on the night shift at the bakery.' We said goodbye and he left. And suddenly, I felt incredibly lonely and very crazy for just being there.

I went up to my room. It was a typical bed and breakfast bedroom, with its kettle, custard biscuits and flowery sheets. I had a poor night's sleep and in the morning wandered around the tiny old-world village feeling tired and with a pounding head from too many martinis. The sun was out, watery, but bright enough to dazzle as it reflected off the snow, and it made my head pound even more. I didn't really know what I was trying to achieve, but I felt that I hadn't yet done what I'd come for. I decided to go back to the house. I got a taxi back to Wardle Brook Avenue and walked up the road towards number 16. I went up the path in front of numbers 10, 12 and 14 that led to the front gate, and up the front path to the door. I knocked and then began to rattle the bolts on the outer door. Suddenly it burst open and I gasped and jumped back. A tall, thin dark-haired man stood in the doorway.

'What are you doing?' he asked abruptly.

I took a deep breath and plunged in. 'I'm a reporter and I'd like to take some pictures of the house for a story. Mind if I come in?'

'You can't,' he said. 'I'm only based here with the council handling the heating enquiries for the estate; it's more than my job's worth to let you in.'

I could see past him, as he stood blocking the doorway, to the stark white walls and pale grey carpet. To the left of the front door was a narrow-stepped staircase and ahead were three separate doors. The furthest was open and I could see the kitchen. For a moment, I saw Brady in there, tall and skinny, preparing a cup of tea and a ham sandwich, just like anybody else. What had made him turn into such a savage creature?

'Sorry, I need the toilet quickly,' I said. I pushed past the man and went up the narrow stairs, and into the small bathroom. It was the same as the rest of the house, small but ordinary, though to Hindley and Brady, when they moved in, it must have been special – the first time they'd lived in a house with an indoor loo or a bath.

On the way back downstairs I looked into each of the bare bedrooms. As soon as I was back outside the man slammed the door behind me, muttering, 'Make it all up anyway – press bastards like you.'

I took out my little camera and started taking pictures of the front of the house from every angle, then I went round the back and took another few. And I took the street, with the New Inn across the road and the rolling hills in the distance.

A couple of hours later I caught the train back to London from Hattersley Station. Linton met me and took me home. He had made it clear he thought I was mad to go, so I didn't discuss it with him.

When I got back, I got the photos printed up and sent one of them off to Brady, with a letter saying 'I've got more of these which I'll send if you like, but I'll need a reply to my letter.'

That was my carrot. The thing I thought might prompt Brady to answer my letters – if he was allowed to. I guessed that he might be curious about the house and the area where he had lived, and want to see it twenty years on.

What a crazy thing to do. I was messing with something far too big for me, far too dangerous. And I wasn't a psychiatrist; I was a misguided girl of twenty-three. But I was determined to hear from Brady, and despite my reservations – and there were plenty – I went ahead. In my mind I was on my way to removing the failure of my life and redeeming it all.

I knew, deep down, that Brady was unlikely to be my real father. But after so many years of focusing on him the connection I felt with him was very strong. And there was something more. Whether or not he was my father, I felt I needed to know the truth about him. I felt such grief, sorrow and deep respect for the children he was said to have murdered. I wanted to know, for sure, if he really had done the things he was accused of, and if he felt remorse. I felt like a detective, determined to get at the truth, for my sake and for theirs.

However, for the next few months I put all of this to the back of my mind. I knew that in all probability, even if the letter and picture was passed to Brady, I would never hear from him.

A few months later, in late 1986, the papers were full of a new story about Brady. He had confessed to the murders of Pauline Reade and Keith Bennett, the two missing children police had long suspected were among Brady and Hindley's victims. That meant there were five in all; five young lives lost.

I was sickened and appalled. But I also felt, in some strange way, that there might be a role for me here, if Brady did get in touch with me. These two children's graves had yet to be found, up on Saddleworth moor.

I wondered whether I could play a part, help in some way, perhaps act as a go-between with Brady and the police, or persuade him to give up more information. I was used to finding things out, through my work, so that was automatically my line of thought. But it remained theoretical, because for some months I heard nothing from him, and I wondered whether I ever would.

The following April, in 1987, was beautiful, with the promise of a long, hot summer ahead. I had a strange feeling all that month, as if something big was about to happen. One afternoon, as I was sitting in the office, an old friend of mine called Freddie phoned. He was an ex-army guy I had worked with at Rob and Gary's agency.

I'd always liked Freddie. He was about two years older than me and from the minute he'd started working with us I had warmed to him. He always seemed wise and clever and we became good friends – I thought of him as a kind of big brother. When I left the agency we stayed in touch; I often phoned him for advice, or we'd meet for a drink and catch up on our lives.

I asked him how he was and he began telling me about a psychic he had been to see. 'He's amazing, Chris, brilliant. You must go and see him.'

I was surprised and not very keen. I was more interested in arranging to meet Freddie for a catch-up drink. But he insisted I take the psychic's number and book a session.

'I don't really believe in psychics,' I protested.

'Just give it a go,' Freddie insisted, so I said I would. Afterwards I wasn't really sure why I'd let him talk me into it. I suppose I thought it would be a bit of fun. I'd go and see the psychic, who was called Mike Baker, and then meet Freddie afterwards to laugh about it over a drink.

It was a few days later, after work, that I made my way to Mike Baker's address, which was in central London, and turned out to be on the third floor of an office building. The receptionist showed me in and a middle-aged, grey-headed man stood up from behind a desk, hand outstretched.

'Christine, glad you could make it.'

He invited to me to sit down, then walked round the desk and shut the door. Then he sat down again and leaned towards me.

'Right,' he said. 'Before I begin, I want you to drop your cynicism. If you don't believe that some are able to read the future for you, then that is up to you, but since you're here, why not keep an open mind?'

'Not likely,' I thought. I was sure it was a complete waste of money and that he was a fraud.

He sat back and closed his eyes. 'You won't be in your present job for long – think of it as temporary. Before October you will be out of the country, somewhere hot, somewhere like Greece. Then you will return to London, and then you'll go again, this time to America.'

I thought of the small sum of money I had in the building society, and wondered how I was going to finance leaving my job and jet-setting it around the world. None of this made sense. I began to think I could have spent the £30 fee on clothes or make-up.

He was in full flow.

'You will go backwards and forwards from America to London, but your base will be in this country. Whatever you decide to do, whatever it is, you will be successful. You are a girl who is looking for something; some sort of answer. Keep looking, because you will find it in the end.'

I looked at the clock on the wall behind him: half an hour had gone past. Only another half hour to go. I was beginning to feel annoyed because it was all so unbelievable. I would never leave my job, I loved it there.

But there was more to come.

'You'll make contact with the media,' he went on. 'Then once contact is made it will never be broken.'

He talked about relationships, telling me, 'There will be someone called P who you will think is the one for you, but he's not, J is. J is the only one who can make you happy. This J is your soulmate. He is self-employed. Can you think of anyone like that in your life? An ex-boyfriend perhaps?'

'No,' I said. I didn't know anyone who was a P or a J. None of it made sense. We were coming to the end of the session and I was extremely unimpressed. Mike Baker opened his eyes. 'Now,' he said, 'I'm going to let you address a question straight to my guide. What I want you to do is to say the question in thought form in your head, then my guide will tell me the answer and I will recite it to you.'

I thought the whole thing was ridiculous, but felt I might as well come up with a question. I thought hard. What was it I wanted to ask, that no one could ever tell me? Suddenly I knew.

'What is the connection between me and Ian Brady?' I asked, in my head.

He paused for a while, and appeared to be listening. Suddenly he looked at me.

'In a week. Does that make sense?'

I felt disappointed. It didn't make sense at all.

Walking out into the weak evening sun, I saw a homeless man wrapped in shabby blankets. I felt so angry at the thirty pounds I had just wasted, and wished I could give it to him instead.

I went to meet Freddie and told him I thought his psychic was rubbish. 'Wait and see,' he said. 'You don't know yet whether what he said will come true.' I laughed. 'It's not very likely Freddie, none of it even made sense.'

After I went home, I barely thought about most of what Mike Baker had said. Once or twice I wondered whether 'in a week' really did mean something. But how could it? No, I was sure it was all the fevered imaginings of a fake. The best thing I could do was to forget it.

9

Is There Such a Thing As Evil?

The following Wednesday, exactly a week after I had visited Mike Baker, a letter arrived for me.

It was a long brown envelope with slightly sloping handwriting on the front, in dark blue biro. It looked official. I glanced at it when I came in late that evening, and decided to read it in the morning.

The next day I didn't have to go in to work until late, so I went downstairs, made a cup of tea and some toast, and headed back up with them. When I reached the stairs I spotted the letter on the hall table, so I popped it between my teeth, and carried on up to my room. It had a Liverpool postmark and I wondered if it could be from a doctor at Park Lane. Probably telling me I can't write to Brady, I thought.

I peeled open the envelope and pulled out a single sheet of white paper, covered with the same sloping blue handwriting. I looked for the signature at the bottom. It said 'Best Wishes, Ian Brady'.

I don't think I registered it at first. Then I thought, no, this is some sort of joke, not after all these years.

It was almost ten years since I had first come across the photo of Brady in the library. Since then I had stood outside

Wormwood Scrubs, written him dozens of letters and visited his old neighbourhood. Yet despite all this I had never really believed I would hear from him.

Now here it was.

The letter was brief. He simply thanked me for my letter and the photos and apologised for taking so long to reply, saying that he had been unwell. He said the photos had brought back memories and that he'd be interested in seeing any others I had.

I felt close to tears and strangely unreal. Almost as if, like Alice in Wonderland, I had just slipped down a rabbit hole into the dream world of childhood magic. That world of fantasy, where the greyness could never reach in and swallow you up, the way it always seemed to in the real world. This was what I had waited for. In my mind Brady's letter represented redemption – both his and mine. This was the beginning. He would trust me, and open up, telling me the truth. And when he did, I would feel that my life had a purpose that transcended all the misery of my past.

I began to feel excited. I had to tell someone, I felt I was going to burst.

I tried Linton's phone number, there was no answer. Next I tried Michael from Greengage House. I said I wanted to meet, to tell him something very important.

He agreed to meet me at lunchtime in a pub around the corner. I got there ten minutes early and sat waiting for him.

'You look well,' he said. 'How's work going? I hear you're doing well.' He put down a pint of lager for himself and a Coke for me.

I pulled a face as I sipped greedily at the Coke. 'It's mostly poking my nose into other people's business and snooping around. And I'm not working till this evening. But let's not talk about work, I've got something amazing to tell you.

'Today it came, a letter from him. I could hardly believe it. Oh Michael, I've finally made contact with Ian Brady.'

Somehow I had convinced myself that Michael would be happy for me. So I was shocked by his response.

'You don't still think he's your father, do you?' he said as he sipped his beer. 'The man whose photo you kept during your time at the orphanage is a fantasy father who could come and rescue you and make all the pain go away. The two are not the same. Ian Brady is a clever, dangerous and evil man. He will get inside your head and mess it up. You're so vulnerable, you're still like a child, and he would see that and torture you mentally. Just leave it, Chris, don't answer that letter.'

He licked at his foam moustache and looked at me kindly. Then he put his arm around me fondly. I shrugged it off. His love always hurt me. I knew I needed someone to care – yet it felt like I was having my head plunged underneath water. I felt guilty that I couldn't just accept it with a smile, but I could not.

I vented my irritation and confusion on him. 'Leave it? You're kidding, aren't you? Why are you against me?'

Michael assured me that he wasn't. 'Brady is dangerous,' he insisted. 'And you're vulnerable and very needy. What could he do except bring you more pain than you've already had?'

I became angry. 'I'm not "vulnerable", as you put it. I've kept a job down now for three years. There's nothing vulnerable about me. Anyway, I invited you here as a friend, not as a bloody meddling social worker.'

The pub was dimly lit, full, and very noisy. Michael reached over and took my hand. I had to strain to hear him over the noise of the crowd and the juke-box.

'Chris, this is a stupid and dangerous fantasy. No one wanted you as a child and you can't face it. You'd be better off facing the truth about the past and moving on. Otherwise you'll be hurt even more. Serial killers are not human, they don't have feelings like we do, they're monsters. And Ian Brady is a highly dangerous man. He's a Category A prisoner – which means the highest security. I'm surprised you've been able to reach him.'

I got up. 'I'm going, Michael. You're spoiling my happy day.'

I walked out. I had been full of hope before I had seen him and now he had made everything dark, cold and isolated, like it usually was.

Not reply to the letter? He had to be kidding.

I made my way round to Linton's house. He was still in bed, so I sat in the huge chesterfield armchair at the end of his bed.

'Guess what,' I said. 'I've got a letter from Ian Brady.'

I held it up and Linton leaned over and snatched it. He stared at it and then threw it back.

'You're mad,' he said. 'You don't know what you're doing. Give up on this before you get in too deep.'

I went home, angry with both Michael and Linton. Why couldn't either of them understand why the letter meant so much to me? Why did they have to pour cold water on my hopes?

Later that night, after work, I sat alone in my bedroom and composed a reply, thanking him for his letter and enclosing some more photos. A week later there was another letter from Brady. The same brown envelope and small, neat, sloping script.

We began a correspondence. Brady wrote to me weekly, sometimes more. Most of the time he talked about books: Nietzche and Kierkergaard and other complex philosophers. He talked about German and Russian politics and other rather stodgy academic stuff. Sometimes he would write for pages and pages, to argue just one point. I kept his letters neatly packaged away, in a shoebox underneath my bed like some dark childhood secret.

He never asked about me, but he did say that he liked my mind and that I was very clever. I wanted to read the books he talked about, to understand what he was saying. I started to order long lists from the library, so that I could keep up with him. He recommended books on the occult, which was clearly a major interest of his. I found the occult books interesting, as they spoke of a world that seemed to me to be more alive than this one. At one point Brady told me to buy a tarot pack. I did, and for a while I would use it every day. I became quite addicted to it.

Brady's political sympathies were all socialist. He admired Vanessa Redgrave, her beauty as well as her politics – she was a member of the ultra-left Workers' Revolutionary Party and this was where our views coincided. I admired both her and her brother Corin greatly.

There was an Indian summer that year. I spent the warm weekends of late August and September down at the end of my adoptive parents' garden, sitting in a stripy deckchair with my feet in a washing-up bowl of cool water, reading the books that Brady had recommended. Or I would go round to Linton's and we would spend afternoons chatting over glasses of dry white wine in his front garden, sitting on dining chairs, with music blaring out of two speakers placed in his upstairs window.

I didn't talk to Linton all that much about my letters to Brady, but I would often lie in bed, sometimes until three or four o'clock in the morning, writing them. It felt to me as though it was part of my deep desire to understand the nature of things, the soul, and what its journey was and whether good and evil really existed.

Despite the regularity of our letters it never occurred to me that I might visit Brady. I knew that no one had been to see him in twenty years, other than his solicitor and Lord Longford. In fact he stressed to me in letters that he never had visits nor did he intend to in the future.

Then, about three months after his first letter, he wrote:

'When you visit, phone my personal psychiatrist Dr Strickland and tell him the date and time you will arrive, I look forward to meeting you for the first time.'

He included details of his psychiatrist, and the number to call.

I wasn't sure what to do. Writing was one thing, but visiting would take things to an entirely different level. I phoned my friend Freddie, the one I used to work with, who sent me to the psychic. He always gave me good advice. I hadn't told him before of my connection with Brady, so I filled him in on the whole story.

Freddie was very unhappy about it, and asked me what on earth I thought I was doing. When I told him Brady had arranged for me to visit, he said, 'That's frightening. Why does he want to see you? Read me the letter.'

I read out the letter down the phone. At the end of it, Brady had said; 'You quote my favourite poem, how did you know? It made me wonder about you.'

'What poem did you quote?' Freddie asked.

'I just picked it; I didn't know it was his favourite,' I said. 'It's by Blake, I used to read it back at the orphanage.

> In what distant deeps or skies,
> Burnt the fire of thine eyes?
> On what wings dare he aspire?
> What the hand dare seize the fire?
>
> And what shoulder & what art,
> Could twist the sinews of thine heart?
> And when thy heart began to beat.
> What dread hand? And what dread feet?

'Don't go,' Freddie said. 'I really don't think you should go there, Chris. Stay away.'

I thought about Blake's famous poem and why Brady liked it. Towards the end of the poem there's a line which says, 'Did he smile his work to see? Did he who made the lamb make thee?' Did Brady think about who had made him, and how he had become evil? If I could find the answer, that would be a result to be truly proud of. My longing to be a psychiatrist was still so strong – and now I felt I had the prize subject all to myself.

I knew that if I went to see Brady there would be no going back, he would be real to me, and I real to him. I might find out, once and for all, whether he was my father. And I might also learn his secrets, and if I did I would be hailed as a hero by all. Yet I felt a cold chill when I thought of the children he had murdered. Would I be seen as condoning what he did if I visited? I loathed what he had done.

I wasn't sure what to do. So I went where I always went as a child when I was in distress, or had a difficult decision to make. To our local church, and Father Michael Fewell. I wasn't a regular churchgoer any more. But I still felt part of the church, and trusted Father Michael.

I slipped inside and looked over at the confessional box. The green light was on, which meant confession could be heard, so I stepped in, taking in the old familiar smell of incense that took me back to childhood.

'Can I ask you something, Father?' I whispered. 'Is there such a thing as evil?'

There was a pause and then the curtain was pulled back and Father Michael looked at me. I had always liked him, with his curly, sandy-coloured hair and soulful, spiritual eyes.

'Yes, Christine,' he said. 'There is, unfortunately, so much evil. What is it that you are concerned with?'

I started to cry. He stood up. 'I've finished the confessions for today, would you like to come and talk to me in my sacristy?' I told him that I would.

I waited for him to disrobe, then followed him through the church and to the small room at the back. I looked around at the large altar candles that lit up his red satin robes. The silver chalices gleamed and the dark wood of the panelling in the room smelled of incense.

Father Michael sat in an armchair opposite me and leaned forward.

'You're very upset about something. I don't know if I can help, but anything you tell me will be kept between you and me.'

I wiped my eyes with the back of my hands and looked at him. Priests had always filled me with a deep sense of trust and security. I saw them as men of God, pure and wise. They were called Father, and to me the sound of the word was like the promise of eternal protection and warmth. He would understand. I poured out the whole story, while Father Michael listened patiently.

'It was OK, well sort of OK until now,' I said, as I finished. 'I mean, I didn't feel that I was doing much harm by writing, but now if I visit him, I just wanted to get it clear,' I faltered, 'that I wasn't being evil, you know. Or condoning the evil that he committed.'

I thought that he would tell me that it was OK, that no one was evil, and that you should not judge anyone, for we were all God's children. So what he did say came as a shock.

'You must not visit him. Leave it to someone like me – or a sister. You aren't strong enough to not be hurt or harmed by the evil he has either connected with or is still inside of him. Forget all ideas of visiting such a person.'

I stared at him, numbly, as he went on, 'You're an unusual girl. It's not often someone so young questions the meaning of existence in the way you seem to. But I suggest that if you want to do something to help humankind, there's missionary work that you can do in Africa.'

He looked at me with kind eyes. He was a good man, whose life had been devoted to Christ. But I felt nauseous and cold inside.

'I'm scared, Father. I'm scared of life. I'm scared of all the suffering, danger, and evil in the world. Is everyone scared all the time, or is it just me? I need to go and look in the darkness and find answers, Father. If I can't then I will despair.'

'Do not feel fear or despair,' he said. 'Pray. Prayer will remove despair.'

I wanted to ask him what you were supposed to do if you felt fear and anxiety overwhelming you. How could you stop that? But I didn't ask. I had heard enough. I thanked him and made my way out to the front of the church. It was all so familiar to me – the smell of fresh furniture polish and the feel of the wooden pews. I slipped into one and sat for a long time, looking at the altar, and wondering what it would be like to live without God. I thought how lonely that would be and how empty.

Yet the choice seemed clear to me. God was on the side of normal everyday people. Killers in prison were on the side of evil. So I could not have God if I was going to go and see Brady. Yet despite what this would mean, I still felt I had to understand why he did it.

Would I really lose God's love? Even though it meant taking that risk, I had to find my answers. I had brought my Bible with me. It was leather-bound, with gold lettering, and I'd had it since I was a child. I tucked it into the prayer book holder in front of me. Then I got up and walked towards the door.

I had taken the decision to turn my back on the religion I had grown up with, and which had played such a big part in my life. Why was I doing that? I agonised about whether I would regret it, and whether visiting Brady made me evil too. But a part of me still felt that I was evil anyway, as my adoptive parents had always said. And if that was true, then what did I have to lose?

A couple of night later I lay in my bed with the window open. A breeze was blowing the curtains around and cooling my hot face as I lay between sleeping and waking. Suddenly I heard voices, whispering my name over and over again.

'*Christine – Christine – Christine.*'

I woke with a start, wondering whether I was dreaming. I got up and shut the window tightly, then climbed back into bed and pulled the covers around my head.

One night a week or two later, I sat in bed writing late into the night, as I often did. The house was still and dark and I wrote by the light of my small bedside lamp, enjoying the quiet of the night. I was writing a long letter to Brady, and when I finished I drew back the curtains and saw that dawn was just beginning to break through the darkness. It was after 4 a.m.

I sat looking around at my things; the letter on my bedside table, the books on my shelf on war, crime and religion and the gold crucifix I still kept hanging over the dressing-table mirror. There were also the books Brady had instructed me to buy – a few on the occult and one by the theosophist Madame Blavatsky.

As I sat there it seemed as if the room faded out, and there was just a haze. I leaned my head back on the headboard of the bed. Then I saw a shape in front of me, shimmering. It was almost as if there was someone there, yet I couldn't see them. Was it a ghost?

'What do you want?' I said in a shaky voice. 'I know you're there. Why can't I see you? Who are you?'

I could still sense it in the room. It was so powerful.

I lay there rigid with fear, eyes wide open. There *was* a ghost there.

Unable to stand it, I tore the sheets back, dived out of bed, and grabbed a jumper, jeans and some old trainers. I pulled them on and ran down the stairs and out of the house.

The street was deserted, the lamps throwing an orange glow into the half-light. I could hear my heartbeat pounding in my ears and I turned to see if whatever it was had followed me. I nearly fell as I turned back and carried on running until I reached Linton's house.

It was five o'clock in the morning by the time I got there. I rapped hard on the door until Linton's sleepy face appeared at the upstairs window. He came down and let me in, then climbed back into bed, without saying a word.

'Linton, I'm frightened. I think I've conjured up some evil spirits.'

'Don't be stupid, how can you conjure up evil spirits?' He rolled over in bed and swore softly when he saw the time on the clock beside the bed.

He got out of bed and padded barefoot downstairs with me.

We sat in the kitchen and as he boiled some eggs and made toast I told him what had happened. I wasn't sure whether he believed me or not, but after we'd eaten, he agreed to drive me back home and to look at my room, to see if he could see anything.

When we got there I made him go upstairs first, while I followed, cowering behind him. The morning sun shining into the room seemed to mock the previous night's fears. I sat on the bed, and wondered if I had been dreaming or imagining things. Or maybe it was tiredness, from staying awake all night. Linton sat across the room, flicking through the books that had been lying open next to my bed. He looked up in surprise. 'Since when have you been interested in the occult?'

'I don't know,' I answered. 'I think it was after I went to see that psychic, and it came true about Brady's letter. Then Brady recommended those books.'

'You shouldn't read these books,' Linton said. 'In the same way that some people are powerfully affected by drugs like LSD, and freak out, you're over-sensitive to this stuff' – he indicated the books – 'and it messes with your mind.'

He stood up. 'I'm going. You'd better get some sleep.'

After he had gone I sat on the bed thinking. He was right. My imagination had run away with me and it was probably because of the books I was reading. I got up and took the books outside to the garden shed, then went back to bed and slept.

Soon afterwards I rang Brady's psychiatrist. He had a very aristocratic accent and I felt he was laughing at me. He asked me why I wanted to visit his patient and I went quiet. The whole call felt very odd. Looking back I think it was perhaps because I had sent in my photo – I think it amused the psychiatrist, given that Brady hadn't seen any visitors at all in such a long time, that he should have a visit from a young woman. However, he agreed that I could come and said he hoped to meet me when I came.

A week before the visit I still hadn't told Linton what I planned to do. He knew that Brady had invited me, but I had only told him I was thinking about it.

The weekend before I took my overnight bag round to his house, as I often did. On the Saturday, we went shopping and I bought loads of chocolate bars and boxes of sweets and put them in Linton's fridge.

'What are those for?' he asked.

'They're for the asylum visit,' I said, nervously.

'You're going then?' he said sadly.

He didn't mention it again until that evening, when we were lying in bed watching some old episodes of *Coronation Street*.

Suddenly he exploded, shoving me out of bed and shouting at me that if I was going to see 'that maniac' then I had better leave his house.

'I don't know what you're playing at,' he said. 'But I can't handle it.'

Sobbing, I took my overnight bag and left. It was pouring with rain and I realised I'd forgotten all the chocolates and sweets I'd bought. I went back and shouted under Linton's window. A few minutes later it opened and the sweets and chocolate bars came flying out and crashed on the ground.

The rain was now so heavy that it was falling in sheets, and I was soaked to the skin. Make-up and tears ran down my face as I grovelled in the wet and puddles for the chocolates and sweets.

I bent my head against the rain and half ran down the street. Huge puddles were gathering in the road as the downpour continued. I only had a light coat, and I hugged it to me as I headed for home, my hair plastered to my head. I heard an engine revving, and Linton's pick-up truck – another of his new 'toys' – drew up alongside me.

'No one's going to want to know you,' he shouted through the window.

I ignored him, my head bent against the rain, and tried to walk faster.

'I said, no one's going to want to know you,' he shouted. 'You're putting yourself outside society if you do this.'

I turned and screamed at him. 'You don't understand. I've got to find out why he did it. I must know if it is his fault. Don't you see I have to, Linton?'

I marched on as Linton sat in his truck and watched me. His window was still open and I could hear Elvis singing one of our favourite songs.

I've lost you, yes I've lost you. I can't reach you any more.

10

The Visit

The train journey up to Liverpool was airless and hot. I had
treated myself to a first-class ticket and apart from one or two
businessmen, their heads buried in newspapers, the carriage
was empty.

I looked as though I was on a business journey myself,
wearing a black suit and black court shoes. I hadn't been sure
about what to wear, but this rather formal and sober outfit
that I occasionally needed for work, felt right.

I had taken two days off and planned to stay overnight and
visit the prison the next day.

For a long time I stared out of the window, watching
endless rows of houses, and then fields and roads, flash by.
Was I doing the right thing? Did I really want to meet the man
who was hated by every person in the country? Why couldn't I
just walk away, and get on with my life? Why did I feel so
compelled to go? And why did I feel as if his fate and mine
were interlinked?

I pulled out the book I had just bought. It was called *Brady
and Hindley: The Genesis of the Moors Murders*, by Fred
Harrison, a journalist from the *Sunday People*. Harrison was
the only person to have written a book about Brady who had

actually met him. And his account was very different from most. Generally Brady was portrayed as a domineering sadist. But according to Harrison's account Brady was schizoid, which meant he had schizophrenic tendencies and was suffering from mental illness. He said Brady had told him of 'the giant bald face of death', a spirit that he had conversed with since he was fifteen. He said the face appeared to him as a half-formed vision in a kind of green mist and he had killed for it to provide 'sacrifices'. It sounded so sinister, I wasn't sure what to make of it.

I closed the book and looked at my watch. Two o'clock. This time tomorrow, I was due to see him. And I was convinced that in that hour I would discover the real truth, the answers I was searching for. I would look at Brady and know if he truly was evil. And I would know too, I felt certain, if he really was my father.

When the train arrived at Liverpool Central I took a taxi to a small hotel where I had booked a room. By the time I got there it was early evening. I wasn't hungry and didn't feel like exploring, so I decided to stay in and get a good night's rest.

I had a lot to think about. Only a couple of weeks earlier the police had found the body of Pauline Reade, the sixteen-year-old who was another of Hindley and Brady's victims. Hindley had taken police to the moors, twice, to pinpoint Pauline's grave and after months of searching she had been found. The final victim, Keith Bennett, had not been found, although Brady had been taken to the moors to show police his grave. Five young lives, cut short in the most brutal way, by the man I was going to see the next day.

That night as I slept I was haunted by terrible dreams of a small child, screaming hysterically, in terror.

'*Help me, help me. I never meant to, I never wanted to. Oh Mummy, Mummy, help me, I'm lost.*'

I reached towards his outstretched hands and pulled the tortured child out of the blackness and towards me. His face was twisted with pain, his eyes fearful and shocked. I pulled him close to me, and whispered words of comfort.

'You're safe now, I won't let them hurt you, you're not alone, I'm here, now. I'll be your Mummy. You are not lost.'

I woke with a start, filled with dread.

I switched on the bedside lamp and looked at the clock. It was four in the morning. I left the light on, and made myself a cup of tea, filling the small plastic kettle on the guest tray from the bathroom tap. I got back into bed with a mug of hot milky tea. I picked up the Fred Harrison book and started to read it again, but this time the account of the murders.

I had never read about them before. I hadn't wanted to face any of the details of their grieving families or their sad deaths. But now I made myself do it. I felt I couldn't go and see Brady without knowing what he did, and as I read tears poured down my face. I burned with guilt, feeling almost as if I was responsible for those poor children's deaths myself.

There were pages of photos, of Brady, Hindley and their victims. I turned the page and saw a little boy, one that I half-recognised. I peered at it harder, until it clicked: it was the lost child that I went to in my dream. The caption said 'Ian Brady, aged seven'.

I lay staring at it for ages. Surely I must have glanced at it before and then subconsciously remembered it.

Why was I dreaming of Brady as a child? How could that possibly have been? It seemed extraordinary and I felt deeply disturbed. I lay awake wondering what life with the foster parents who brought him up from babyhood had truly been like. What had made him the way he was?

Eventually I fell asleep again, only to wake a short while later, at six. I felt terrible. I went though to the bathroom and threw up. I'd had a nervous stomach since childhood. Whenever I felt anxious or scared I got sick. And now I felt both.

I pulled back the heavy beige curtains. The air smelt of summer – freesias, lily of the valley and freshly mown lawns.

I needed to talk to someone. Linton was still furious with me, and I hadn't told James or any of my other friends about the visit. I phoned Freddie, hoping he'd be understanding.

'I'm in Liverpool,' I said. 'I'm going to visit Brady today, and I feel so nervous. Am I doing the right thing? And should I take him something? Can you think of anything?'

'Look Chris, this whole thing turns my stomach,' he said. 'If you're going through with this, don't phone me again.' He paused and I started crying.

I was using the public phone in the hallway of the hotel and three burly lorry drivers walked past. 'All right Blondie?' one of them said, winking.

'I don't know why I want to go and do this, but I have to, Freddie,' I said. But the phone went dead. I put the receiver down and looked at my face in the mirror above the phone. I looked awful, with make-up in smears down my face, and dark circles under tired and puffy eyes.

Another friend gone. How much was I losing, in this crazy quest?

I could smell the eggs and bacon being served up in the dining room, but I couldn't face food. I went up to my room, re-did my make-up and packed my bag, then I left the hotel.

It was ten in the morning. I had four hours to wait before visiting time began. I made my way to the nearest coffee bar and sat with a coffee and the papers. There was an article about Brady, as there was most days at that time, because the hunt for the two remaining bodies on the moors had sparked fresh media interest.

I couldn't face reading any more about him. I put the paper down and sat, watching people in the street outside, most of them shoppers, carrying bags and chatting to one another. They were normal decent women, the kind I longed to be. But I wasn't normal or decent, I knew that. I was a bad girl, a wicked girl, an unwanted girl.

I sat there so long, frozen to the spot at the small formica table, that I lost track of time. I looked up at the clock: it was quarter to two. I jumped up.

It was five to two by the time I got to the bus station and asked which bus went to Park Lane. The bus driver told me it would take nearly an hour to get there. I started to panic.

Luckily there were several taxis waiting at the station. I jumped into one and it was just after ten past two when he slowed down and went through the huge iron gates of Park Lane Hospital for the Criminally Insane.

Park Lane was situated in the suburb of Maghull, and was one of only three secure units for the criminally insane – the others being Rampton and Broadmoor. Park Lane was built in the early seventies as an overspill facility for Broadmoor, in Berkshire, which was built over a hundred years earlier. Today Park Lane is known simply as Ashworth Hospital, though it is still a high security facility for criminals who are considered to be criminally insane.

Inside the front entrance there was a large reception area. I was asked to sign a visitors' book, then I sat down to wait my turn in a smallish room with a sofa, cushioned chairs and huge notice boards warning of prosecution if anything was smuggled in to the prisoners.

A voice came over the loudspeaker: 'Christine Hart to see 490, Ian Brady.' I got up quickly and moved towards a door that slid upwards. Beyond it was a security cubicle, where I passed over the sweets and chocolates I'd brought and was searched thoroughly by a guard. After I was cleared I was directed towards another door. A buzzer sounded, the door slid upwards to open and I found myself inside a different, very tranquil world, in which time seemed to stand still. Another uniformed guard was waiting for me. The look on his face was stony.

'This way,' he said briskly, and I followed him as he walked quickly along a cold, grey corridor and into the garden. It was large and very basic, with no bright flowers or exotic blooms. Dotted around were benches and on most of them sat old men with bent backs, muttering to themselves and swaying backwards and forwards.

We walked past a number of small grey buildings. From one I could hear a man screaming, in a high-pitched voice, through the window. I hesitated, and the nurse glanced back at me, then snapped, 'Come along, I haven't got all day.' I was taken to Newman Ward, where Brady was kept for his own protection. I had read that he'd been beaten up several times since he had been at Park Lane. In the end, they moved him to the old men's ward, where the inmates were mostly too feeble to beat him up. Nontheless he remained in his room most of the time for fear of further reprisals.

We entered the building through a sliding door, which closed behind us before another opened in front of us. Then I was led into the ward and asked to wait outside the office, in a long corridor that smelt of disinfectant and school dinners.

There had been no sign of the psychiatrist I'd spoken to. A short grey-haired man came out and ushered me into the office.

'So you want to meet Brady, do you?' He didn't look friendly.

'Yes.'

After a minute he turned and called out, 'Get Brady'.

I was ushered into a room that reminded me of the 'quiet room' at my children's home. The walls were white, and bare, and there were four or five sad, shabby green armchairs dotted about.

A guard sat on a chair at the other side of the room. My mouth was dry and my legs felt wobbly and I was glad to be able to sit down in one of the armchairs. I turned to look at the guard. He was staring at me with undisguised contempt.

I shifted around in my seat and my clammy palms stuck to the seat of the chair. My stomach started churning, the way it always did when I was nervous or scared. And I was very scared – of the warders and nurses, with their granite stares, and of the moment when Brady would walk into the room and I would have to face him.

The seconds ticking by felt like hours.

'Does he see a lot of people?' My voice came out reedy and thin. The guard was silent, and I didn't think he'd heard me. Then he said coldly, 'Just his solicitor'.

The closed door was behind me and I kept turning towards it. My mouth was so dry I kept trying to swallow.

The handle turned, and I jumped. The grey-haired man from the office came in. 'OK, you can go in now. He's in the room at the end of the corridor on the right.'

I wasn't sure if he meant me to go alone, but I looked around and the guard was right behind me. We went out of the door and turned down the corridor. The ceilings were low and the walls were painted a dull orange, with green carpets. The décor looked new, and it was brightly lit, yet not remotely welcoming or pleasant.

This was his reality, I thought. Orange walls, low ceilings, and the smell of school dinners and disinfectant.

I could see his door. I felt I was barely breathing. This was it. I was about to come face to face with a man who knew the true nature of hell.

I had been told that he barely came out of his room. The guards took him his food. He was like a monster that no one ever saw, locked away in his lair.

I was standing outside the door. I took a breath, tried to ignore my pounding heart, put my hand on the handle and opened it.

He was sitting in a chair facing the window, through which the sun was shining. He was broad-shouldered, which surprised me. From his photo I had expected a slighter man. He was wearing a cheap navy polyester jacket over a black woollen polo-neck sweater, with blue denim jeans that were so worn out the material looked almost threadbare. His hair was dark and slicked back in a Teddy boy style, as it was in the pre-jail photos taken over twenty years earlier.

He turned and looked towards me. He had dark glasses covering his eyes, one lens pale, and the other dark, which had a bizarre effect, as I could only see one of his eyes. I must have stood there for a few minutes as he looked at me, trying, I suppose, to work out why I was there and what it was that I wanted from him.

The guard, who was still behind me, tapped me on the shoulder. 'Psychiatrist's doing his rounds, you'll have to go back to the visitors' room.'

I presumed he meant that I should go and Brady should stay, so I was surprised when Brady stood up and walked towards me. He was at least six feet tall and my anxiety increased. I had thought he would be ill, or weak, or small, but he appeared nothing of the kind. He was a tall, broad, man and I felt even more out of my depth. His room was smaller than an average size bathroom. A few biscuits, spread with what looked like cream cheese, sat gathering dust on the floor beside the bed. There was a bite taken out of one of them.

Brady walked slowly down the corridor in front of me towards the visitors' room. I noticed his trousers were way too short and his jacket miles too tight, so that his arms and legs poked out. He was walking slowly and deliberately, with a slight stoop, and at one point he faltered and swayed against the wall. I wondered whether this was because of the drugs I had heard he was kept on, but later I learned that it was because he had a bad knee. I followed him into the rooms and sat in the same chair I had used earlier. He sat down opposite me and the guard sat by the wall directly behind him, which meant that I could still see his contemptuous stare. I felt desperately uncomfortable.

We sat in silence for several minutes. I had no idea what to say. Nothing I had prepared in advance felt right. I couldn't come out and ask this strange figure if he might be my father. Nor did it seem appropriate to ask him trivial questions about the food and what he did all day.

Brady had removed his dark glasses when he sat down. But he didn't look at me, he had his head down and seemed to be looking at his hands, which lay crossed on his knees, his large white fingers intertwined. His face was also white, with a sallow tinge, like parchment. He had a Roman nose and his mouth was turned down at the corners, while his lower lip jutted out. He appeared not to have shaved – I could see stubble across the lower half of his face.

I looked down and started fidgeting with the hem of my skirt. I could see the clock on the wall, the minutes were ticking by and still neither of us had spoken.

After twenty minutes he spoke, and my impression, from the effort it appeared to demand of him, was that he wasn't used to talking. He spoke in a slow soft drawl, almost a whisper, and he seemed to have difficulty in pronouncing his words. I supposed that this too was the effect of the medication he took.

'Did you get here all right?' He looked at me as he spoke, and I had the impression of very intense, dark grey eyes, before he looked away again.

I could feel my face burning hot. 'The traffic was bad,' I said.

The guard behind snorted softly in derision. I felt stupid – stupid for being there and stupid for not having anything to say.

I realised that the photo I had kept for so long, and which had brought me comfort as a lost and abandoned teenager, had nothing to do with this man in front of me. That man, the one in my picture, belonged to a fantasy world in which I felt safe and protected. This man was a stranger.

I wanted to go.

He was speaking. 'They want me to go back to search for the other body again. They're looking in the wrong place. I've told the police I can help them find it.'

He was talking about Keith Bennett. He had already been taken out to search for the little boy once, but he clearly wanted to go again.

It was horrifying to hear this. The room swam in front of me. I thought I was going to pass out. I felt drenched with sweat and dizzy. I stood up and looked at the guard. 'Can I go?' My voice was trembling.

Without looking at Brady again, I headed for the door. I could just leave, and forget that this ever happened. Suddenly I longed to be miles away, somewhere cool, safe and clean.

I had to wait for a guard to escort me out to the gate, so I stood in the corridor. Brady got up and followed me to the door. 'Thank you for coming,' he said.

I turned away from him and heard him begin the slow walk back down the corridor towards his room. The relief I felt as I walked out through the swing doors was indescribable. It was as if I had been holding my breath and could finally let go. I felt like sobbing.

I walked back through the gardens and into the reception building. The guard escorting me was different and unlike the one who brought me in and the one in the visitors' room, he seemed friendly and happy to chat, and it was clear from his remarks that he had read my letters to Brady.

'You can't help but feel horrified by what he did,' he said. 'The people in here ignore him mostly. But he was beaten up the other day, on his way to the shop we have here. Five on to one and he fought back – but he still ended up with scars. '

He went on, 'You're interested in good and evil and whether he's sorry or not, aren't you? It's very important to you – isn't it – that he should be sorry.' He smiled at me so kindly.

'He found your letters about good and evil and the soul's journey fascinating. So did I.'

'I was wrong to write,' I said. 'I realise now that there is no excuse for what he did.'

We had reached the outer door, which would take me back to the front drive and the gates.

'Your letters are why he agreed to see you. Everybody looks at him in the same way, but you saw him differently.'

I didn't know what to say. I was still unable to take in that I had come face to face with Brady.

I shook hands with the guard. 'I was a stupid kid,' I said, and turned to walk out.

Once outside the front gates I found the bus stop that would take me back into the city and sat on a bench to wait. I breathed in the smell of wet earth and damp hedgerows and felt I had been released from a kind of prison myself. I was hot and sweaty and I took off my jacket. The sun burned into my face and relaxed me a little. When the bus arrived, half an hour later, I sat upstairs at the front, with the small window open beside me, grateful for the cool breeze. An hour later I was on the London train, and the further I travelled from Park Lane, the greater my sense of relief. Whatever crazy quest I had been on, it was time to give up. The following day I was back at work and glad of the familiar office routine as I made notes on the healthcare swindles, bank fraud and surveillance files on my desk.

After work I went to the pub with James to talk about the cases we were working on and two important new clients from the Sudan. We chatted over chilled white wine, then went next door to the chip shop and bought hot chilli sauce kebabs. My visit to Brady began to feel like a distant dream, something that wasn't real. This was what was real, my life in London, my career in the security industry, my hopes for marriage and children.

I got the tube home and by the time I reached my front door I was exhausted and longing for bed. I put the key in the lock and slipped quietly inside, careful not to disturb my adoptive parents, who would long since have gone to bed.

I glanced at the hall table, and saw the letter, with the sloping handwriting on the front, sitting there. My heart started to pound. It hadn't occurred to me that he would write again. And certainly not this soon. He must have written it as soon as I left.

'I sit alone in my room, a lot of time, sometimes I can go for weeks and I don't need to speak, because there is no one to talk to. I am sorry for your wasted journey. You are very, very beautiful, but I am sure you know that already . . .'

I tore it up and threw the pieces in the bin.

11

Front Page Story

Several weeks passed, summer turned to autumn and as I got on with my life I began to feel calmer. A couple more letters arrived from Brady, but I ignored them. He said that he had registered me with the authorities as a visitor he was willing to see, and that I was welcome to go and see him again at any time. But I had no intention of taking up his offer. I made my decision: I was going to break off contact with him. I began to feel good about the future. I was normal now, just like any other girl my age.

I was still living between my parents' home and Linton's, spending the week with them and the weekends with him. Familiarity kept me in the relationship with Linton, and at home, too. Over the past couple of years my parents and I had come to a more comfortable place. I was able to come and go as I chose and they no longer imposed their rules on me. I hadn't so much forgiven what they had done in the past, as put it away, out of sight. Perhaps because deep down I still longed for them to love and approve of me.

What I really wanted, more than anything, was to meet someone I could settle down with, and create a life in which I

felt happy about myself. I longed for the safety and respect-
ability of a husband and children. I wanted to be like every
other girl, and to escape the unhappy legacy of my past.

Then something happened that changed everything, and left
my hopes for a peaceful, ordinary future, in shreds.

One Sunday in early October, I climbed out of bed and
padded barefoot downstairs in my pyjamas to make myself a
cup of coffee and see if anyone else was around.

The house was quiet except for the grandfather clock
ticking away in the front room. I realised my parents must
be at church. I tried the door to the front room but it was
locked. Even though I was an adult, my parents still locked the
doors of their bedroom and all the downstairs rooms, apart
from the kitchen, whenever they went out. It always made me
feel as if they didn't trust me and thought I'd run off with any
cash or valuables left lying around.

I went into the kitchen to make breakfast and saw the
Sunday papers were lying on the table. I didn't usually bother
reading them, but I started to look idly through them. My cold
toes kicked against the table leg and I could smell the French
coffee beans that I had ground, bubbling in the percolator. I
drizzled maple syrup over a stack of pancakes and tucked in
greedily.

My parents always bought a serious paper and a red-topped
tabloid. As I flicked through it I saw the usual mix of gossip,
celebrities and shock-horror stories. Then I turned the page
and saw the headline of the story on page five. For a second
reality seemed suspended. What I was reading seemed so
beyond the bounds of possibility that I almost convinced
myself I was imagining it. The headline said: 'Mystery Girl
Visits Brady'. The story went on to outline Brady's fascina-

tion with a beautiful, blonde woman in her early twenties, who had been writing to him for some time, and who was the first visitor, apart from his solicitor and Lord Longford, he had allowed in to see him for twenty five years.

That's wrong, I thought. Fred Harrison, the author of the book I'd read about Brady went, for a start. And who was this blonde? It had to be someone else.

But I knew.

I read the last sentence of the story; 'as yet this girl has been unnamed.'

It couldn't be. It just couldn't be. I read and re-read the story, hoping to spot something that might make me realise they were talking about someone else. But there was nothing.

I hadn't realised that my contact with Brady *was* a story. Surely the papers only wrote about famous people, not everyday people – not people like me. How could anything I did matter to them? But suddenly it seemed to. My private world, a secret I had told to only a very small handful of trusted friends, was now something millions of people were reading about. And I had absolutely no idea how they'd found out about it.

I sat there for ages. I had no idea what to do. The only thing that made it bearable was that I wasn't identified. They didn't know my name. Could they find out who I was? Surely not. But then they'd found out about my visit to Brady, and even my letters to him.

I had no idea what to do. Who could I talk to? My adoptive parents had never known about Brady and I wanted it to stay that way. And the people I'd told – Linton, Freddie, and Father Michael – had all told me to stay away. Would any of them sympathise with me now?

What seemed especially hard was that I had walked away from it all, and thought it was over. I had decided not to see or write to Brady again. I wanted a fresh start to my life, a new direction. Now the story was in the paper, and if I was identified, not just my friends, but everyone in the country would turn against me.

For the rest of the day I paced about in my room, trying to decide what to do. I rang Linton, who said, 'Well, you shouldn't have visited a serial killer. Now you're for it.' This only frightened me even more. That night I didn't sleep; I lay wide awake, sick with anxiety, and sobbed into my pillow.

All the old feelings of being evil and unwanted came back with a vengeance. I had thought I might be able to lead a normal life. But if I was named or, God forbid, photographed, then my life would fall apart. Brady was known as the most hated man in British criminal history. So what did that make me? How bitterly I regretted ever having anything to do with him. How had it all started anyway? Why had I ever written to him? I had just been a sad, lonely and unloved little girl clinging to a straw. I felt terrified.

On Monday morning I got up very early. I had a plan, of sorts. I would phone my old friend Freddie. He had been angry with me for going to see Brady, but I was sure he would forgive me. He had always given me good advice in the past, he was sharp and clever. I would tell him the whole story and he'd know what to do.

I didn't want to phone from home, so I went out to a nearby phone box. On the way I went into the newsagent's, which had just opened. I flicked through all the papers, checking that there were no more stories about me.

'You have to buy them before you read them,' the newsagent said. 'Sorry,' I muttered, and I put them back and left.

Freddie answered the phone sleepily. 'Christine, why are you ringing at this hour?' he said.

'I'm sorry Freddie, but I need your help, I'm in real trouble.' I told him about the story in the paper. 'What shall I do, Freddie?' I wept.

He was silent for a moment. Then he said, 'Look, the best thing is to disappear for a bit. There probably won't be another article, but in case there is, just don't be around. Go up to Scotland for a week or two. Why not go to Glencoe or Rannoch? You've always admired it in the pictures I've shown you. It's nice and remote. By then this will all have blown over.'

Freddie was a Scot. Trust him to recommend I flee to his home town, I thought. I was still terribly upset but I was also hugely grateful.

I thanked him and said I'd ring him when I'd decided where to go. I opened the door of the phone box and walked slowly back home. It was still early, only half past six, and barely anybody was about. It was one of those mellow, warm autumn days. I began to feel a little better. Freddie was right, all I had to do was disappear for a bit, and it would all go away.

When I got home I looked out my savings book. I had a few hundred pounds put away; that should last me for a bit. I slipped it into my handbag and began to pack clothes into a small case.

At nine, when the agency opened, I phoned in and told James I had a few personal problems and needed a couple of weeks off. He laughed good-naturedly. 'If it weren't for the fact that you're so good at this job I'd tell you to get lost. As it is, make sure you get back here as soon as you can.'

I promised him I'd be back at my desk in a fortnight and he wished me well.

Next I went to the building society, drew out two hundred pounds, and checked on the times of the coaches from Victoria to Scotland. A coach left at ten each morning for Glasgow and another at four for Edinburgh. I decided I'd go to Glasgow the following morning. I spent the rest of the day quietly at home and that night I got a few hours' fitful sleep.

When morning came I woke with a surge of apprehension, but I told myself I had nothing to worry about. In a few hours I would be sitting on a coach bound for Glasgow and I would be safe.

At six-thirty I went round to the newsagent's to see if there was anything in the newspapers. This time I bought a couple of them, to make him happy. Although Brady was in the paper still because of his visit to the moors, there was nothing about me. Thank goodness. I began to relax a little more as I walked back home.

As I stepped inside the front door I heard the phone ringing. It was still only seven – who would call at that time? My mother was up and she handed the phone to me.

It was Freddie. 'I'm going today,' I told him. 'I've got my case all packed.'

He sounded a bit distant. 'Christine, look, I've been think-ing. I'm not sure going to Scotland is the best plan. I've got some ideas and I think we should meet for lunch and talk it all over.'

I was surprised, and touched. He really was trying to help. Perhaps he'd come up with a better plan than Scotland. If not, then I could take the afternoon bus to Edinburgh. I'd take my suitcase with me and go straight to Victoria.

I told my parents I was off on a work trip – they were quite used to me going away and didn't think anything of it. I prayed they would never know the real reason.

Freddie had asked me to meet him at The Red Lion in Ealing, a huge newly refurbished pub, with a big outside eating area. The weather was still warm and when I got there dozens of office workers were enjoying an outdoor lunch. There was no sign of Freddie, so I pulled up a chair at one of the white plastic tables.

Fifteen minutes later Freddie appeared. He hurried over and said, 'Christine, I'm really sorry, but I can't make lunch after all. Things are really busy at work and I can't get away.'

Something about his behaviour was odd. He wasn't meeting my eye, which was unlike him. I felt uneasy.

'That's a shame,' I said. 'I guess I'll go back to plan A and go to Scotland, if you haven't got a better idea.' I tried to give him a hug – we always hugged when we met – but he moved quickly away.

'Got to dash – sorry,' he said.

I stood watching him walk away. I was puzzled. The whole thing seemed odd. Then I saw them. Two men and a woman, sitting at a nearby table. They had been talking, but now they stopped and turned to look at me and I saw that one of them was holding a camera with a large flashgun.

The next few moments seemed to happen in slow motion.

As they got to their feet and came towards me I saw Freddie, behind them, watching. Everything fell into place.

'Not Freddie, not my friend, not this.'

I wanted to cry, but instead I grabbed my case and ran. I could hear my three pursuers running behind me. I headed for the nearby main road and dodged through the traffic. Cars beeped at me but I was oblivious.

Then I saw a red double-decker bus at the stop a few yards ahead of me. With a huge effort I lugged my suitcase towards it. As I got there it was beginning to pull away. I threw the case onto the platform and grabbed the pole, but I couldn't get on. The bus drew away with my suitcase on it and I stood in the road and let out a sob of helpless fury. Then the bus slowed down again at some traffic lights. I sprinted towards it and managed to jump on just as it started moving.

I looked out of the back window and saw one of the three reporters – that's what I assumed they were – in the road behind the bus. He'd been running after me, he was rather overweight and was sweating and panting.

I put the suitcase in the rack downstairs then climbed up to the top deck and sat on the back seat. The conductor, a tall West Indian, came to collect the fares.

'You look as if you just seen a ghost,' he laughed.

I managed a watery smile. I'd have preferred a ghost.

I'd got away – but was I safe? I found it hard to think straight. Should I try to get to Scotland? The bus was going in the wrong direction, towards my home. I'd go back there, lie low for a bit and decide what to do.

I wanted to ask Freddie how he could do this to me. What has made him betray me? I knew he didn't like me contacting Brady, but to tell the papers my secret he must really despise me. Had he ever been my friend?

It didn't occur to me that I could just refuse to comment if they caught me. I thought I'd have to talk to them. For the next few minutes I stared out of the window, waiting for the pounding of my heart to slow down. I glanced out of the back window, wanting to reassure myself that I really was safe.

Behind us was a green Jaguar. I peered down at it, and my stomach did a somersault. Both the men who had chased me were sitting in the front. The girl was probably in the back.

I turned round quickly and started to cry and shake uncontrollably. I was scared out of my wits. Who were these people? They seemed so ruthless and so frightening. There was nothing I could do: the only exit on the bus was the back door and they had it covered.

The conductor passed by and saw my tears. 'Are you all right love?' he asked kindly. I nodded.

I was afraid that one of the people in the car would board the bus and corner me. I had to get off. We slowed down at a roundabout and I ran downstairs, grabbed the case and jumped off.

I dodged around people walking along the busy main road and managed to slip down an alleyway in between the shops. I crouched there amongst some dustbins for almost an hour until I was certain the coast was clear. Then I went back out to the road and got on another bus which took me close to home.

I got off the bus and started walking. It was only a few streets away, but I was tired and my suitcase felt terribly heavy. I turned the corner into my road when a horrible thought occurred to me. What if they knew my address and were waiting for me?

I began to run towards the house, the suitcase thumping painfully against my ankle. I wanted to get inside as fast as possible. I reached the house, and as I ran down the front path and fumbled with the key in the lock I heard car doors slam and the reporters came running across the road. I got inside, slammed the door shut and collapsed on the stairs, sobbing and out of breath.

'Please let them go away,' I whispered. Thankfully my parents were out, but they could be back at any minute. Then the woman shouted through the letter-box.

'Christine, we know you believe Ian Brady's your father, why don't you tell us about it?' She banged on the door.

A man's voice came through the letter-box. 'Look love, if you don't let us in and tell us the story, you'll have everyone in Fleet Street outside the door. The wolf pack, they call them. We're your friends; we only want to help you.'

I moved from the stairs through to the kitchen, then jumped as I saw one of them at the back door, trying the handle. I put the bolts on the door then walked away backwards, never taking my eyes off him.

I went up the stairs and crouched down on the floor like a cornered animal, crying and shaking. They were still banging on the front door and shouting through the letter-box.

Eventually the banging stopped. I waited a while then tip-toed down to the front door. Had they given up and gone? I turned the handle slowly and pulled it open just a crack to see if their car had gone. As I did the door was pushed open and one of the men came in.

'Look, Christine,' he said, softly. 'We don't want to hurt you, we're on your side, but if you don't tell us your story, you'll have the whole of Fleet Street out here.'

I started to cry again. 'Can't you just leave me alone?'

'Who else lives here?' he asked.

'My parents,' I said. 'And I don't want them disturbed. My father has a weak heart.'

'Tell you what,' he said. 'We'll take you up to our offices, and we can all have a chat about it there. How about that? We already know from your friend Freddie about you and Brady, and that you think he's your dad, so you might as well do the story with us.'

'Look, Brady's not my Dad, Freddie's wrong. I grew up in an orphanage,' I said, wiping my eyes.

The man – this was the portly one – glanced at the other two reporters, who'd followed him in. 'So you grew up in an orphanage believing he was your father, did you?'

'No, I . . .'

I stopped. How could I explain?

'They told me my father was in prison,' I said. 'But they didn't say that it was him.'

'You just thought it was,' the woman said. 'But why? Did you come from the same area?'

'Well, my Mum lived in Hull, and he was in Hull in borstal. She gave me up because my father did something terrible and he was in prison. That's why she left me alone in the world. When I thought he was a child-killer I forgave her. I under-stood it. But I was a kid. It was . . .' I was going to say nuts, but they weren't listening.

It was enough for them. They persuaded me to go with them, promising that they'd do a fair story and that I was better off with them. I went, mainly because I was desperate to get them away from the house before my parents came back.

I sat in the back of the green Jaguar, exhausted and emotionally wrung-out. I had no idea if I should really be going with them or not. I felt I had no more fight in me, I had put myself in their hands and now I had no idea what was ahead.

It did pass through my mind, as I sat slumped in the car, that there was a terrible irony here. I followed people for a living, and now I had been followed – and caught. Until this moment I'd had no idea how awful it was to be chased by people determined to trap you. However, there was one crucial difference. The subjects I followed were always political and moved in the worlds of surveillance and counter surveillance, so they were expecting it, whereas I was taken completely by surprise.

The driver – the younger man who was the better-looking of the two – wove in and out of the traffic. I caught the eye of a girl in the car next to ours. She looked happy and carefree, and at that moment, I would have given anything to swap places with her.

We got to the newspaper's offices and they took me inside and up in the lift to the news floor. We went into a small office at the side of the huge open-plan room full of desks and reporters, and one of the men got me a cup of tea.

'We'd better introduce ourselves,' he said. 'I'm Nick, this is Piers and this is Cathy.' Nick was the older one with red hair and a public school accent. Piers had a beard, a slight cockney accent and smooth Kurt Russell good looks. And Cathy was dark blonde, slim, about thirty and immaculately turned out. They all had an air of sophistication and a kind of hard edge about them. They scared me, the last thing I wanted to do was talk to them.

How could I explain to these tough-as-nails reporters that I felt different to others, as if I didn't belong and I was inferior? Or that I had made a connection with Brady because I had thought he was abused as a child and I wanted to explain that to the rest of the world. Or that thinking of him had eased my loneliness though those teenage years in the orphanage? Or that I'd pretended – even made myself believe – that he was my real father because he'd had the same life as me?

I couldn't tell them all of that, just as I couldn't explain that my visit to Brady had woken me up, made me realise what I was doing, and that I'd walked away from it. That I had found the reality of the man I met too overwhelming to want to do anything but run a million miles from him and his dark lonely world, his horrific memories, the missing boy on the moor. All of it.

I sat there looking at the grey light filtering through the unwashed windows, the thick red carpet, the air-conditioning and the strip lighting and I knew that if I tried to explain they would look at me as if I was crazy. Freddie had told them a story, and that was what they wanted.

They all went in and out, conferring with various people in the office. Then a man called Ted came in. 'We're going to take you to a nice hotel,' he said. 'We'll look after you there, and that way no one else in Fleet Street will bother you.'

By this time I felt I had no will of my own, I simply went along with what they wanted.

They drove me back to my parents' house, where I collected my suitcase. My parents were in the front room, and as I'd already told them I was going away on a job, they weren't surprised when I appeared, grabbed my case and left.

They looked so old and as I said goodbye I felt terribly sad. We had at last, after all the years of hurt, reached a more comfortable place with one another. Now it was all going to end. By the time the press had finished with me I was quite sure they would never want to speak to me again.

Back in the green Jaguar we headed for a hotel. I told Nick I couldn't sleep alone as I was scared. He offered to sleep on the sofa in my room, to keep me company. I was grateful, but he fell almost instantly asleep and I was left wide awake and restless.

I looked around at the pink walls, pink curtains and matching dusty pink bedding. I went into the bathroom and looked at myself in the mirror with loathing, and wondered how I had managed to get myself into such a mess. I couldn't cry; I had no tears left. I felt exhausted and numb.

I went back into the room and lay on the bed. They were going to say that I was the daughter of one of the worst serial killers in history and there was nothing that I could do to stop them. How had I come to make such an inescapable horror of my life?

I felt totally at the mercy of the three reporters. I thought about begging them, pleading with them: 'Please don't ruin my life. It is so ugly and awful already.' But I was sure they wouldn't take any notice. They had their story, and they weren't about to lose it.

I wanted to sleep, but every time I drifted off I'd wake minutes later with a severe jolt. Sleep was impossible, so I gave up and just sat there, waiting and dreading what was to come.

It was half past eight in the morning when I heard a sharp knock on the door. By that time I was nauseous and aching after a third night of virtually no sleep.

Nick came in. He must have woken up earlier and gone to chat to Piers. 'Oh good, you're up,' he said. 'Look, what we want you to do is go up and see Brady. We'll fly you up there, we want you to hand him your birth certificate and ask him if he's your father. Okey dokey?' He smiled at me as if he were asking me to make him a cup of tea.

I started to cry again. My eyes were too sore to rub, so I just pressed them with the back of my hand. The idea of going up and seeing him again, especially as I hadn't replied to his letters, was a terrifying one. As for asking him about being my Dad – I just didn't think I could do it. I felt exhausted and manipulated. I just wanted the whole nightmare to go away.

Nick started to get impatient. 'We just want to know the Moors Killer's reaction to the possibility of him having a beautiful blonde daughter. Why are you acting as if it's all such a big deal?'

I sat down on the bed and looked up at him. 'I've told you, he's not my father.'

At that moment Piers came in. 'The photographer's here Nick, and he's brought Sue with a couple of dresses.'

A tall dark curly-haired man came in the room with an array of expensive looking camera equipment round his neck and carrying a huge silver case and a tripod. Behind him a short blonde girl with spiky hair came in with a heap of clothes over her arm.

'Hi, I'm Sue,' she said. 'You come and sit over here and we'll get going.'

She started pulling creams, and lotions from the large pink bag she'd brought.

'What look do you want – what's the story?' she called over her shoulder to Ted, who was across the room, talking to Piers and the photographer.

'Make her look as sexy as possible, Sue,' he said.

Sexy? Why on earth would they want me to look sexy? How did that go with the story?

Sue worked on my face for about fifteen minutes, applying gold shadows and crimson lipstick from the huge selection in her large silver toolbox. Then she pulled out some tongs, plugged them in and started painting my nails with scarlet nail polish.

After she had teased my hair into what felt like curls, she held up a dress and told me to put it on. I went in the bathroom, pulled the black and silver dress on, turned to look at myself in the mirror, and recoiled in horror. I had never worn a dress that gave me that kind of cleavage before. I looked like an over the top soap starlet.

I should have refused to put it on, wiped the gunge from my face and walked out. But I felt wrung out and incapable of fighting back. It was as though I had lost my own will and was that abused child again, numb and obedient. I had no idea I could just say no. It never even crossed my mind. The world of the media seemed so powerful. I did have power in my own little ex-army world of surveillance, but in this alien world I felt like a child.

I unlocked the bathroom door and came out. 'That looks great,' Nick said.

'God,' I whispered, 'please don't make me wear it. I look like a kissogram.'

Sue shot me a sympathetic glance. 'Try it back to front to hide your tits a bit – you're very busty,' she said cheerfully.

I did, and it was a slight improvement. Nick seemed to be losing his patience again. 'I suppose it's OK, but for God's sake smile. It's not the bloody end of the world.'

The photographer had set up his equipment. He sat me down under a couple of huge lights and began taking shots. After a few minutes he stopped. 'It's no good. You look as if you're going to cry. I can't get a good shot with you like this.'

Nick dialled room service and five minutes later a porter arrived at the door with a large bottle of vodka, a jug of fresh orange juice, a glass and some ice. Nick poured me a drink. 'Here,' he said, 'this will help to relax you'.

Since I'd had no sleep and nothing to eat, the drink soon began to make me feel light-headed. The photographer began again and eventually he was happy.

'Right,' Nick said. 'You're on the one o'clock flight to Liverpool. Piers is going with you, so get changed, there's a taxi waiting.'

I changed back into my jeans and T-shirt but there was no time to comb my hair straight, or wipe off the heavy make-up. Piers and I got into a black cab and he sat silently beside me, as we headed for Heathrow.

The cab driver had seen Piers' press card. He spoke to me over his shoulder.

'I've seen you.'

I looked over at Piers in horror. 'What does he mean?'

'I've seen you,' the driver said again. 'You're one of those page three girls, aren't you. You're my favourite you are.'

I had to laugh.

'Look,' I said to Piers. 'This is stupid. I don't want to go. Really I don't.'

'I wouldn't put you through this,' he said. 'But you know what Nick's like. If you don't do this, he'll go ahead and print that you're Brady's daughter for definite. This way you've got a chance that he won't print that.'

'He can't just say that,' I protested.

'He can, and I can't stop him. That's why it's best to go and visit Brady and show him your birth certificate and see his reaction.'

My stomach churned with fear. Yet there was a glimmer of hope. If Brady said that I wasn't his daughter and there was no way I could be, if he insisted that the whole thing was ridiculous, then they wouldn't have a story. And I could go home and pretend this whole nightmare never happened.

12

The Bridge on the River

Our flight was delayed and by the time we came into the arrivals hall it was two-thirty. I knew that visiting hours ended at four. We were met by a local reporter, a plump man who ushered us out to the car park where his ancient white Cavalier waited. I turned and stared out of the window as we drove, my insides bubbling with anxiety. The reporter had no idea how to get there and he and Piers were poring over a map.

The lack of sleep and the two vodkas I had drunk earlier were making me feel sick and dizzy. I hoped we'd get there too late. But at 3.45 they dropped me at the end of the drive leading up to the hospital, and drove off up the road, where they said they would be waiting for me when I came out.

Once again I walked up to the guard behind the desk, gave my name and told them I was a visitor for Ian Brady.

He said, 'We have two Ian Bradys here – which one do you want?'

Was he joking? I didn't know what to say. But he knew who I had come to see.

'In any case you're too late,' he snapped.

'I've still got ten minutes, haven't I?' I said nervously.

He looked at me with distaste, picked up the grey phone in front of him, said something and slammed it down again. 'You've got five minutes,' he said. A buzzer sounded in front of me and a young guard stepped forward to escort me to the security hatch.

Once again I was searched. I had to take off my white cowboy boots and hand over a bottle of orange drink that I had in my bag.

The guard escorted me through the grounds to Newman Ward. Neither of us spoke. My boots crunched noisily on the gravel.

As soon as I walked into the ward I caught sight of Brady, crossing the hall area with a small white plate of fish fingers, chips and peas in his hand, presumably on his way back to his room from the dining hall. It was odd, somehow, seeing him doing something so mundane.

I was shown into the visitors' room and a minute later Brady came in and sat down opposite me. He didn't seem at all surprised to see me there, just before the end of visiting time, wearing over-the-top make-up. But I felt horribly embarrassed.

He leaned forward and offered me a cigarette. I shook my head so he took one himself. I lit it with my lighter. He nodded and exhaled then looked down at the floor. He looked nervous and sat forward, his shoulders hunched and his hands grasping his bony knees. He looked down at the floor, and said nothing.

He was wearing exactly the same clothes as last time; the black polo neck, worn blue jeans and the navy polyester jacket. His face was clean-shaven and hair brushed back, teddy boy style.

The young guard sitting across the room said, 'Ian, why is she late?' He spoke loudly, emphasising every syllable, as you might to someone who was deaf or unable to understand. 'You know visiting hours, Ian, why didn't you tell her?'

Ian could have said that he hadn't known I was coming, but he remained silent.

'My train was late,' I said quietly, blushing.

He glanced up at me. 'Her train was late,' he repeated to the guard in a monotone voice. The guard went on about how rules had to be obeyed, still talking in the same domineering manner.

Brady put out his cigarette and seemed bored by the whole scenario. He leant back in his chair and looked at me curiously. After I had ignored his letters since my last visit, he must have wondered why I was there.

I looked at him. How could I tell him about the trouble I was in? How could I say I was terrified in case they said I was his daughter? I certainly couldn't show him the birth certificate which was in my bag, he'd think I was crazy.

I didn't know how to explain why I was there. I asked him if he got lonely. It was an unkind thing to say, since the answer was obvious, but I was nervous and agitated and not thinking straight.

He kept his eyes down and drew heavily on his cigarette, then he looked up at me – an expression of contempt on his face. A cold chill went through me and I felt afraid of him. I fidgeted in my seat, wanting to go.

The guard got up – our time was up.

I went towards the door, and Brady followed me out. Without thinking I held out my hand to him – perhaps in apology for my earlier question – and he took it and squeezed it. I looked up, surprised, and he smiled.

His smile took me by surprise. It was open and friendly, and seemed to me to say that the grim man who had sat in the visiting room with me wasn't real. The smiling Ian looked almost happy, as if he wasn't bothered by what the guards said. His smile also disturbed me, because it gave the impression he felt I had made a connection with him, and that wasn't what I wanted. I felt he was playing a game with me, toying with me, by suddenly smiling like that.

I turned away and was escorted through the swing doors and back to the security gate. I made my way out to the waiting car outside.

As soon as I got in, Piers began badgering me to find out what had happened.

'Can I talk about it later,' I said. I was tired and everything felt unreal. And I had no idea what to say about the visit to Brady. I needed time to invent an answer that would get me out of this mess.

The local reporter made me stand outside the gates of the hospital, while he took photos, then we headed back to the airport.

All I wanted to do was to get home, sleep and wake to find it had all been a nightmare. Piers kept on and on asking me what Brady had said, but I fobbed him off. When we got back to the hotel, I shut myself in my room and flung myself on the bed.

I am a bad liar at the best of times but I knew I had to make it work; I felt my whole life depended on it. I had to stop them from printing their story.

The door opened and Nick came in. 'How did it go?' he said.

I told him I had shown Brady my birth certificate and that he had said, 'Why are you showing me this? I don't know of any Olivia or of any love child.'

I thought I'd been pretty convincing, so I was surprised when Nick grinned and said, 'You're not very good at it, you know.'

I looked at him, wide-eyed. 'What do you mean?'

'You had five minutes in there, barely enough time to say hello. Now did you show him the birth certificate or not?'

'No,' I said timidly. 'I'm sorry, but it seemed a bit ridiculous. And if he didn't say anything then there isn't a story, is there?' I hoped I was right. He had caught me out in the lie, but if there was no story then soon this would all be over. I felt relieved.

Nick looked surprised. 'Of course there is. Even without your visit to Brady there's a big story. In fact your visit won't even be in the story this week, we had enough to go on without it. You're on TV advertising the paper on Saturday. You'll be on every half an hour, in the commercial breaks until eleven thirty.'

I stared in disbelief at Nick. 'I'm what?'

'You're on TV. It is our week for advertising so we're using the best photograph of you, then a flash-up picture of Ian to give a hint of the story.

My stomach was churning. 'What story?'

' "The Devil's Daughter" is the headline. It's on the front page,' Nick announced proudly.

Piers had come in by then. 'Nick's a big Dennis Wheatley fan. He was the one who thought it up,' he said, grinning.

My last hope that this crazy story might all evaporate, that I'd be able to go back to my old life in peace, had gone.

'You can't say that, it's not a joke, it's my life, and if it's going to be on television everyone's going to see it. My parents will see it, they'll chuck me out and I'll have nowhere to live. I'll probably lose my job. James, my boss, will go mad – and so will my friends.'

'It's too late, I'm afraid,' Piers said. 'You've given us the story and the pictures, of course we're going to run it. It's a great story. It's going to be the best front page we've had for a long time, and there will be page two and then a centre spread. You look absolutely stunning in those pictures we took, they make the whole piece – it's just like beauty and the beast. And that piece of shit sure is a beast.'

Cathy came in at that point. Surely she would understand how I felt.

'They're going to say that Ian Brady's my father and I can't stop them,' I said. 'It's going to ruin my life.'

'I wouldn't write to or visit Ian Brady for a million pounds and anyone who does deserves what they get,' she snapped.

She was right. Why did I do something as crazy? I thought I knew why, but suddenly all my reasons seemed unimportant. I had done it, and now I had to stomach the consequences.

The following couple of days I spent alone in the hotel room. On Saturday I didn't dare turn the television on in case I saw the advertisement.

I didn't sleep much, and when I did I had nightmares. I saw people chasing me and beating me over the head with clubs and my face covered in warts and looking hideous, shining out from the front cover of every newspaper, with headlines saying, 'This Girl is Ian Brady's Daughter'. I'd wake up sweating and look round the hotel room and wonder where I was.

By Sunday morning I was so frightened that I felt disconnected from everything. The phone buzzed and it was Nick, sounding bright and breezy. 'Have you seen it yet?' he asked.

I went hot and cold then numb. I couldn't bear to think about what everyone would think of me when they saw the paper. My parents would be horrified.

'I haven't seen it,' I whispered. 'I don't want to. I'm too scared.'

'Why?' said Nick cheerily. 'It's a very good story, and you'll be pleased to know they didn't use my headline.'

I wanted to sob with relief. 'Didn't they?'

'No. So there's nothing to worry about. You'll like it, you really will. You stay there and I'll get them to send a copy up to you.'

When the paper was delivered to my room I sat on the bed and unfolded it. My face covered most of the front page. And the headline, while not as bad as Nick's, wasn't much better. The story went on to say that I believed I was Brady's daughter.

I flung it down on the bed, picked up the phone, and dialled Nick's room number. I swore and screamed and sobbed. He and Piers were sharing a glass of champagne – and they had just ruined my life.

Nick told me to come to his room. I did, still sobbing and shouting at them. They sat me down, gave me a drink and told me to calm down. I didn't know how to feel towards them. They were the ones who had done this to me, yet as I was certain no one else would be speaking to me, I felt very dependent on them, too.

Piers took my hand. 'Listen, we're going to take you away for a bit, out of the country. They're going to run the second part of the story next week, so we'll help you lie low until then.'

'You mean that's not the end of it?' I gulped down my drink.

'No, there's a second part. About your visit to him. But don't worry, we'll look after you.'

I hadn't felt I had a choice about any of it since the moment the reporters had cornered me. And I certainly didn't feel I had a choice now. What else could I do? On the Monday morning Piers took me to get a passport. We went to the photo machine in Euston station to get my photos done. A young French boy was watching us, and as my photos came out of the machine he grabbed them. 'Can I keep these and tell people you're my girlfriend?' he asked.

Piers began to laugh and rustled the boy's hair. 'No you can't, that's what I'm going to do.' He took the photos back.

In the cab on the way back to the hotel I looked over at Piers. He was so good looking. Did he really mean what he had said? I was startled, and, despite the situation, a tiny bit thrilled.

The three of us – me, Nick and Piers – headed for Dover in Piers' blue Rover company car. At Dover we took a ferry to France, and Nick and Piers immediately settled in the restaurant with French wine and cheese.

I picked up a gossip magazine. 'Look at this,' I said to them. 'It says here that this girl did a deal with the *News of the World* for fourteen thousand pounds for her story. I didn't know you got paid for stories.'

Piers and Nick exchanged glances.

'Famous people sell stories, not ordinary members of the public,' Piers said.

It seemed odd to me, but I didn't argue.

By the time we disembarked Nick was in a good mood. 'Right,' he said. 'We'll drive down to the South of France and then lie back on a beach, somewhere exorbitantly expensive.'

Piers seemed more cautious. 'No, I think we'd better stay in the Northern region, in case we're needed.'

'Piers is a bit of a brown-nose to the editors, but never mind, we'll try not to let him spoil it for us,' Nick joked, as Piers grinned back at him.

As we drove through France, the sun came out and both Nick and Piers were in high spirits, laughing and joking. I began to relax. Awful as my situation was, there was very little I could do. Here I was, driving through France with two mad reporters – I might as well make the best of it.

'I want you to think of me and Piers as family for the week,' Nick said. 'You're with your Uncle Nick and Aunt Piers and you're going to have fun, because I'm going to make sure you do.'

Despite myself I was touched. Not many people had ever invited me to think of them as family.

Despite Piers' reservations, we did head south, the windows open and his only tapes, Simply Red and Genesis, playing loudly. The two of them took turns driving, and all three of us took turns lying on the back seat sleeping.

When it was Piers' turn he drove at 100 miles an hour, his elbow casually on the open window, the white sleeve of his shirt billowing out. Phil Collins' 'Invisible Touch' was playing loudly on the car stereo. The air outside was getting hotter and hotter and the sun was scorching my skin through the window.

I could smell his lemony aftershave, mixed with the musky scent of male sweat. We talked and laughed and I found myself feeling attracted to him. He was sophisticated and clever and seemed like the kind of man I had never met before. It was a strange contradiction – here was the man who had put a story in the paper that tore my life apart, yet I felt very drawn to him. And the further from England we got, the easier it was to put all my worries and fears behind me and enjoy being with him.

Finally we reached Provence, and our hotel. It was gorgeous, a small manor, set on the side of a hill, overlooking a river and a huge bridge, the Pont du Gard. My room was white, with dark wood and a beautiful bathroom.

Here we spent a few days which seemed almost idyllic. Nick and Piers no longer seemed like hard-nosed journalists, they were kind and funny and we laughed a lot. It was hard to remember that this trip, which was turning out to be so enjoyable, was being paid for by the newspaper.

Every evening, after a delicious French meal in nearby Avignon, the three of us, heady from the wine, would link arms and walk over the bridge to the secluded campsite buried in the trees opposite the hotel. There we'd sit outside the log cabin bar and drink fifty-year-old brandy while talking endlessly about life, literature, religion and philosophy. Then we'd walk back to the hotel, singing and laughing.

One evening the three of us were in the hotel, looking out over the bridge, when Nick said, 'Doesn't it look Greek? Like the Parthenon.' Suddenly a shiver ran down my spine as I remembered the psychic and his predictions. This was the second one to come true. First I heard from Brady within a week, and now here I was in a hot country, 'like Greece', as he had said. What else that he had said might come true? Was Piers the P he had said I would become involved with?

It seemed that he was. That week I fell a little bit in love with Piers, and he with me. Nick joked that he had a crush on me, which made me blush, but in fact he did, and I returned it. I don't think either of us had expected such a thing to happen, given the circumstances in which we met, but to our surprise it did. I felt as if fate had brought us together and despite Nick's hints that Piers was a womaniser, I believed that I would change him. The chemistry between us was so electric that I believed he was as blown away by it as I was. And I wanted and needed to be taken care of, and Piers seemed to be offering just that. We had a wonderful time. He was sophisticated and good-looking, he seemed to be everything I had been looking for, and two nights before the end of our stay we became lovers. Sense might have told me that it couldn't last, but after all I had been through, I didn't want to look any further than this moment.

Inevitably the time came to leave and I think we all felt sad. It had been such a lovely, and unexpected, week. I wished it could have lasted much longer. I certainly didn't want to go back to face the horrors that lay ahead, but I hoped that Piers would stand by me and help me cope.

As the two of them took turns to drive, I sat looking out of the window. The bright sun of the south became weaker and eventually gave way to the grey gloom of the north, and my spirits slowly sank as my fear of what lay ahead loomed large again.

On the ferry, I slept for what seemed like hours. When I awoke we were already back in England. Piers was out on deck and Nick sat next to me, writing a letter. I felt immediately that he had changed. The funny sweet Nick of our trip had given way to a brisk, cool businessman with work on his mind.

We disembarked from the ferry and drove from Dover up to south London. Nick stopped at a phone box and insisted that I phone my adoptive parents to tell them I was coming home while he and Piers waited for me in the car.

My mother hung up, as soon as she heard it was me. I re-dialled, and this time it was my father. 'We gave you a chance, and you've proved you were what we thought you were. A bastard child with bad blood who has brought us shame. Your stuff has been thrown out, and if you call here again, we will phone the police. We want nothing more to do with you.'

He hung up, and I walked back to the waiting car.

'What are we supposed to do with you?' Piers said. 'The story's over, it's in print tomorrow, there's no need for us to keep you.'

I didn't know what to say. None of us spoke as we headed for Nick's house. When we got there they both got out and stood talking behind the car.

I heard Nick say, 'This is for you,' and he handed Piers a bottle of brandy he had picked up from duty free. Then, without a word to me, he walked towards his house.

Piers got in and started the car. 'Is Nick meeting us later?' I asked.

'Don't be silly,' he laughed. 'You'll probably never see him again.'

I opened my mouth to say, 'But that can't be true, he didn't say goodbye,' but I closed it again, shocked.

Piers headed for Earl's Court. 'There are plenty of small hotels here,' he said. 'I'll pay for the first night for you.'

Piers stopped the car in front of a small bed and breakfast hotel. He went in and booked me a room, then helped me in with my case.

The room had peeling yellowed wallpaper, the stink of stale sweat and a single bed with a paper-thin mattress and eggshell blue nylon sheets.

Piers sat down on the bed next to me and handed me his work phone number. 'If you're keeping in contact with Ian Brady, then I'd like you to keep me informed.'

I had almost forgotten about him, with everything else that was going on. I wondered what he had made of the story.

'There won't be any contact with him,' I said.

He put his arm round me. 'Look, I'll take you out one evening this week, to a nice nightclub I know – Bootleggers. Loads of celebs there. That'll cheer you up. I still want there to be an "us". You know I'm falling in love with you, don't you?'

I stood up and turned away to wipe away tears that had started running down my face. I didn't want him to see them. He turned to go, then looked at me.

'You're very brave, do you know that? And I admire you for it.'

He left, and I lay on the bed, wondering how I had come to this – I was back in a dreadful bed and breakfast hotel, little better than the one I'd been dumped in when I left the children's home.

Despite my misery, I was so exhausted that I slept deeply that night. The next morning I dressed and went out to find something to eat, and to get the paper. I bought a copy, and an egg sandwich, and headed back to my room.

This time my story filled the centre pages. There was another tacky picture of me, in the glossy make-up and low-cut dress I had worn for their photo-shoot. And the story was all about how I had visited Brady. The whole thing made me feel cheap and shabby. I lay on the bed and sobbed.

I needed someone to talk to. I took some change from my purse, went down to the pay phone in the foyer and dialled Linton's mother's number. A few weeks earlier his phone had been cut off after he failed to pay the bill, so we'd passed messages to each other through her. He was close to her, and I liked her very much, and hoped she might be a sympathetic ear, now that I was in so much trouble.

When she picked up the receiver her voice was cold and harsh. 'I don't want you near my son again. Linton has gone up to Scotland with Jem, until this blows over. He never wants to see you again.'

She hung up, and I leaned my head against the wall and cried. I was feeling real panic. I dialled the number of a friend from work who I went to lunch with now and again.

'I didn't think you'd phone. Do you realise what sort of trouble you're in?' she said.

I choked out between sobs, 'What trouble?'

'Look, someone's just come in. I've got to go,' she said, and put down the phone.

Was there anyone left who would talk to me? It seemed I had become public enemy number one.

I dialled the work number Piers had given me, and a voice said 'Newsdesk'.

'Is Piers there? I have to speak to him,' I said. The person on the end of the line promised to get him to phone me. He did, and I sobbed down the phone that no one would speak to me.

'There's a letter at the office for you, from Brady,' he said. 'I'll pop it over tomorrow.' Then he said he had to go, and hung up.

I had never felt so desperately alone and sick with fear in all my life. Everything swam and tilted in front of me, as if my world was rocking and I was just about to slip off. I went back to the grim little hotel room and lay on the bed and cried some more, then slept fitfully.

On Monday I got up and went down to the lobby to phone work. I was due back that day, but needed another day off, to find somewhere to live. I got through to James, who told me I was fired.

He was very apologetic, but he said he had to do it. 'You were on the front pages of a national newspaper saying you are an employee of a London security firm. You know how important it is to keep our profile low. You had a lucrative career as a spy ahead of you, but I'm afraid you've blown it. None of the ex-Government agencies will touch you with a barge pole now you're mixed up with the press. You're out in the cold, my lovely. I'll pay you until the end of the month. Goodness knows what you're going to do with your life now. You've been very, very foolish mixing with newspapers.'

I was so shocked that for a moment I couldn't speak. Surely he wasn't going to take my job away from me. I began to sob.

'Please don't leave me like this. I need you. The agency is my family, James.'

But he was adamant that I was no longer employable. He hung up and I wanted to die. James had given me a sense of security. Now I was alone. Outside everything that was respectable.

I spent the day looking for a flat and had no luck, when I told them I was currently unemployed. I came back to the bed and breakfast at about seven o'clock and paid for a further two nights. The receptionist handed me a letter in a long brown envelope with a note attached to it and I took it up to my room.

It was the letter from Brady. He said:

'You know, I do remember an Olivia. Of course, to prove you were mine conclusively, I would have to take a blood test. I'm glad I have found you.'

The note attached was from Piers, 'I opened it by mistake; we're running a story on it.'

I ran downstairs to phone him.

'You can't,' I said.

He started to laugh. 'He thinks he's your real father. It's great, isn't it?'

'It's because of that story,' I said. 'But it's cruel to pretend things like that to someone who's all alone in the world.'

'He's a monster. It's a good story, and it'll go in next Sunday under the heading "Brady Admits He's Her Father". Now, what are you going to say to the Moors Murderer in a reply?'

'I'm not replying,' I said quietly.

I knew I couldn't stop the next story appearing. The whole thing now seemed to have a momentum of its own.

While the last thing I wanted was another story, and I was furious with Piers for opening the letter and using it, something about Brady's letter touched me. I hadn't expected him to respond in this way. He hadn't complained about the stories in the paper, or accused me of using him, as I feared he might. I had expected that he'd either be angry or dismissive. Yet he was neither, and instead he had suggested he knew my mother. Did he really believe he could be my father? But I felt sure that if he really did remember an Olivia it wasn't my mother. This was just a desperate act by an incredibly lonely man clinging to a long lost hope for a family.

I had a week to find a place to live before the next story came out. I decided to go to Ealing. I knew the area well, through my work. If no one I knew would speak to me, at least I could live in a familiar area, and I hoped that might stop the strange disassociated feeling I kept having.

By three in the afternoon I'd had no luck, so I started walking towards the shopping area, to get something to eat. I was just about to cross the road when I heard someone shout out of a passing car. It was the two girls I had been friends with at school, Philippa and Ellen. Of course, I remembered, they lived around here. I let out a shout and went running towards the car. It was so good to see their familiar faces. I could see there were two men in the car too – presumably their boyfriends.

I reached the car and leaned towards the window to say hi to Philippa. Too late I saw her face twist with contempt, as she spat at me. 'I've got children, I've got children,' she yelled. 'Are you mad? How can you have anything to do with that monster? Did you think you were clever? And they called you beautiful – what a lie – you aren't beautiful, you looked like an evil slapper tart.'

I turned away from her and stood with my head down as they drove away. Badly shaken, I walked into a sandwich bar. A group of girls who had been talking animatedly stopped as soon as they saw me. I tried to tell myself I was imagining things. I bought a sandwich and glanced back at them. They were still staring.

I took a deep breath and went over. 'Do I know you?' I said.

'I'm a secretary at your old agency,' one of them said. 'You left before I came but I've seen you up there visiting Freddie.'

'Oh I see,' I said. I went and sat at a nearby table with my back to them. I could hear them sniggering and I caught tail-ends of their conversation: 'Hope she got paid well for it. Imagine doing that. She must be mad.'

Unable to eat, I got up, and walked out, my face burning. I walked along the street, terrified that at any moment someone would jump out of the crowd and start shouting or hitting me. I scanned all the faces around me, ready to run if I did see anybody I knew.

Then a hand grabbed my arm and a woman I recognised as a friend of a friend from way back, said, 'Everyone's seen the paper. They all think you're really sick.'

I pulled my arm free and ran along the high street, in and out of the crowds, tears running down my face. Breathless, I stopped in a shop doorway. I felt odd, and was afraid I might faint.

A young man tapped me gently on the shoulder. I jumped, terrified. 'Are you okay?' he said. His voice seemed to echo, as if he was miles away.

I nodded, and ran again, panic overwhelming me.

I don't know how I made it back to my hotel room, but somehow I did. For a while I sat on the bed, still trembling. Then, unable to face anything more, I climbed into bed to try to sleep.

A couple of hours later there was a knock on the door. I wondered if it was Piers, and got up to dress, calling out that I'd open the door in a minute. But I heard a key turn in the door and pulled the bedcovers over me as a thickset, swarthy man walked in.

'I'm the manager here,' he said. He had a heavy accent. 'Have you got a job? I could fix it for you to earn a lot, working for me in my clubs.'

I stared at him as what he was suggesting sank in. 'You mean I could work as a prostitute?' He grinned. 'There's no need to put it like that. You could earn a lot – you're a very beautiful girl.'

I turned away from him and started to cry.

'I was only asking,' he said. He pulled out a pen and paper, scribbled down a phone number and left it on the table, then went away.

I phoned Piers early the next day. Part of me still hoped that Piers really did care, that despite the way he had behaved he meant all the things he said about loving me. I told him what had happened and that I had to see him. He said he could come over that evening.

He finally arrived at nine. I sat on the bed and cried and he put his arm round me. When I'd poured out all my troubles, we went out to Bootleggers nightclub, where Piers held my hand and told me he loved me and wanted us to have a future together.

We drank champagne and ate grilled tiger prawns, which he fed me across the table as we talked about what a wonderful time we'd had in France. Then we went back to his airy flat in South Kensington, where he put on Matt Munro and we both sang along to our favourite songs and then made love as the sun came up. We both loved the poetry of Sylvia Plath and Ted Hughes and he read Ted's to me as we lay in each others arms and I read Sylvia's.

At that moment and other times like this, I felt he really did love me. But just as he was being warm and loving and I felt more trusting, he would suddenly say something cutting and become very distant. I never truly knew where I was with him, so I didn't dare to let my guard down and tell him that I loved him.

The following day Piers helped me to move to a small hotel in Bloomsbury, where I stayed for the next three or four weeks. I had no job and was living on my savings. It was a difficult, depressing time and I had no idea what I was going to do. Piers was the only friend I had and he came to see me whenever he could. My only escape was when he drove me, in his green Jaguar, out into the Surrey countryside, where we would walk and stop off in pretty pubs.

I hoped that we might, after all, have a future together, until one day he landed a bombshell. He mentioned casually that he was going on holiday with his ex-girlfriend. Not only that, but they were going to Pont du Gard, where he, Nick and I had been together. A place that I thought of as special to us.

He insisted that the holiday had been booked before we met, and that they wouldn't be sleeping together.

'I have to go,' he said. 'But it isn't what you think. I've fallen in love with you, you've cast a spell over me.'

I kept silent, and he left.

I realised I had to make a decision about what to do. I couldn't stay indefinitely in cheap hotels, or hanging on for Piers. I had a little money left, but it wouldn't last forever.

I went out and walked up Kensington High Street, towards Knightsbridge. I realised that no one in the world cared what happened to me.

The sun was shining and I kept lifting my face towards it for comfort, trying to pretend I was back in the South of France, where all the fears and pressures of life had been suspended.

I passed a travel agent with a board outside and I stopped. It said, 'New York – One way flights £100'. In the window was a great big poster of the Statue of Liberty. I walked in and bought a ticket.

'Do you want a return?' the girl asked.

'No,' I said. 'I'm not ever coming back.'

I went from there to the American Embassy to get a visa. There was a long queue, and when my turn came the tall blond official smiled as he handed my stamped passport back and said, 'Have a nice time out there, ma'am.'

I went back out into the sunny street, feeling a mixture of fear and excitement. My flight was two days later. With all my possessions in my small suitcase, I got to Heathrow on the tube. Last-minute doubts flooded in. What was I doing? How would I earn a living?

I hadn't told anyone I was going. Who was there to care? But I wanted someone to know. At the last minute I rang Nick in the newspaper office.

'You can't go without telling Piers, he's in love with you.'

I remembered the warning Nick had given me about Piers being a womaniser.

'I don't trust him, Nick. You said . . .'

'I know I did, but he's gone on you. Don't walk out on him. You need someone and so does he.'

But I told him my mind was made up.

'Look, you little waif,' he said. 'Phone me at least once a week, OK?'

My flight was being called. I picked up my case and ran through to the departure lounge. An hour later I sat on the plane watching the fields shrink to the size of postage stamps. This was it. A new start, a new country and a chance to put all the mistakes and horror of the past behind me.

13

America

As the coach from the airport took me into Manhattan, I sat staring out of the window, wondering what on earth I was going to do next. It was all very well to run away from the nightmare back home, but now I was in a strange country, with no job, no friends and very little money. How on earth had I got myself into such a mess, and what kind of future lay ahead of me? I was tired, frightened and sad.

I got off, clutching my tatty suitcase, and looked around at the drab street of nondescript shops and diners. This wasn't the picture of New York I'd had. I flagged down a yellow cab and asked the driver to take me to the very centre.

After ten minutes we turned into Broadway and I gasped. This was what I'd been waiting for: the brightly-lit theatres, the famous restaurants, huge neon signs, wide boulevards and smart people hurrying in every direction. I sat in the back of the cab as the radio played Michael Jackson's 'Bad' and the driver wove in and out of the traffic, honking the horn at anyone in his way along the wide busy throng of 42nd Street.

I could see people dressed as cowboys and others in gold lurex or sparkly outfits. And there were black guys gathered around glowing braziers on street corners, just like in the *Rocky* films.

The taxi driver screeched to a halt, jumped out, heaved my suitcase onto the pavement, took the twenty dollars I held out to him and then sped off. I was in Times Square, the epicentre of one of the greatest cities in the world, and I didn't know a soul.

I had no idea which direction to go in. I decided to cross the road, but when I was halfway over a car skidded to a halt inches from me. As it dawned on me that they drove on the other side of the road here, the driver honked the horn loudly and leaned out of his window. 'This is New York baby, wakey, wakey,' he shouted.

It was mid-November and by now it was early evening. Dusk had fallen, making the lights of Manhattan even brighter, and it was growing very cold. I'd packed my coat in my suitcase in case it was too bulky on the plane, so I stood shivering in a T-shirt and jeans, as people bumped into me or pushed past me.

I wandered up a few side streets and eventually found a small hotel and booked in there for a few nights. By ten o'clock I was in bed. I had barely spoken to a soul, and I felt scared and rootless. I had been told by a woman on the plane not to go out after eight at night, but there was no way I could sleep and suddenly I thought, 'I've just arrived in New York and I'm in bed! What am I doing?'

I got dressed, pulled on my white cowboy boots, put on some make-up and brushed my hair. I put ten dollars in my pocket, stuffed the rest of my money under the mattress, hid my handbag behind the shower curtain and headed back to Times Square.

The whole place was buzzing, like one big party, and even though I was alone I felt exuberant. Music seemed to be coming from just about everywhere, while good-time girls in brightly coloured mini-skirts paraded up and down the street in front of the limousines that cruised slowly past.

Nervously I went into a dimly lit bar, slid onto a stool and ordered a beer, which was handed to me without a glass. A man with a Texan accent shouted over to the barman, 'Her drink is on me.'

I smiled my thanks, but was a little anxious that he might expect me to join him. I heard him say to his friend. 'We have some very exciting women in New York City' and nod over at me. Even though I didn't want to talk to him, it lifted my spirits.

I finished my beer and went back out onto the street, in time to see a man in a white suit standing up in the sunroof of a passing car, blasting out a tune on a gold trumpet.

I suddenly felt a surge of loneliness. I tried to cheer myself up with a hot dog covered in mustard and, determined to experience the night life, went into one of the many nightclubs I passed. A middle-aged man with fair hair came and sat next to me at the bar. His name was Ed and he was in New York on business and staying at a hotel around the corner. He bought me a Bacardi and Coke and, when the throbbing music allowed, we exchanged small talk.

As the night wore on I had several more drinks and began to feel slightly drunk and maudlin. So when Ed grinned at me suggestively and nodded towards the erotic video being projected onto a huge screen he didn't quite get the reaction he expected. I leaned forward on the bar, put my head in my hands and started to sob quietly.

Startled, he apologised for any insinuations he had made and rapidly disappeared. Wiping my eyes I made my way back to the hotel room and went straight to bed where I lay staring into the darkness and wondering what on earth I was doing in New York, all on my own, not knowing a soul.

The next day I went out and bought a local newspaper, then stood at the phone in the small foyer of the hotel, ringing round to find a room to rent.

I got two stock replies. Either 'The room's gone' or 'If you haven't got a job, you can't stay here'. I was close to giving up when a friendly sounding voice answered the phone. When I told him my predicament he said his name was Joe Vaz and added, 'Get your butt over here now, and rent my room. I like the sound of your voice, English.'

'Over here' turned out to be Manhattan Island. I had to get the train all the way downtown to the end of the line at South Ferry and then take the lone yellow Staten Island Ferry over to the Island. I stood on the deck of the dusty old ferry and marvelled at the vast Statue of Liberty as we sped past it. It was breathtaking and I felt so alive, standing there on the deck, looking at a marvel I had only ever seen in films.

Joe, it turned out, resembled the late comedian Roy Kinnear, except with a Brooklyn accent. He took me in his small battered white van to view rooms in the three houses he owned in different parts of the Island.

The houses were run-down and the rooms were small, dark, dank and very depressing. My face fell further with each visit, until Joe said, 'What's up with you? You look like you're going to cry. Do you want some of this?' He pulled out a large plastic bag of marijuana.

'No thanks,' I laughed. 'I hate that stuff. Even the smell of it makes me feel paranoid.'

After rolling himself a large joint, he shoved the bag back in his pocket, started the car again and, telling me he had one more house to show me, drove back up towards the ferry terminal and along a road which ran along the water's edge. He pulled up in front of a large white clapboard house that stood alone on a hill sloping down to the water.

The house reminded me of the one in the film *Psycho*. And to make it even less inviting, it was surrounded by a scorched front garden and a barbed-wire fence with a huge metal gate.

Joe explained that before he bought it, it had been a half-way house for old men, most of them senile, from the psychiatric home in Port St George. Some of the locals hadn't liked the idea of the old men living there so they'd tried to burn it down – with the residents still in it. The garden and the base of the house were charred and it made the old house look very sad. Even the bushes were reduced to blackened stalks.

We wiped our feet on the dusty mat on the porch as Joe unlocked the door. A tatty old swing-seat stood nearby and I pushed it. Thick dust and tiny moths flew off it as it creaked back and forth.

I followed Joe up three carpetless flights of stairs. I thought we were at the top of the house, but he opened a battered white door and behind it was another steep flight of stairs. At the top of those was a single attic room.

I took in the almost bare room, the ancient double bed and the dark wooden crucifix pinned high on the wall. It looked like a room a priest or a nun might have, mysterious and quiet, cut off from the whole rest of the world. The effect was even more enhanced by the oil-lamp which was the only light.

For some reason electricity had not been brought up to the attic.

The room was spartan, dusty, and a long, long walk up from the street, but I felt I could live there. And besides, it was just about my only option. I walked over to the window, which looked out over the harbour, and the traffic of boats coming and going from the Island – the only reminder, from this silent, solitary attic, that there was a busy world outside.

Joe was happy for me to move in straight away. He drove me back to his house, which was just along the front. I met his assistant, Manny, who carried out repairs on the houses, and handed them my cash, counting it out on the table. It was all I had.

Joe looked at Manny and said drily, 'Now we have her money we can rent the room to someone else. You know what to do with her. She's a foreigner – no one will miss her.'

He began to laugh. But it reminded me I was as vulnerable as a mouse in a cat convention, all on my own in a strange country. Manny drove me back to the house and, despite their jokey manner, I half expected him to take me somewhere out of the way, as Joe had said, and put me out of my misery. Back in the dusty attic I unpacked my case and hung up my clothes in the small wooden closet, and tried to make it feel a little like home.

The other residents of the house were three old men who lived in rooms way down below me. They were all that remained of the original halfway-house occupants. Joe had told me a little about them before he left. The first he called Frankie, because the old man thought he was Frank Sinatra. He had spent all his life in homes, and he was Joe's favourite; he'd come over regularly to chat to Frankie and make sure he was all right.

On the bottom floor there was a Mexican man of about sixty-five called Miguel. And the last of the three was an old Jamaican man called Eli who lived on the middle floor. He was forever ironing his clothes, Joe said, and he had to put the ironing board up in the hallway as his room was too small. Eli was the only one who worked, and he was on permanent night duty.

It was a daunting, if not terrifying prospect, living in a house with three ex-mental patients. But I badly needed a place to live, and Joe had promised me that none of the three would harm a fly. But the real reason I stayed was that I felt numb. If I'd been able to feel properly I'd have run a mile from such a place.

As it turned out, the old men really were harmless, but the area certainly wasn't. One night, as I went to buy some milk, I was chased by two rough-looking men who had heard my English accent in the shop. 'English bitch, why don't you fuck off back to Maggie,' they shouted. I ran to the house and they sped away in their car, but if they'd wanted to get me, all they had to do was to kick open the door of our house – the security was non-existent.

For much of the time the three old men in the house were my only companions. None of them grasped my name; they would all call me 'English'. Sometimes when I couldn't sleep I would bum cigarettes off Miguel, who was short and scruffy and barely ever left his room, peering round his door before disappearing inside again. No matter what time I knocked – and often it was two or three in the morning – he always answered his door with a smile, clutching two or three stale Marlboros.

Late at night, standing at my window, I often saw Eli leave for work, his old body stooped over as he shuffled down the road through wind and rain and snow. I never did discover what he actually did.

Within a couple of days of moving in I found my first job as a waitress in a restaurant in Manhattan. Over the following weeks I had a series of similar temporary jobs, some waiting tables, others washing up. The jobs were mostly dull and routine, but I loved commuting over from the Island on the ferry each day. It only cost a dollar, and most of the Island's residents commuted to work. I would stand on deck, the wind in my hair, marvelling each day anew at the magnificent Statue of Liberty guarding the harbour entrance and the sun rising behind the city's skyscrapers. In the evenings I would gaze at the myriad lights of the city twinkling behind us like a handful of diamonds.

Looking at those stunning views I told myself I should have felt excited and happy. Here I was in New York City, making a new start and a new life for myself. So why did I feel so flat and empty? Why did nothing around me really touch me? It was almost as if everything around me was part of a dream and I had woken to find I was the only person left in the world.

The answer was that I was terribly lonely. For all the people bustling around me each day, I had no real friends. I went to work each day then came home and sat in my room alone. The only people I spoke to, mostly in passing, were Frankie, Miguel and Eli.

On my birthday, which fell a few days after I arrived, I walked past restaurants, staring in at all the families and friends eating out together, laughing and having a good time. I bought a pink iced cupcake and went and sat on a bench and ate it.

A few weeks after I arrived I rang Nick. I had promised to let him know where I was, and it was good to hear a familiar voice. He asked me if I was all right and I said I was fine. He said to keep in touch and asked if he could give my number to Piers.

I had missed Piers desperately, even though I'd done my best to put him out of my mind. He had betrayed me, and I had run halfway round the world, partly because of him, yet I couldn't just stop loving him. In my lonely New York life I thought of him all the time, and a couple of weeks earlier had sent him a poem I'd written for him. Not because I thought we'd get back together, but because I was thinking about him.

A couple of days later Piers rang me. He had news. 'I've been promoted to chief reporter.'

'Oh,' I replied, wondering if he wanted me to congratulate him.

'Look, about us. I made a mistake – I shouldn't have got involved with you,' he said. 'You are beautiful though. I got the poem you sent me. I keep it in my wallet.'

He went on. 'I've been listening to Genesis. Do you remember the Bridge on the River? That place.'

'Yes, I remember our place in France.' I felt sad.

' "In Too Deep". That's the track. Do me a favour. Play it and think of me from time to time. I'm not a bad guy. You don't know me. No one does.'

I sighed. We were so far away that it seemed unnecessary for him to say it was over. I had ended it, by leaving. Perhaps he just needed to be the one who said it. I told him I understood and he offered to send me money. I had none, but I told him I was fine and to keep his money, and hung up.

I felt proud of myself for refusing his money. It hadn't been easy to say no, or to end the call, when at times I still ached for him. But I was still angry too, and I knew I had to be strong and let go. Piers had behaved dreadfully to me and I needed to stand up for myself.

When Christmas came, five weeks after my arrival, my loneliness grew deeper. As families celebrated all around me I wanted to hide away, ashamed of my loneliness, my emptiness. I wanted to go to sleep and wake up to find it was all finished, the pain over for another year. But there was no such release. I sat in my little attic, listening to Christmas carols on the radio and trying to believe that one day I might have a family of my own to celebrate with. I tried to imagine the warm feeling of acceptance and belonging that I had never truly experienced. But imagining it hurt even more.

Sometimes I stood by the window and looked out at the boats, their tiny lights crossing the harbour in the dark, and wondered who was on them. I prayed that anyone who was alone at Christmas would not feel the pain as intensely as I felt it that long lonely night.

New Year was almost as bleak. I knew no one and had nowhere to go to celebrate. I hoped that in 1988 things might be different for me.

In the New Year I trudged around the streets of Manhattan and finally found a restaurant that had needed someone permanent, Café 43, on 43rd and Broadway. The people there were friendly, and allowed me to relieve the monotony by doing different tasks and varying my shifts.

By late January the snow was so deep that I had to buy Wellington boots to wade through it in the front garden. After work I'd huddle under blankets in my armchair, reading, when I wasn't trying to stuff sheets and towels into the gaps where the windows were broken. The draught at night was so fierce that even buried beneath layers and layers of bed covers I'd be shivering.

I felt very downhearted. My life seemed empty and I wondered how it had come to this. I worked at a boring job simply to keep myself fed and a pretty pitiful roof over my head. Everything seemed frightening and desperate.

There were times when I felt so low that I thought about suicide. Who would miss me, I wondered? Wouldn't it be easier to just leave this miserable existence behind? But something – perhaps a shred of hope that there might be a different future ahead – stopped me from taking that final step, and I struggled on with life.

Now that I was in a permanent job I had made friends with some of the other waitresses and we sometimes went for a drink after work. But, like the girls I had made friends with on the bus at school, they were casual friends; there was no real closeness. My real and adopted mothers had poisoned my view of women so much that I feared them and feared getting close to them, so I kept them all at arm's length. But there was a high price to pay for my isolation.

Nick stayed in touch. I would ring him at night, because of the time difference. I'd stand in a call box in Times Square, shivering and sipping hot tea from a plastic cup, regaling him with stories of my poverty and desperation. He would sympathise and then make me laugh, which made me feel so much better and more human.

After a while I began finding stories for him and sending them over. I had seen him and Piers in action and I realised that this was something I could do – you didn't need qualifications to be a reporter, just a quick wit and an eye for a story. And of course I was already trained as an investigator. In my spare time I began selling stories to another, daily newspaper, as well as to Nick, and I even went along to a few court cases which were of interest in Britain, and wrote them up.

One of them was the Howard Beach trial. I got to know the black family whose son had been beaten to death by a crowd of rich white college boys after he wandered onto the beach where they were partying. I gave the copy to the *Guardian* and was thrilled to see it made a few paragraphs. The money I earned was very welcome, though not enough for me to give up my café job, and I began to think reporting was something I might pursue as a career. I hoped that one day I could become an investigative journalist, do something worthwhile with my life and help others by exposing injustice.

One morning I was heading down the garden towards the gate, muffled up in my coat, wellies and several scarves, when Eli, who was sweeping the snow off the porch, called out to me, 'English, there's a letter for you.'

'There can't be,' I shouted back. 'I don't know anyone here.'

I didn't want to stop – I had about three minutes to get to the bus stop a hundred yards down the road, before I missed the bus to the ferry. And there wouldn't be another for an hour.

'It's from England.' He stopped sweeping and leaned on his broom to look at me.

Surprised and curious, I turned and ran up the steps past him and back into the dusty little kitchen. There, amongst the junk mail, lay a long blue airmail envelope, addressed to me, in familiar neat, sloping writing.

I picked it up, then leapt down the steps too quickly, skidded on some ice and fell straight into a pile of snow. I got up and dusted myself down, just in time to watch the bus to the ferry speed past the end of the garden.

Eli stood on the steps and rocked back and forth with laughter, 'I guess the letter was worth it.'

I smiled at him. 'It's from my Dad.'

The words had come out before I even thought about it. Perhaps because I had been so desperate for contact from someone, anyone, who might care. And now here was a gesture from a man who had been announced to the world as my father, and who had even hinted that he might believe himself to be.

At this stage of my life, in exile, as I felt myself to be, the smallest kindness meant an enormous amount.

I think there was another reason I told Eli it was from my father. I wanted to let him know that I did have a family, that I did belong somewhere.

Brady had sent the letter care of the newspaper, and Nick had forwarded it, after – as I later discovered – opening it and using it for another story.

I read it while I waited for the bus. It was a brief letter, asking how I was and what I was doing. I had vowed to break off all contact with Brady. But now that I was across the ocean, it felt somehow safe to write back. That night I sat and wrote to him, telling him I had come to America to escape all the misery at home.

After that he wrote to me almost weekly. His letters were often about books, poetry and ideas. But he talked of personal things too, telling me how much it had hurt him that his mother gave him up because he was illegitimate. He remembered his childhood as one of great pain, being fostered out to another family because his birth mother did not want him. He had thought that the family who he had been living with had been his own, until they told him that he had been dumped with them.

He said that at Christmas he got no presents, as his foster mother always said, 'Your real mother's coming to give you your presents.' But she never did, so he ended up with none, sitting watching her real children excitedly tearing theirs open.

He told me he had pretended not to care, but it had mattered a lot. He talked of feeling that he had never quite belonged in this world, so that by the time he was seventeen or eighteen everything seemed increasingly unreal. 'That is where it began to get dangerous,' he said.

As he talked about himself and began to open up about his unhappiness as a child, I felt I began to understand more about him. But I didn't think of his letters as an insight into the mind of a killer: to me they were simply a lifeline from someone who cared, when no one else did. A reminder of home, a long way from the cold reality of my new country, where I was struggling to survive.

By March it was still minus two and bitterly cold. I'd taken to warming myself up before bed with a cup of hot chocolate and brandy. More often than not Frankie and Eli would come into the kitchen as I was waiting for the milk to warm. There was no heating in the kitchen and they'd stand shivering in their shabby dressing-gowns, eyeing the bottle of brandy on the table, until I offered to make them a hot drink too. Soon it became a nightly ritual and I'd take each of the old men a cup of hot chocolate and brandy before bed.

I felt a bit like Wendy with the lost boys. These sad old men, sitting alone in their tiny rooms, seemed very lost, and I couldn't help wanting to offer them a little bit of comfort and caring.

Most of my evenings and weekends were spent alone in my own small room, and I often passed the time by writing letters to Brady. But earlier that week I had been handed a leaflet about a meeting at a Spiritualist Church on Fifth Avenue and I decided to go along.

The meeting was the following Sunday, in a dusty old Victorian building next to the church and it was run by Reverend Ron Fredericks. He began by telling us to write something on a piece of paper. Then he took each piece of paper, held it in his fist, and told us what it said. It was impressive stuff, and very entertaining. He reminded me of the old music hall magicians like Houdini, with his black attire, spiffy looks and conjuring tricks.

Next he made us all sit in a circle, blindfolded us and asked us to put a personal possession in the centre. Then we took turns to pick up an object and try to tell who it belonged to, and a bit about that person.

The first few people got it all wrong, and there was lots of laughter and joking. Then my turn came. I picked up a bunch of keys and immediately saw, in my mind's eye, the red headed woman who was sitting opposite me, walking down a corridor full of paintings.

I said, 'These are your keys, do you own an art gallery?' She looked startled, they were indeed her keys and she said she had been in an art gallery just before the meeting.

Reverend Ron told me to say a number between one and a hundred. I shut my eyes and listened and heard a man's voice say the number five, which I repeated out loud. He smiled and said he had put that number into my head. 'You're telepathic too,' he said excitedly.

I laughed. I wasn't sure I wanted to be.

After the meeting Reverend Ron took me for a coffee in a local family diner and invited me to take part, for free, in a course he was running. He told me I had the talent to work as a psychic, and could be up and running in less than a week.

I thought of the psychic I'd been to see, Mike Baker, and said, 'Oh no, I don't want that, thanks.' Somehow the idea just didn't appeal to me.

But Reverend Ron said to me, 'Whether you decide to use your powers or not, now you know you have them you will have no choice. You'll get messages. You can't just turn these powers off, it's a gift. Schiller once said in a poem, "Take back thy dreadful sight. Take back thy terrible gift." And it is. Terrible.'

It was hard to know what to think. I had already suspected I had some psychic ability after reading some of the occult books and books on Madame Blavatsky, but I had never tried to use it or encourage it. I didn't want to start seeing things or hearing messages. Despite what Reverend Ron had said, I hoped I could ignore the whole thing.

Unfortunately, I couldn't. One night, a week or two later, I lay awake reading *The Godfather* by Mario Puzo until two o'clock in the morning. The book fascinated me because it was about how immigrants had coped with coming to America. Eventually I put out my oil lamp and lay in the darkness, trying to get to sleep, when I heard something tapping on the window. I got out of bed and peered into the darkness, but I couldn't see a thing.

I got back into bed, but a few moments later I felt the room start to shake and shudder. I leapt out of bed, terrified, and went down to Eli's room on the next floor, where I banged on his door until eventually he opened it and peered round the door.

'Eli, did you feel the earthquake?'

'This is New York, not California. We don't have earthquakes,' he said.

I looked at him in surprise. 'Well, I just felt a really huge tremor, as if the whole house was shaking and rocking back and forth.'

'I haven't felt a thing,' he said. 'Perhaps it was a big truck going past.' He was looking at me oddly in my thick white granny nightdress.

I wanted to ask him to come and check my room, but he said goodnight and closed the door.

I made my way back upstairs and re-lit my oil lamp before getting back into bed. It must have been ten minutes later when the rocking and the shaking started again. I sat up in bed and looked around me, and then realised with horror that it was not the whole house that was shaking, it was just my bed. It seemed as though my mattress was jumping around all of its own accord. A deep, icy fear came over me. The shaking stopped and I sat, holding my breath, waiting to see if it would start again. Suddenly I heard a loud whisper come from the corner of the dimly-lit room, from the direction of the crucifix on the wall. I strained to hear it again, telling myself I must have been imagining things.

I didn't sleep for the rest of the night, and I was hugely relieved when dawn broke. I thought of what the Reverend Ron had said and realised that perhaps he was right – I was becoming more tuned to other levels, and simply could not shut things out.

I never went back to the spiritualist church, but not long after that I had a powerful dream. I saw a long, dark path covered in snow, with dark forests on either side. I started walking along it, following footprints in the snow. Eventually the footprints trailed off and I had to forge on, making my own way. Gradually it got darker and more frightening. Furry creatures and winged insects flew past me brushing, against my face. In front of me hung large brown hairy moths with huge wings and yellow fiery eyes glowing in the dark. Then I heard a noise behind me. I turned, and saw a huge column of ice, with a young boy trapped inside it. There was such suffering and pain on his face that I wanted to smash the ice and free him. But I was powerless to help him. And as I stood watching I heard a voice talking to me, reciting some sort of poem. '*For that he was a spirit too delicate to carry.*'

The voice urged me to carry on and I kept walking. Now there were other paths leading off the main one, and I could see beautiful scenes of enchanted landscapes and castles and palaces and hear the laughter and merriment of people there. As I walked on I grew more and more despairing. I felt stupid for not taking one of the other paths and enjoying the lovely things I could see. I realised that others had made this choice, and I was alone on my path. I began to think that I must be mad, stupid, and crazy.

Then, just as I was about to give up hope it started to get warmer and I saw light shining ahead. And I knew that this was a home for all the unwanted, the misfits and the lost. I turned and I called to the boy in the ice and I could see him running towards me. I grabbed him by the hand and dragged him with me. He was crying with grief over his actions, and I was crying with relief. And God welcomed us home and looked down on everybody with the love and protectiveness of a Father. Behind us, there were shouts and cries of joy as everyone followed us into this world this home, where we all truly belonged, where all of us were wanted and accepted.

It was so beautiful that when I woke, I lay in bed and sobbed because I'd had to leave and come back to the harsh reality of my life.

I remembered straight away what the poem was that the voice had recited to me in the dream.

> *And, for thou wast a spirit too delicate*
> *To act her earthly and abhorred commands,*
> *Refusing her grand hests, she did confine thee,*
> *By help of her most potent ministers*
> *And in her most unmitigable rage,*
> *Into a cloven pine; within which Rift,*
> *Imprisoned thou didst painfully remain . . .*

It was from Shakespeare's *The Tempest*. I remembered it from my early school days, it had always been my favourite.

The dream left me very thoughtful. It seemed to be the story of the long and lonely path my life had chosen. But I also felt it gave me insight into Brady. I felt he had been the boy in the ice, not evil in himself, as a child, but imprisoned in a rift, as Shakespeare had described.

A few days later I found a copy of the play in an old shop on 53rd Street and sent it to Brady.

Over the next few months my life carried on in much the same vein. I continued to work in the café, and to sell stories to Nick and one or two other British papers in my spare time.

I went out from time to time, but made no close friends, so when I wasn't working I mostly wandered around the city, exploring.

Sometimes I would go to the second-hand bookshops in Greenwich Village and sit on the floor at the back reading the biographies of interesting and unusual people.

A lot of the girls in the café said I was so pretty that I should go in for acting or modelling. I approached an agency, who took three photos of me. The owner said she wanted me on her books, but I would have to get a good portfolio together, and that it would cost 1000 dollars. I saved and saved and eventually went back with all the dollars stuffed in my purse.

This time a different photographer was there – a student who wasn't trained. His photos weren't nearly as good as the first ones I'd had taken, and too late I realised that the whole thing was a scam.

I sent the three lovely photos to Brady and wrote a letter in which I said, 'Life – it's not really worth it. I feel I'm in the space where I want to slip into the cold water on the ferry ride back to this awful place I feel I can never escape.'

He wrote back, ' "*Now more than ever it seems rich to die, To cease upon the midnight with no pain.*" *Looking at these photographs you have sent me you seem too beautiful for this world. I intend to die by my own volition. It's the wisest thing to do.*'

He understood my pain in a way that scared me. As if he was a psychiatrist and I was a patient. At times like this he felt closer to me than anyone had ever been. I felt like lying down and listening to what he was telling me.

His favourite topic was the afterlife. ' "*Darkling I listen; and for many a time I have been half in love with easeful*

Death." *Death is my friend and I shall shriek with laughter when I meet it finally and for the last time, spitting into the face of my enemies. Suicide is an act of bravery. Why fear it?'*

When eventually the summer came it was the hottest weather I had ever known. I got a deep tan, and loved hanging out in the city, which was full of tourists and pulsating with music. I loved the smell of hot dogs mingling with that of the over-heating tarmac on the roads and the strange sight of the bluey-white smoke billowing out of the street drains along the sidewalk.

All too soon it was autumn again. The weather cooled and I wondered if I could face another freezing winter. At least in summer I'd been able to get out and explore a bit, but in winter it was back to my lonely, cold room. My only contact was still the weekly letter from Brady and occasional calls to Nick.

One evening I stood outside on the ferry, returning from my job in the café, and watched the lights of Manhattan Island getting smaller and smaller. I leaned over the edge of the ferry, looked into the blackness of the water, and sobbed. I had spent so much time alone, feeling outside and alienated. Why couldn't I mix with others? What was the block that stopped me from relating to them?

I leaned right over the edge of the boat; there was no one else on deck. Would the icy water blot out my misery, and numb me so I couldn't feel any more of the endless heavy weight of isolation? Ian Brady was right, I thought. Don't fear the reaper. The poetry he had quoted me went around in my head. Keats.

The wind was whipping my hair against my face, making the loose strands cling to the wet streaks my tears had made. If only, oh, if only there was someone in the world who was like me or who could understand me so I would not feel so alone. Perhaps their was a tribe of us, scattered around the world, all not fitting in and feeling confused, and scared and lonely.

'Look at the way the water lashes up against the side of the boat, and the sea looks like it's dancing.' A tall, blond man was standing beside me, looking back at the island, then down at the water.

I looked around me, as if with new eyes. He was right, the water looked beautiful – but I hadn't noticed. I turned, but the stranger had gone.

It was then that I decided to go home. Something dark seemed to slink away from me – failed, yet he would return again some other time.

The next day I rang Nick. He owed me several hundred pounds for stories of mine which had been used in the paper. I told him I wanted to come back and he promised to send me a ticket. 'I'll meet you,' he said. 'And you can come and stay at my place.'

It would be a start and I was grateful. I didn't know what kind of reception I might get from everyone else, but whatever I might have to face back in England had to be better that the empty, lonely life I was living here.

14

The Tiger's Cage

True to his word, Nick met me from the airport and took me back to his lovely penthouse flat on Kew Green, where he'd made up the spare room for me. He'd turned out to be a real friend, and I was grateful. He told me I could stay as long as I liked and, relieved at having no pressure to find a place of my own, I began to enjoy being back in England again.

Nick was a good companion. After so much time alone it was good to have someone to talk to in the mornings and over dinner. And he helped me out with work too, driving me in to his office in his red Stag sports car and giving me stories to work on. I learned about the workings of a paper and hung out in the 'Stab in the Back' – this was the nickname given to the local pub by the hacks – with him after work each evening.

Piers was often there, with the long-term girlfriend he'd taken to France, the one he'd told me he had finished with. One evening he came over to me and pulled out the poem I had written for him.

'I keep it in my wallet, always,' he said. He asked me for a drink, but I said no. Though I still had feelings for him, I knew we couldn't go back to what had been.

By the time I had been back for about three months, I still had no idea what the future held for me, or what I should do. I knew I couldn't stay with Nick forever, and that I needed to find a full-time job. But I was afraid of starting again on my own.

One evening a group of us went to the Wine Press, a little wine bar near the newspaper's offices. Propping up the bar was a good-looking Welshman, who introduced himself to me as Rhys Evans. He worked for a rival paper to Nick's and the two of them exchanged friendly banter.

Rhys and I got talking, and later that evening he invited me to go for a curry with him. Over the meal we got to know one another. He was clever, funny and great company, and I realised I hadn't felt so drawn to a man in a long time.

Within a month of our first meeting Rhys had asked me to move in with him – he had a lovely large, antique-filled flat in Bloomsbury. I packed up my things, thanked Nick for his patience and hospitality, and began a new phase of my life.

Rhys was a busy tabloid journalist and he taught me a lot about the job. I often drove him to interviews and assisted him, and I became proficient in the ins and outs of tabloid journalism. When we weren't working we would wander around the museums and private parks of Bloomsbury and go to little Italian restaurants. It was summer, and we enjoyed long, warm evenings together, just talking and sipping cold wine.

It was one of the happiest times of my life, a rare time when I felt cared for and loved. I began to believe that we might have a future together. We talked about marriage, and my dream of a loving husband, kids and a stable home began to feel like a real possibility. Only one thing worried me – and that was how little Rhys had told me about himself. I longed to know him better, but whenever I asked him questions he was closed and said little.

One day when he was out, I went through his drawers to try to find out more about him. I knew I shouldn't be doing it, and that he'd be furious with me, but I was desperate to find a way to get closer to him. Of course it was a mistake, I came across a photo of an ex-girlfriend of his, a girl called Debbie, whom he'd mentioned to me once or twice. I felt very upset he had kept it and over dinner in a smart Indian restaurant in Covent Garden I attacked him about it in a really childish way.

'I've never seen such a big chin on a girl. Didn't it make it hard to kiss her? Are you sure, you're not gay Rhys? I'd be worried I was gay if I were attracted to a woman with a chin that big.' I went on and on in a bitter, hurt whine.

Deep down I was terrified that he would return to her. I wanted him to say she was awful and had been a mistake, but he didn't. He was angry, and he said, 'Firstly, you had no right to go rummaging around in my drawers. And secondly, your trouble is you don't know what pretty is.'

I tipped his plate of Tandoori chicken over him and ran out crying. I wasn't looking where I was going, and I ended up getting lost in a maze of dark alleyways for hours.

It had been a silly, pointless row, and we should have made up. But I couldn't get over my jealousy of his ex, and the next day I told him I was moving out. Rhys bought me a huge fluffy white seal to try to make me stay, and then cried when I refused. But I felt numb, and told him I needed to leave him and survive on my own.

So reluctantly he drove me to a very grotty bed-sit in Streatham that smelled of stale cabbage, with a meter in the corner and damp carpet. Rhys couldn't believe I would leave him, and his smart flat, to live there. He told me I was his last chance at a real relationship.

'I'm not your last chance,' I said guiltily.

'You're the last chance I want. It's the seal, isn't it? It's come between us – I knew it would,' he said. It was an attempt at a joke.

I looked at him. He was a good man. But I was so afraid he still had feelings for his ex that I wanted to hurt him by ending it. It was perverse, but I couldn't stop myself.

He left, and for a moment I was tempted to run after him. But I thought of Debbie, and imagined how I would feel when he finally left me to go back to her, as I believed he would, and I kept my resolve. That night I went to sleep in my flea-bitten second-hand, single bed. Alone again.

Looking back, I can see that it was my own insecurity that made me destroy a lovely relationship. I just couldn't believe that anyone would really love me, or want to put me first. To me, there had to be a catch.

Back in bedsitland, and now aged twenty-five, I needed a job and a better place to live – fast. So I went back to the work I knew best, investigating. I wasn't sure if I'd be able to find work, after what James had said. But two years had passed since then and luckily for me most people don't remember what they read in the newspapers. I found work with an ex-SAS guy called Charlie Scott who ran his own agency, and for the next few months I kept my head down and worked long hours doing spying and surveillance jobs. We worked mostly in teams of four or five, using walkie-talkies, and I learned a lot through working with several highly-trained ex-SAS men.

My new boss was nice, and he took me on a few weekend shooting trips at Bisley, where mostly ex-army people competed against one another in shooting ranges. I turned out to be a great shot and I won a fair few bets with people who'd been shooting far longer than I had.

Around this time my ex-boyfriend Linton reappeared. He got in touch and it turned out he had been looking for me for some time. He regretted cutting me off and wanted to know if we could see each other again.

For some months we met as friends. He was still living with Jem in their odd set-up, and it was good to see them again. After a while Linton asked me to move back in with them, and I agreed. It was far nicer than the bedsit, and the three of us always got on well, misfits that we were.

Linton and I were back together, but I found it very hard to be close to him. We had sex once a week; I couldn't bear it when he touched me sexually, but I liked the cuddles that would follow. I would fall asleep, while he would stay up all night lifting weights to the strains of Rocky, and watching videos. Then he would sleep all day while I went to work.

I suffered a lot from depression. Black clouds would descend on me from nowhere and the abuse I suffered as a child at the hands of my adoptive father came back to haunt me. I felt dirty and despoiled and knew I would never be able to be comfortable with my sexuality. I was afraid that I would never let a man get really close to me, or be able to have a child. I feared that I was so dead inside I would be a useless mother and a child of mine would end up in care and have the life that I'd had. I felt bitter and angry and each day seemed to be an ordeal. I hated life and living, I could see no meaning or enjoyment in it.

I was still in touch with my parents, but only sporadically. I'd phoned after I came back from the States and my mother had answered and said, 'What do *you* want?' It really hurt, but I swallowed it.

In November that year, around my birthday, I decided to go on holiday on my own. Linton was never a good traveller and I wanted to go to Morocco.

I stayed a few days in Tangier then, eager to explore and short of cash, I stood beside the highway and hitch hiked.

An Arab man in traditional dress pulled over. I told him I wanted to see somewhere interesting. We drove across the desert for two hours and ended up in a small village called Tafrout. The man told me I could stay at the house of a friend, introduced me to the family and drove off saying he would be back in a week.

I got by on my smattering of French, the girls of the family painting my hands with henna and me painting their faces with the cherry lip glosses and glittery silver eyeshadows that I had in my suitcase.

Before the week was out I was ready to move on, so hitch hiked again in the direction of the desert. This time four German men offered to take me to Quarzazate, past the Atlas mountains.

I sat squashed in the back with two of the men, as the driver smoked a huge joint and laughed as he drove perilously close to the edge of the mountain road. The other three men also seemed to find it hilarious that we were driving inches from a sheer drop.

After a stop to eat a meat tagine in a roadside café we drove on. As night fell, one of the men reached over and stuck his hand up my skirt. The others saw, and roared with laughter.

Terrified, I seized my chance when the car slowed. I opened the door and threw myself out onto the road, rolled across and fell into a muddy ditch. The car screeched to a halt and the men all got out. I got up and kept running and running on into the darkness. Eventually I came to a wood, where I crouched, hardly daring to breathe and sobbing quietly. I could hear the four men shouting as they searched for me. I knew then that I had been quite a precious cargo to them.

I waited over an hour and when I was sure they had gone I made my way out of the woods, through a dark field and along a dust track, until I came to a clearing, where three men were packing some equipment, next to a barn. The men, two young and one older, sat me down but we couldn't make ourselves understood. I was dirty and scratched and must have seemed in a bad way and I hoped they would get me some help.

I was waiting for them to take me to a car and drive somewhere I could get help. I had my handbag with me, but my suitcase had been left in the boot of the car.

Instead of taking me to where I could find help, to my horror the men pulled out a blanket and urged me to lie under it on the floor. I was certain I was going to be raped, by each of them, then killed. I cried into the rough smelly blanket and waited for it to start. I could hear my father's voice, *'Men do that to her. It's not them. It's her. She's a temptation. She's one of those bad women.'*

My body went rigid and I could hardly breathe. I shut my eyes.

The minutes ticked into hours and the hours ticked by and I waited. From the corner of my eye I could see the two young men cuddling the older man under another blanket. One of them laughed as he saw me watching and unable to contain myself I let out a howl like an animal. The older man got up and came over to me. He leant down and laid his hand gently on my head. I stopped my howling and he went back and laid down.

Dawn came and I had never been so pleased to see daylight arrive.

A car arrived, driven by a fourth man, and the older man ushered me into it before getting in himself, with the two younger men. We drove for a very long time and I sat in the back swallowing hard and sobbing. I had no idea where they were taking me.

I could barely believe it when we arrived at a large hotel. The older man got out of the car, helped me out and signalled towards the hotel.

I don't think I will ever forget his face, which was filled with kindness and concern. I leant forward and wept on his shoulder, then I reached for my gold crucifix. I realised later that he must have been Muslim – but in the moment I didn't think.

'Please take it – please have it. It's a thankyou.'

He shook his head and pressed it back into my hand then smiled. He touched my shoulder and then he walked off, turning once to look back at me standing staring after him. His kindness had been exactly what I needed after my ordeal.

In the hotel they spoke English and I was able to arrange my journey home.

When I got back Linton was disgusted. 'It's your own fault for hitch hiking. Acting like a nutter.' He would say no more, but I needed someone to talk it out with – I was still suffering from shock. I went to see my mother and tried to tell her. 'I'm not interested in this,' she said, as if I had done something dirty.

My father cast me a look from his armchair as if I had been somehow up to something and been caught out. Then he stared into my eyes, longingly, as if he was in love with me but couldn't have me. I got up. I couldn't take this.

I went back to my room and poured out the whole story to Ian Brady in a letter. I felt better afterwards. I waited for a reply.

His reply came. 'If you ever go back to Morocco again I will break off all contact with you. Understand.'

The word 'understand' was underlined in red biro.

He followed it up with a phone call. 'You're going to get yourself killed.'

I didn't know what to reply.

'I've three minutes,' he hissed.

I still sat silent, until a deeper male voice said, 'That's it – break off the call.' I heard the click and then the line went dead.

I threw myself into work. I knew there was something inside me that hated myself. That wanted to get into cars with strange men and risk awful things. That felt I was bad, evil and because of that I deserved to die in pain The critical voice in my head always sounded like my mother's. Cool and controlled and speaking as if she was merely telling me 'how it was'. I was low and bad and the world would be a better place without me.

I bought lots of books on childhood abuse and incest. I would buy them and then stand outside the shop, breathless, in the throes of a panic attack. Sometimes I would shove the books straight into a nearby bin even though I'd spent a lot of money on them.

I grudgingly attended some groups with other women who had suffered from sexual abuse at the hands of their fathers, and friends of their fathers. It never occurred to any of us to go to the police about our fathers. We loved them and were fiercely loyal. We were – all of us – ready to believe it was we who were at fault. Most of the time in these groups we just sat and cried – shooting each other looks of sympathy.

It didn't occur to me that I was the way I was because of the past. I just thought I was a bit nuts and most of the time I played up to it by acting the dumb blonde so that people would like me and not be threatened by me like my mother was.

There weren't many people I could be myself with, and exchange ideas with, but one of them was Jem. Despite his menial role cleaning windows, he had been privately educated and had then graduated from a top university. He was extremely bright and well read, and like me, he was on a search for life's meaning. He liked to read books about theosophy, interpretations of the Bible and philosophy.

It was Jem who took my side when I told Linton that a spirit guide, an invisible presence who told me he was called Michael, was coming to me almost every night. I felt horrified and hid under the bedcovers. Linton promptly whisked me off to the Priory Clinic, where I saw a psychiatrist called Mark Collins.

Dr Collins gave me a clean bill of health, but Linton was derisive on the car journey home. 'You're not a schizophrenic – great. You carry on chatting to your ghost at night then. Go for it, Doris Stokes!! I can't believe he let you go and didn't section you.'

Dr Collins had been very interesting. He had told me, 'It's not an illness to experience what you have. Schizophrenia is very different, it's a very serious disease. And one that you haven't got, my dear.'

'What do you think is happening to me?' I had asked him.

He had shrugged. 'Don't know. The other side? No one really knows, do they? Where do we go when we die? Evaporate, or go to another level? And are some people here aware of that level? Very probably.'

Jem had another explanation. 'There are people like you in one of my books,' he said. He gave me a book called *The Outsider* by Colin Wilson. It had been big in the sixties, and was about people who didn't fit into society for one reason or another. Jem felt himself to be one of them, and he thought I was too. I read and loved the book and we both wanted to meet Colin Wilson. So one day, with Linton, we decided to go down to Cornwall, where he lived, and visit him. We wanted to ask him if the three of us were outsiders or not, and how to live with that and find the happiness we could never achieve.

We packed the car with a picnic of Old Jamaican chocolate, scotch eggs and bottles of ice-cold lemonade and set off on the four-hour journey to Cornwall with Jem, as always, in the back seat of Linton's sports car. When we got there I went and knocked on Colin Wilson's door. He was charming, and invited us in. He remembered me from the press stories and during our visit I went for a long bracing walk with him and his two Labradors across the hillside and talked to him about Brady. He said I should write a book about my life as an outsider and call it *The Female Outsider*.

We all went to the pub that night and Colin talked eloquently of books he had read and we had a lively and interesting conversation as we sipped the champagne Colin had bought us. Afterwards we went back to his house, where his wife Joy made us cauliflower cheese and we drank burgundy from a crystal decanter, with his two grey parrots flying around us.

I thought that evening, as I had thought before, that Jem was a lovely, bright and attractive man, and that if he hadn't dropped out, he might have made himself a good life. Once or twice I even wondered if he had been the J the psychic Mike Baker had referred to, the man who I should really be with. He had so much going for him, but he didn't know it, and I knew a relationship between us would be impossible.

After that we went several more times to visit Colin and became good friends with him. He let us all stay in the chalet in his garden. Colin told us we were all outsiders, which only confirmed in our minds that we didn't fit in with conventional society.

For the next couple of years Linton, Jem and I rubbed along together, as I continued to write to Brady. I felt that I was one of his very few links to the world, and that he had come to rely on me, so that I couldn't just walk away. And whenever I did decide not to reply he would find a way to suck me back in, by saying he was lonely or sick.

By this time I thought of him as four different people. One by one they emerged from his letters. One was a cold and ruthless intellectual. Another, which I called 'Christie' was like the character Richard Attenborough played in the film *10 Rillington Place*, a misfit in pebble glasses. A third I called Ice Man. This was the aspect of him that was sub-human and capable of real horror. And the last was a child, a boy of about seven, who was terrified of rejection. This was the one I identified with, and reached out to.

I had wavered several times, wondering whether to continue the association, but Colin Wilson's comments had encouraged me. Perhaps I really could contribute something useful to society's understanding of a criminal like Brady. I still had a strong personal interest too. I had come to believe that I could cure myself of my terrible depressions through him. I thought that if I could work out why he committed his crimes, then I could understand what my adoptive parents did to me, and thus somehow be free of them and their legacy

It was warped thinking, because even if I had understood Brady, that wouldn't illuminate my parents' behaviour. And even if it did, and I understood them, I would still have to live with their legacy. There would have been far easier, more effective ways of helping myself, but I didn't know about them yet. I had been sucked into a dark whirlpool of something sticky and inescapable. And because of it, my distance from the real world was increasing. I felt like the elephant man because of the abuse, unable to befriend others, and so afraid of rejection that I felt it would kill me. And with Brady, I had taken a wrong turning and I felt trapped in my past. I badly wanted someone to help me, but no help was at hand.

A few days later, Brady sent me a letter inviting me to visit him. He hadn't invited me since the visit I'd made which had been prompted by the newspaper. The reason he wanted me to come, he said, was that his conditions had been improved and he was now allowed a visit with no guard present.

He said, somewhat cryptically, 'You will be alone with me. How does that make you feel? *Afraid I might bite you?*'

I had to think long and hard about whether to go. I was stunned that the authorities had agreed to it. I told myself that my interest was now professional, and that I might be able to ask him useful questions. I felt that alone with me he might spill out his secrets; something he couldn't do in letters. I wasn't afraid of him, because after what I'd been through as a child, I was pretty numb, and felt very little fear of anything. It was as if life was something that passed me by and I stood looking at it from the other side of a thick glass pane. Looking back I know that I would be afraid now. But back then I wasn't. So I went to see him.

Once again I got the train up to Liverpool, and made my way to the hospital. Once again I was asked to wait, then searched. At this point a man came and introduced himself as Brady's personal psychiatrist. This was the man I had once spoken to on the phone, the one I had felt was laughing at me. He gave me that impression still. He shook my hand and then told me he would escort me over to Newman Ward. On the walk there, through the gardens, he didn't say a word. I imagined that, having read all my letters to Brady and his to me, he knew why I was there. I wondered about what had made him want to be a psychiatrist, and whether it was, like me, to cure a sick parent.

Once inside the ward he said goodbye and waved me towards the visitors' room. I expected to have to wait, as before, while Brady was called. But to my surprise he was already there, his tall frame squashed into a rather small seat, facing the door. I went in and said hello, and sat down opposite him. This time there was no guard with us, and as we sat silently, I began to wish there was. Awkward as that had been, at least it had provided a focus of sorts.

Brady was smoking. He hadn't shaved and yet he smelled of Hai Karate aftershave. He was wearing the same clothes as before, jeans and a faded navy jacket, although he was thinner than before. His hair was now almost entirely grey, and it was wavy and well combed. After a few minutes he produced a piece of paper, and told me he had made a list of topics he would like to discuss. I took the piece of paper and looked at it. There were fifteen topics, which I thought typical of him. He was always very meticulous.

We began with poetry. I liked Shelley, he liked Blake. He told me he was reading Shelley and that Shelley's poetry made him think of me and the way I saw life. 'Shelley was mad, of course,' he added.

'Well, I'm not,' I said, indignantly.

'You're different,' he said. 'Different from other people. We're both different to others.'

I felt uncomfortable with the comparison. I didn't want to be like him, in any way. I wanted to ask him why he had said he knew my mother. Had he done it to keep our connection? Because he didn't want to be alone? Surely it had been a lie; he couldn't really have known her. But somehow that lie had made the idea of him being my father real. It had stuck with me.

I didn't have the courage to bring it up. But Brady gave me an opening when he said, 'You are angry, Christine, and feel dead inside. So you seek out men who can act where you cannot. It is why you write to me. You are looking for the devil. Years all alone in here have made me a great student of humanity'.

I was shocked. 'That's not true,' I said. 'I'm here because I thought you were my father.'

'No, you're not,' he said. 'You are fascinated by me because of what I did.'

'No,' I said.

I began to feel sick and said so. Being alone in an airless room with a man considered by most rational people to be a monster, was beginning to take its toll.

Brady attempted a joke. 'I must be losing my charms if I make you want to throw up.' He got up suddenly. 'Hang on. I need to go and get some medication. I'll be five minutes.'

When he returned he looked dizzy and distracted.

'I'm sorry to disappoint you,' he said. 'Coming here in search of The Great Beast. It was not me – you see.'

'What wasn't you?'

'It was another who did it. The killings.'

I felt sick again. 'Why did they convict you? Are you blaming Myra Hindley?'

'Who do you think it was?'

'I don't know.'

'Come on.'

'I don't know.'

He leaned forward and whispered, 'The Devil. And you saw that. You saw his hallmarks, didn't you? Not many did. But you did. That's why you're here. To meet the Devil and ask him: why? Ha. Why? Why are you so bad, Devil? Ha.'

I swallowed hard. He was scaring me.

'I'm not the Devil,' he said. 'I'm sorry to disappoint you. I am weak, my little owl. The Devil is strong.'

I fidgeted in my chair. Was he right? Had I been searching for the Devil? I knew that inside me lurked the demons of my past. My mother's intense hatred of me. My father's crucifying betrayal. They fed on my negativity and fear. A small part of me felt almost disappointed. I felt I needed a devil to slay my demons. I was afraid that they would stay forever. I looked around me, then at him. I was on the right track. The Devil was definitely around here somewhere.

As I stared hard at him, studying the pale face and the moist red lips, I caught sight of some hidden part of him that seemed immensely broken and sad – then as quickly as it had shown itself it vanished.

'I had foster parents, just like you did,' he said. 'Don't let it ruin your life. Forget the past. You mull it over and over. I know. I know.'

I didn't reply, and for a moment there was silence.

I got up to stretch my legs and stood over by the window. He appeared to take it as a cue. He stood up, came over and stood facing me, looking almost excited. He was very tall and towered over me. I felt intimidated.

'We went to the seaside once,' he began unexpectedly. 'Myra kept going near to the sea. I told her, "Keep away from the fucking sea." It was wild, you see, and dangerous. She ignored me. She couldn't hear me. I came up behind her and put my hands around her throat. I said to her, if you disobey me then I will kill you. I had such power over her. My power was her terror of me. Myra couldn't leave me. She was in her own prison. She knew what I was capable of – see? She knew that I meant what I said. I don't ever threaten – I just do.'

He stood there for a while, then said, 'I will never let you go. You know that, don't you?'

I felt terrified. What did he mean by that?

We were both standing close to the window. Suddenly he gripped my arms on either side, a powerful hold I couldn't break.

'Still your father's little girl?' he said, staring into my eyes. I felt cold with fear. He was playing with me.

'I remember your mother Olivia. I told you that, didn't I?' He brought his face close to mine. 'You don't believe I'm your real father any more?'

'Yes, of course I do.' I was shaking. I wasn't about to disagree.

'Prove it to me that you believe I'm your real father, with a kiss.'

I could smell his breath very close to my face. Mint and tea.

Obediently I leaned forward and kissed him on the cheek. But he grabbed hold of me, pushed me hard against the window, pinned my arms by my sides and kissed me full on the mouth, his large tongue searching hungrily around in my mouth. I was horrified, yet too shocked and frightened to stop him. I felt like a rag doll.

He brushed strands of hair away from my wet, red face and looked intently into my eyes. I felt dizzy, and overwhelmed by the intensity of his scrutiny. I could see a blue vein on his neck throbbing rapidly. He shot me a long, potent animal-like stare of pure threat. Then he pulled away, sat down and reached for a cigarette.

I still stood by the window. I felt as if I had stepped outside normal human boundaries and been sucked down into an inky dark hole. He lit the cigarette with my gold lighter that sat on the table. He looked at the cigarette and flicked at it, then blew a thin stream of smoke out into the room. 'You don't know what it's like to be chronically untouched for years and years. You don't know what loneliness is.'

I wondered was that his way of apologising for kissing me like that. Loneliness – the great excuse.

He seemed angry and I was reminded of my adoptive mother. I had been so afraid of her anger, I had never been able to stop it.

'I know what it's like to be lost and alone,' I said.

I remembered a letter he'd once written to me. He'd said that things he hated still brought on his killing rages. Suddenly I wondered why, after reading that, I had still come. Like a lemming.

'You'll never betray me, will you?' he said. 'Never mention this to anyone. Us.'

What 'us' did he mean, I wondered.

He stood up. 'I've a very strong circle of friends outside – IRA men, gangsters – you know. The result of years in the joint.' He pulled on the cigarette and held the tip of it between forefinger and thumb, like a villain in an old black and white movie.

It was dark in the room now. The authorities seemed to have forgotten me. I looked at him and felt that I was seeing him properly for the first time. I caught a glimpse of a place beneath humanity, of his anger at everyone and everything within society. Something about him reminded me of a deadly teenager who always carried a flick knife and was a danger to anyone who crossed him.

'Did you carry a flick knife as a teenager?'

He seemed surprised, and pleased. 'Aye – a sharp one,' he said. 'I was never without it. Slit anyone's neck if they looked at me wrong. That was just the way that I was.'

He began to laugh. 'There was this old tramp once . . . no, you don't want to hear – or do you? I think you do, my hen. I think you do.' He took another pull on the butt of his cigarette, then ground it out on the floor with his black brogue.

I felt overwhelmed. It was as if I had run and run from my past, and yet had ended up back in the same place. I had doubled back on myself and stood facing the house of horrors of my childhood.

Then the door opened and a woman guard came in. I felt exposed and awful. I wanted to catch her eye, and have her smile at me, but she ignored me.

'Ian, come on, she has to go now. Tell her to leave.'

'Aye, I will indeed.' He didn't look at her but his loathing and contempt were palpable.

She left again.

'When Broadmoor was short of staff one time, they rounded up all the local tramps,' he said.

It was a joke, but I didn't get it. 'Did they?'

He laughed. 'Yes they did.'

He carried on laughing and at that moment he seemed to be really enjoying something about me, but I couldn't work out what, and I didn't like it. Looking back I think he was laughing at me, because I hadn't understood his joke. It was dark outside and despite my numbness I could feel the flame of fear prickling insidiously at the back of my neck. I had been studying a tiger in a cage, and enjoying my power. Now, forgetting my weakness, I had climbed into the cage. I was at the mercy of Ian Brady, the Monster of the Moors. I had no idea how to get out of his dark and crazy world.

The visit had gone on far over the allotted time. I reached out my hand to shake his goodbye.

He looked at me with contempt and then leaned unbearably close to me.

He pushed his finger underneath my chin and pulled up my face so he could see into it. His finger hurt me.

'Who are you? Just who the hell are you? And darlin', what the fuck are you doing here? In this khazi?'

I felt like someone caught stealing silver in the house of a maniac. I didn't know who I was. I didn't know why I was there.

'Is this a trick – part of a press stunt?' he spat, his head cocked to one side.

'No, no of course not. I'm just a person.'

He had me pressed up against the wall with his body. I had thought him thin but I was wrong, he was heavy. He laughed, 'Don't kid yourself.'

'What do you mean?' I looked at him, surprised.

He laughed again and leaned away from me. 'You're nothing as odious as that, my little owl.' His anger had dissipated and he was looking at me cheerfully.

I blinked fast. This would soon be over. I wanted to say, why? Why did you do it? Please, just tell me why?

But I knew he would never tell me. I had been treading water for years. Getting nowhere. Acting like an idiot. The Walter Mitty psychiatrist.

A male guard came in and turned the light on with a brusque click.

'Please, I need the toilet – I don't know where it is, will you show me?' I said, screwing up my eyes in the sudden harsh white light.

I looked in his eyes to see his reaction to me being there. His contemptuous look said: Serves you right, you silly bitch.

He led me out of the room, and showed me into a small toilet. It had no light and I could barely see. It was icy cold after the heat of the visiting room.

I stared at myself in the small mirror. A sleepwalker in a nightmare. I looked around me. It reminded me of the hospital where my Uncle Edward had been.

I had clung on to this man – a stranger – when I had lived in New York and had nothing. Before that, in my kids' home. I had clung on for dear life – to this. It was madness. I was mad. Tears ran down my face. I'm mad. I'm mad. I wiped my face where he had kissed me. I remembered his anger towards me and I started to shake uncontrollably. I felt lost in the darkness. With no hope of a way out.

When I came out of the toilet the communal area was quiet and empty. The guard had gone, Brady had gone. I looked around me. Outside, it was pitch black. Inside, the room was dimly lit by a lamp in the corner. I could hear voices behind closed doors a long way off. They had left me in here. I fought with breathlessness and claustrophobia as I went over to the double doors that led outside and shook at them violently. They were locked. I was locked in the asylum for the night. I could hardly take this in, the guard had gone off, he had forgotten me.

There's no way out. This is a prison.

Panic rose up inside me. I wanted to cry, but I knew that if I did I would never stop. My heart beat so loudly that it scared me. Then I gasped in shock as I heard a tiny rustle come from a dark corner behind a long dirty yellow curtain. There was someone there, skulking behind the curtain, peering at me. He jumped out. He was short and bald and his squashy, pale face looked deranged. I was so afraid I thought I would vomit. I turned and shook at what I knew was the office door, gripping the round handle and shaking it hard. 'Hello, hello,' I shouted as I rattled the knob.

No one came. I spun round and the whole place seemed to swim before me. The short, bald inmate walked off down the corridor. I felt certain he was going to Brady's room, so I followed him down the corridor to the dimly lit room on the left.

The man went into the room and a voice I recognised shouted, 'Get lost!' in a strong Scottish accent.

The man came out, and I took a breath and went in. Brady was sitting on the bed and he looked shocked to see me.

He mumbled almost to himself. 'So. You like it so much you're staying.'

'Yes, they said I could stay,' I said, with a show of bravado that masked my fear. I felt almost as if I was on a spying job for James.

I sat on the small bed next to him, my heart still beating heavily, feeling breathless. He reached into a drawer beside his bed and pulled out two photos – one was of a large stag on moorland, the other was of Eileen Donan castle in Scotland, covered in snow. 'Have these,' he said. I imagined he didn't have a lot to give.

'I've been to the castle,' I said, as I tried to calm down. 'It's magnificent.'

I looked around at the small, dark room, which was lit by a yellowy bare bulb. A small window showed the black of night. It was as claustrophobic as a coffin.

I was still frightened but my thinking was also incredibly clear. It was as if all my consciousness was focused on being there in that room. I was alert. I remembered in letters he had described his psychiatrist as 'an idiot I play games with. It's my only sport.' In twenty-five years he did not feel he had been helped. Why not?

At the time of his arrest a police detective in Manchester had announced to the waiting press. 'We know you've all stuck on the question of black magic – but we can state categorically – this case contains nothing involving it.'

It was never again mentioned.

I thought of his letters to me. The advice to get a ouija board, to read the Tarot, to study Blavatsky and Crowley, theosophy and the occult.

I had assumed it had been an interest he had developed in prison.

He wasn't truly mad, I thought to myself as I looked at his ramrod straight back sitting dazed and upset on his thin mattress. He had been someone broken by his parents and numbed into ice who had been dabbling with the dark arts. From the books I had studied I was sure of it, and convinced that he had created a satanic cult. He had been practising black magic. Something normally found in places like California, not England in the sixties.

It wasn't a psychiatrist that Brady needed. I thought of Father Michael. He was such a powerfully spiritual priest – could he be the one to help? Exorcism was still a rite practised by very devout priests in the Catholic Church for sick individuals who had housed a diabolical evil inside them and given it life.

Brady sat silent on the bed beside me. Sweat had formed on his upper lip. He looked pale and desperately unhappy. I stood up and put my arm around his shoulders, as a nurse might. It seemed right. He turned slowly and looked at my arm as if it were something detestable. Deliberately he lifted it off him.

I knew to push him to talk about things inside his head would disturb him further, so instead I said, 'You're not mad.'

He didn't flinch. 'I've always been mad.'

He changed the subject and suddenly seemed to cheer up. 'Do you like the stag? I had a dream last night – I was the stag and they were trying to break my antlers.'

I looked at the photo. 'I love Scotland. I cry when I go up to the Highlands. All that beauty makes me weep.'

He looked at me for a long while and I wondered again why he had pushed away the comfort I had offered him. He spoke quietly. 'What would you have done if you'd met me – you know – back then – out there? Would you have liked me? Like a friend?'

I took a breath. 'I would have run to the cops at the first sign of – you know – that side of you. But you met someone who liked your sickness, who thought it was great that you were a taker of lives.'

'It was my bad luck meeting Myra,' he said.

I felt angry. 'Worse luck for some.'

He got angry back. 'Worse for the dead? Oh, and I'm not dead? This is worse than dead.'

I felt scared again. All of a sudden I realised where I was, and how bizarre it was. Because my visit had started late and run late the authorities had forgotten me completely.

I said, 'I've really got to get out. I'm sorry. Goodbye.'

Something in me felt exhilarated, knowing I had the freedom to walk out of the coffin and he did not. Something cruel inside me enjoyed feeling powerful. He was weak. Now I was in control. I wasn't trapped after all. I was going to walk out and go to a pub and have a cold beer and wash off the stale smell of this funeral parlour full of ghouls.

But Brady hadn't even heard me. He was leaning forward, his head in his hands. 'I'm fucking DEAD. I'm not dead? I'm dead. I'm DEAD.'

I slipped out of the room while his head was still in his hands, and walked down the corridor, my designer heels clacking on the floor and his desperate shouts echoing behind me.

Not knowing where to go, I stood in the corridor for what seemed like an age. Someone saw me and went to get a guard, who showed me out. I wanted to scream at him, 'Thanks for leaving me. I've seen and heard things I shouldn't have had to see and hear.'

I was escorted to the gate, and walked down the drive, knowing I wouldn't be back.

As I made my way to the station I was reeling from the visit and all that had happened. Alone with Brady I had glimpsed, for the first time, the madman in him, and it had frightened me terribly. Yet thinking about him trapped alive in that little room made me feel as if I could not breathe. The only escape he had was into his head, and in there were all the memories of what he had done.

I felt bad. I had got close to him. He would remember me. Need me, maybe. A Scottish accent whispered in my head, 'You're getting out of nowhere. You're as trapped as I am. There's NO way to fly away, my little owl.' And then I heard that harsh laughter.

As I sat on the train home, suicidal thoughts and a feeling of heavy black depression welled up in me and I felt I could barely breathe. Ian Brady, Moors Murderer, locked away for twenty-five years in solitary confinement, had kissed me. Kissed me in a needy, male way, full of passion and hunger. My head spun and I wanted to cling to someone. A man nearby had headphones on. I could hear the song. It was Elvis, and it reminded me of Linton. 'Suspicious Minds'. *I'm caught in a trap . . .*

The journey passed in a blur and at Victoria station I jumped off the train, and then had to lean against the side of the railings, feeling dizzy. I saw small boats in front of my eyes bobbing about on a river. I blinked and held on to the railings until I could see the station around me again. I thought of Linton. I would have to tell him about the kissing. I had to tell someone. I felt dizzy, sick and scared.

When I got back to the house I told Linton what had happened. His reaction was even worse than I had expected. He slapped me – hard.

I stared at him in shock, tears pouring down my face. My lip was swollen and bleeding. I started to gulp in large mouthfuls of air.

'I feel really weird,' I said. 'As if I'm not here, all strange and floaty, and I can't hear properly.'

Jem appeared in the doorway looking worried. 'Sounds like she's in shock. We should take her to accident and emergency, or call a doctor.'

Linton was still furious. 'Oh yeah, and tell them what? Oh Doctor, she's a little bit shocked because she's just let the Moors Murderer slobber all over her, but perhaps you could give her some tablets and she'll be all right in the morning.'

He grabbed me by the shoulders and started to shake me hard. I went a deathly shade of white and my knees buckled. 'I want to take the silly little witch to get a lobotomy.'

He turned to Jem. 'Get a case and put her clothes into it. The whole point is that she will never be all right in the morning.'

I began to sob again. 'But he's squashed in a little coffin of a room, buried alive there, and it's so awful.'

'WHO GIVES A DAMN ABOUT AN EVIL PERSON SUFFERING?' Linton bellowed. 'I want you out. Get her case. NOW.'

Linton left, and a moment later Jem appeared. 'He wants me to help you pack and take you round to your parents'.'

My parents? I thought sadly. I would feel more comfortable picking a house at random, knocking on the door and asking a bunch of strangers to put me up. I begged Linton to let me stay, but he was adamant.

A short while later Jem put my case into the back of the truck and climbed in beside me.

'Linton was really in a good mood tonight,' he said. 'He was looking at small boats. He was going to buy one and call it after you. As a surprise.'

I felt oddly calm sitting beside Jem, even though I was sure he too thought me sick and confused for visiting Brady.

'There's a part of you that's normal and in shock at having anything to do with a monster like Brady,' he said, unexpectedly.

I stared at him. 'So, if there is only a part of me that's normal, then what's the other part?

He looked at me in surprise, as if no one could possibly be interested in anything he had to say.

'Well,' he began. 'If you really are interested.' He hesitated. 'I've read a lot about this. Psychology really interests me. I did a module in it when I was at Durham. It's unconsciousness. For some reason, most of your brain is unconscious when it should be conscious.'

'Do you think someone who had a lot of unconscious rage would feel like a powder keg waiting to explode?' I said. 'Do you think that they might feel that everything in life was ashes in the mouth and not be able to feel the life that's going on around them, and feel alienated and different from other people?'

'Of course,' Jem said.

'I'm sick, Jem. I can see that, because of what I just did. I'm so very sick and no one will help me and I'm all out of escape routes.'

'No, there is a real escape,' Jem said. 'It was pioneered back in the seventies, by someone called Arthur Janov. He wrote a book about it called *The Primal Scream*. It's still at an experimental stage; but it is a kind of radical therapy. John Lennon tried it back in the seventies. It can be highly dangerous; it caused psychosis in some patients and suicide in others.'

'Oh, that sounds great,' I said. 'I end up psychotic, if I'm not already.'

'But it's a gamble for more life; when the alternative is a living death, isn't it?' Jem said excitedly. Jem's enthusiasm reminded me of a film, *Escape From Sorbibor*, in which a few Jewish prisoners in a concentration camp overwhelmed the guards and then shouted to the other prisoners, 'Go, run for your lives. Go tell everyone what is happening here.' Yet half of them were so conditioned to their horror that they stood, immobilised and unable to make a get-away.

He helped me lug my suitcase to the door of my adoptive parents' house, then walked back to the truck and shouted over to me.

'By the way, the therapy's not in this country yet. You'll have to go and live in the States. Los Angeles, actually.'

I wanted to run from what he was saying but I had no more energy in me. 'What does this experimental therapy do anyway?' I asked feebly.

'Opens Pandora's box.'

He cast me a long thoughtful look with his intelligent, silvery-blue eyes. Then he climbed back into the truck, and was gone.

15

The Primal Journey

I contacted the Primal Institute and they told me I could come for an initial appointment in three weeks' time. Determined to go through with it, I drew out the £3000 I had in the bank and bought a ticket to California.

Before I left I wrote to tell Brady I was going. I was so used to writing to him weekly that, incongruous as it seems looking back, it didn't occur to me not to. He wrote back: 'At least find somewhere safe to stay. Be careful out there, trouble is easy to find. Write soon, you keep me alive just by bringing the outside world in to me.' I put his letter in my bag, and a few days later, boarded a plane.

Los Angeles was as beautiful as in every film I had ever seen. Rodeo Drive and the shops full of designer clothes. Sunset Boulevard, so wide and lined with palm trees. Hollywood Boulevard with its sparkly glamour. The hot white beaches of Santa Monica and Malibu. I gazed out of the window of the cab and let the hot sun burn into my face and smelled the salt as it came off the sea.

The yellow cab took me to a cheap motel in Santa Monica. That evening I went for a walk along the beach, by Santa Monica pier. I walked barefoot along the frothy surf's edge and let my toes dig into the hot white sand. Here I was in America again. I had brought all my savings, and I had nothing and no one to go back to. This was it for me. The end of the line.

I looked once again at the letter I'd been sent, which I carried in my pocket. 'Interview to possibly commence Primal Therapy, subject to psychological suitability. Please attend to see resident doctor on Monday at 11 a.m.'

The sun was baking my skin, so I pulled off my top and stood on the beach in my green bra and knickers. I felt the sunshine was a good omen. Tomorrow I would begin. Tomorrow someone would come, as to Miss Havisham in *Great Expectations*, and rip down the dusty curtains in the dark, airless room and let the daylight shine through. Tomorrow someone would throw open the gates and tell me to run, and I would run.

The next day, after a Danish pastry and a gallon of hot coffee in the motel, I got on the bus from Hollywood to Venice beach and then made my way to the address I'd been given, Cotner Avenue. The Primal Institute, with its striped canopy over the door, looked more like a pizza parlour than a clinic offering radical therapy. But their letter had made it clear that they were deadly serious. 'This is not hypnosis or a drug-induced mind control,' it had said. 'But there must be a strict adherence to the rules. For twenty-four hours before the initial session, you must remain in total isolation, with no smoking, no drinking or socialising.'

Now I was standing on the steps of the Institute I felt terrified. Was Primal Therapy all a con, or worse still, a cult I would be drawn into? I was tempted to turn and run, but having got this far, I decided I had to find out. I pressed the buzzer and a small youth came to the door, took my name and told me to go through to the first room on the right. A long white corridor stretched ahead, with doors leading off it.

The room I had been directed to was so small it was like a cell. The effect was enhanced by the pale grey padded walls with scuffs and hand marks all over them. What on earth had gone on in here? Did they lock the worst of the patients in rooms like this? I was getting more nervous by the minute. Perhaps I'd made a terrible mistake.

I turned to go, and collided with a man who was coming into the room. He looked like Barry Bostwick, the drop dead gorgeous actor who often used to play the swooning hero in Danielle Steele films. Tall, well-muscled and tanned, he had green eyes flecked with gold and a mop of dark blond curly hair, greying at the temples. He was wearing a T-shirt with black jeans and black leather boots.

'Christine Hart?' His voice was deep, with a New York accent.

'Yes,' I said, feebly.

'Come this way.'

I had no idea who this man was. An assistant, perhaps? He led me down the white corridor and into another of the claustrophobic little rooms.

'Sit down.'

There were no chairs, only cushions on the floor. He pulled one over for me, reached up and dimmed the lights a little, and then sat on another cushion, a couple of feet away. I felt so intimidated by this very good-looking man that I could hardly get the words out.

'I'm here to see the doctor.' As I spoke, realisation dawned. 'Oh God – it's you isn't it?'

He smiled. 'Yes.'

Doctor Barry Bernfeld, I had been told, had been practising primal therapy for twenty years and was an expert in his field. I hadn't imagined he would be so young and attractive.

'Are you OK?' He looked at me, calmly.

I wasn't, but I nodded, and he went on.

'I just want to start by telling you that I've read the story of your life that you wrote and sent over to us. I think that the way you have defended against your pain is so sensational that you may not be ready for what we can do for you here.'

'I don't understand.' I was surprised by the gut-wrenching feeling of despair that washed over me. Surely I hadn't come all this way, and invested my hopes and my money, only to be turned away?

'Well, let me try to explain. You see, your symbolic stand-in for your father was defending against his pain, instead of feeling it, when he killed. This tells us that his past was much more horror-filled than the person who becomes a drug addict or an alcoholic to block past pain. Do you understand?'

'I don't think that was the whole thing, with him.'

'Whatever, it was definitely the starting point. And your ability to overlook his crimes tells me that your repressed memories of your childhood are also probably pretty near the same level of horror as his.'

He smiled at me with such warmth and acceptance that it made me feel uncomfortable. It was as if he could see inside me, to a part of me that no one had ever recognised before.

'We always, always recreate past situations,' he said. 'The life we lead in adulthood can be used as a history lesson about our childhood. Abuse victims always blame themselves, you know. The level of hate energy they carry around with them is phenomenal. And it gets directed either outwards, towards others, or inwards towards the self. So in the worst cases you get either homicidal or suicidal feelings – they are one and the same.'

I wriggled on the cushion; the room was making me claustrophobic.

'What are you feeling?' He sounded concerned. I managed to whisper that I felt I was going to retch.

'Just let whatever it is trying to come up, come up for you. What I meant was that you have blotted out the horror in your childhood, and denied it. What you think happened is a hundred times less horrific than what really happened.

'Denial *always* plays a part in severe cases of abuse; the ego cannot take the reality. So the child will "forget" what happened. And this denial is what causes all the problems; not the pain itself but what we do to run from it – the acting out.'

I was beginning to see what he was saying.

'So you mean people say they had a good childhood, but sometimes that's not true at all, right?'

'Right. In the case of murder something very wrong has happened in the person's childhood. With child murder something very wrong and sinister can always be found with the killer's caregivers. Child murder is symbolically murdering childhood, so usually the level of abuse the killer suffered is horrific. And as like calls to like, the same can be said for a young girl who could allow herself to become so close to such a violent and evil force as a serial killer.'

He was talking about me. I was deeply shocked, and yet I knew that what he was saying was right.

'Do you think that you can help me to become normal?'

I felt my insides roll, as if something huge inside me longed to come rushing to the surface. It felt like an ocean of need – the need to be seen, to be understood, to end the years of surviving all alone.

'Your orphaned childhood has made sure that you will never be like most others who have been socially conditioned,' he said. 'You missed out on all of that; no one has taught you how to behave. However, I can help you bring out all that repressed shit inside that is making you blind and try to free whatever is at the core of you.

'I can see that you are holding in a great deal, and it must be making you very tired. What we try to do here is bring the numbness back to life. We try to thaw you out so you can become a feeling individual instead of a half-dead robot searching for stronger and stronger sensations in order to try to escape your suppressed memories and feelings.

'Our main concern is that we do not thaw someone out to a reality that they cannot face. For instance, do you think that Ian Brady would be able to survive the therapy here?'

'I don't know.'

'No. He has no real concept of what he's done, or of the utter horror he brought to the lives of others. He knows he is mad, but he cannot really comprehend that madness. Only when you can feel something can the reality of it sink in and allow real change to occur. There's no way he could face what he has done, because no human mind could possibly cope with the guilt; it would push it into insanity. It's why he's kept on heavy medication. He was insane when he carried out his crimes and he will die insane, still unaware, on any real level, of the pain that he caused.'

'Does that mean that he is going to die without being sorry?' I asked. 'Because he can't see the evil of his actions?'

'That's right. And I don't think that you see the reality of evil actions either. But if you remain here you will no longer be able to overlook evil acts – they will disgust and horrify you as they do others, who haven't been made blind. You will be as disgusted by Brady as you should be. You've had to split off from the human, feeling and seeing part of yourself, because that's the part that remembers.'

I was afraid to hear the answer, but I had to ask. 'Do you think I'm crazy?'

He smiled. 'No, in fact quite the opposite. I think that you are extremely intelligent and well meaning. You simply have an inability to see evil in focus. There is some kind of block in you. Someone or something evil in your past that you had to not see, in order to survive.'

I was stunned. Here was someone who saw me so clearly, and yet who accepted me, and who saw only good in me. The impact of his warmth and insight was so profound that I felt overwhelmed, and afraid I might pass out. I sobbed quietly into my hands.

He leaned forward and took my hand. For a moment I thought of Jesus, and what it would be like to be touched by his hand. 'Most people think they feel but they do not,' he said gently. 'Here we change all that. Every defence is dismantled brick by brick. If you are willing to go ahead with the therapy then I think we can help you. I'm going to take you apart piece by piece and then I'm going to rebuild you.'

Relief flooded through me. After a lifetime with no one on my side, I realised that I needed someone so very badly.

Someone who could see good in me, who didn't dismiss me as worthless or bad.

At the end of the session Barry asked me to return the next day for another session with him after which, he said, I would be joining in the group therapy. And he asked me to go and watch the film *When a Man Loves a Woman*.

'If you feel unreal or spaced out you can phone me,' he said. 'Let me be your anchor to reality.'

I walked down the road until I found a patch of grass where I could sit down. I felt very shaky, and at the same time as though a door had been opened to a future I had believed would never be mine.

I pulled out Brady's last letter and stared at it. Sometimes if you lean on someone for so long you think that without them you will somehow cease to exist. Now suddenly I felt as if I was watching a scary thriller, one in which you see a lunatic who is involved with an evil serial killer, then realise, with horror, that the lunatic is you.

It wasn't easy getting through the twenty-two hours to my next appointment. So much had been stirred up in me. I caught the bus to Venice beach where I wandered around and made friends with some artists from Germany. They talked about Gauguin, Van Gogh, Cézanne and Degas, and how, if you looked closely, light was in everything. I loved the way they saw beauty in everything, and I sat and painted with them – it was to be the first of many evenings spent in their company.

In the evening they'd light beach fires and do a dance of gratitude to the setting sun, their drums banging madly and bodies gyrating wildly as the big fat orange ball of the sun slowly made its way down over the horizon. This thrilled me and one day I joined in, holding up my hands and cheering as the sun disappeared, and shouting out, 'See you tomorrow, my friend.' I loved the Venice beach life; I spent hours there and my hair turned blonder while my skin became deeply tanned.

Despite this welcome distraction, I found my thoughts and fears so disturbing that I did phone Barry, who was calm and reassuring.

In our session the next day I asked him, 'Do you care about me?'

'Very much,' he answered.

Once again I was in tears. 'I keep waiting for you to be mean to me. People always are. If you let them see that you're weak or vulnerable they hurt you.'

'No, not everyone,' he said. 'And you are going to learn here that although the world is full of people who can be cruel, you just do not invite these people into your life, as friends or lovers. Do you understand? Like a killer. Someone like that is cut off from the humanity in him. He really cannot have warm or caring feelings towards anyone or anything.'

'He cared about his rabbits – well, one of them especially.'

'A rabbit?'

'He had lots of them when he was a kid at his foster home. He asked his foster mother to cover the hutch to protect them from the frosts, but she didn't and he found them lying there on top of each other, frozen. He gave them a funeral and left a letter in the box they were buried in for the small black one.'

'How do you feel towards the child he once was?' Barry asked.

'I guess pity. I feel compassionate towards the orphaned child. He was brutalised and unwanted and I know how life-wrecking that is.'

'Do you want to hold and comfort the child?'

'Oh yes. I want to hold him and try to protect the vulnerable mind of a child from damage and de-humanisation.'

'How old would you like to see him?'

'Oh, seven or eight.'

'Why?'

'He lets me hold him. Up in a coach all through Glencoe, and on the ferry as it pushes through the water to get over to the Isle of Mull. He has slipped under the ropes that say, *Staff only* and he is right up at the front of the boat. So excited. I want to stop it.'

'Stop what?'

'He is an innocent boy. I don't want him to grow up in the nightmare.'

'Grow up to cause all that pain, you mean. Do you think it's in him at this young age?'

'It's in him. He needs to cry. So much pain, so much rage and darkness in the child. It is an icy twin within him. So dangerous.'

As Barry guided me through the therapeutic drama in which I saw Brady as a vulnerable, hurt child, who had suffered great pain, he encouraged me to tell the child what he would grow up to become, and to recognise that I could do nothing for him.

By the end I was wrung out.

'Whatever happened to him was such a shock that it pushed his already smashed human mind over the edge and into an animal state.'

'You've a very exceptional mind,' Barry said. 'It's almost as if you could see what happened. Like you have a sixth sense. How long have you been like that? Do you use it in your work as an investigator?'

'I see stuff now and then – have premonitions – nothing so strong it will help me win the lottery,' I said. 'I met a priest in New York. One of those cranky Spiritualist churches. He could do it too and he tested me with keys – asking me to say who they belonged to. And he sat opposite me and planted numbers into my head.'

'You picked the numbers he was thinking out of his head.'

'Yes, it was easy. He said he could have me giving people readings in a week.'

Barry looked at me solemnly. 'Well, I can't see you with a tea towel around your head and reading tea leaves. However, you do see evil as familiar and known, and you see warmth as alien and unknown.

'I want to say something that is important,' he went on. 'You should have never been anywhere near a serial killer, Christine. Let me criticise your British authorities over and over, they have let you down. The adoption authorities let you down by not making sufficient checks on your parents. The British Prison Authorities let you down by allowing you to be alone with a category A serial killer. It's obscene. A beautiful, vulnerable young girl alone with a dangerous monster.

'We sit around Charles Manson, one of our most notorious mass killers, with five or six armed guards. He is permanently in chains – even as he eats his meals. Britain tends to be liberal in its views, but serial killers aren't predictable. Brady could so easily have killed you. There was a threat in the letter he wrote you. "You will be alone with me. Are you afraid I might bite you?" It must have been read by them, yet they let an unsupervised visit go ahead and let him, in a way, bite you. I can't believe it. It was so unfair on you.'

Once again I wanted to cry. I had only ever been criticised for my contact with Brady. Now at last someone was offering me an insight into why it happened, and more than that, was condemning the authorities for letting me down.

Barry hadn't finished. 'You saw Brady and you felt the situation was familiar, because being with a sick, good-looking man who did evil things *was* familiar. Your good-looking father was so sick that he did what he did to you. It's why you tore the page out of the book, and thought: this is my father. It was familiarity you felt, not the recognition of your long lost criminal father.

'The Moors killings were representative of your life, Christine. This good-looking young couple who should have been planning children of their own went and took children off the streets by pretending to be mummy and daddy. But instead of helping them they tortured and murdered them. Like bogeymen. Do you see any likeness in what happened to you?'

He looked at me tenderly. 'You went to Ian Brady for help, Christine. You see, if someone taints you, and being tainted stops you from living life, where else do you go to get untainted, but back to the one who tainted you. You couldn't do that, you were stuck in care, and then your father was old and ill, but Brady was there instead. You never wanted to cure him, Christine, or sort out his problems. It was *you* that you wanted to cure. You thought he had all the answers in the secrets of his murders. You thought if you made him hand over the photos of the grave of the missing boy – if you could make him into a good man – you would find your buried answer. It's all symbolic. You're a girl who's looking for your answer. You're searching for the key.'

A shiver ran down my spine, as I thought of the psychic, Mike Baker, and what he had said to me. 'You're a girl who is looking for an answer. Keep going because you will find it.'

'You've been running the wrong way, Christine,' Barry said. He waved his hand around the room. 'These walls , this place, this is your key. This is what you've been searching for. You're a bit neurotic and damaged by your past but don't worry, we can knock that out of you. I'm pleased with your mind, it's an excellent one. God knows what you could have done if you'd been brought up by loving folk.'

'I've always felt very angry about my life and sometimes I felt angry just at humans in general – you know, people just walking down the street.' I said. 'I thought it meant I was a psycho?'

'Justified anger,' he said. 'That's OK, we'll get to it and we will erase it.'

Erase it – Jesus, it was all I knew. Where would I be if I didn't have my anger? 'But I like my anger,' I told him. 'It makes me strong, it's my identity.'

'It makes you a fighter, a survivor. But wouldn't you rather be living, experiencing, a woman, maybe a mother and a wife?'

'You mean wear a creamy cowboy hat instead of a black one,' I joked.

'You jest?' Barry said. 'You, who have been sticking up for a famous serial killer all over England – who have been willing for the press to say you may be his daughter. You can joke about sticking up for a killer? Because you sure as hell were made a fool of when it came to payment by the press who made a mess of your life and used you to make up a front page story.'

'I wasn't interested in money,' I said quickly, stung by his words. 'I'm not an idiot. And the effort was worth it. I wanted people to understand that we make serial killers by the way we treat children. We are the hate factory. Armed with that knowledge we can stop it happening again. Teachers in schools, foster parents.'

He leaned back. 'No, I'm sorry. I don't believe your altruism – you're not there yet. You are sticking up for yourself, Christine. *Your* hatred. *Your* anger. *Your* dislike of people you cannot relate to. *Your* alienation. And it's OK to hate. Contact that hate and let it out safely and you will be free.'

'I don't want you guys to use me like a guinea pig and make me go mad, Barry,' I said carefully, watching his handsome face intently.

He smiled at me then said, 'How can you go where you've been for years?'

I looked at Barry and realised I would have to trust him. I had never really trusted another person because people had always let me down. But now it was time to trust. And I was afraid. I knew the therapy was dangerous and might unlock unbearable feelings.

But it was a gamble I would have to take.

A couple of days later I was due to start my first therapy group session at the Institute. And I was terrified – of being exposed in front of others, of what might come up and of sharing Barry. Alone with him I had felt safe, but as I sat with him and twenty other people I felt he was abandoning and mocking me.

I tried to hide behind a large man called Jay, who was eating pretzels from a paper bag, but Barry introduced me and then began talking about Brady. The reaction in the room was instant.

'Scum like Ian Brady deserves to be fried on the chair.'

'How could you visit a monster like that? You must be completely insane.'

I closed my eyes and tried not to hear what they were saying. I was so frightened I felt I no longer existed, and there was only the fear.

'A killer. Why'd you go see a killer, for Chrissakes?' a balding man called John, with a whiny voice like Woody Allen, piped up.

A large blond man looked at me. 'I can see how someone would think they were so low and worthless that the only one they deserved to make friends with was a street beggar or a serial killer.' He turned and lay down on the floor face downwards and sobbed his heart out and I could hear him saying 'Like me, like me'.

Five or six people got up and walked out of the room. Two others jumped up then turned and faced the padded wall behind them and started pounding on it with their fists. And expressing their hatred for me. 'Fucking witch, fucking fucked-up witch.'

Barry stared at me from across the room, calm amidst the chaos. I felt I was going to melt in agony and drip into the floorboards. Hurt and sadness such as I had never felt, flooded through me. Great surgings of paranoia, anxiety and panic pushed up into my head, which felt as though it was floating somewhere up near the ceiling. I could hear a voice somewhere saying suicide, suicide.

Barry spoke up from across the room. 'The woman that I see in front of me, is not the real you, she is merely a mixture of your defences and a false self. It is why your life is empty and meaningless. The sane woman is the insane one and the insane one is the sane one.' I swallowed hard. Everything was shaking and rocking and there was nothing and no one to cling on to any more.

What did he mean the real wasn't real? I felt as if I would disappear. I had no idea who I was. I was nothing. Nothing.

There was a punch bag in the corner of the room and John was laying into it. His parents had taken away his dog when he was nine and he was back there, shouting, 'Don't you touch my dog. Take anything, you can beat me bloody, Mummy, but hurt my dog and I'll smash your head in.'

By this time the whole room heaved with fury. People were jumping up and going crazy, hitting the walls and screaming out threats of revenge to their cold distant mothers and violent brutalising fathers. Others rolled around the floor, screaming and crying hysterically.

As I watched and listened it was as if something awful and forbidden and frozen started to loosen itself from a mooring within me and wind its way up inside my body. I jumped up and joined the others. Fists clenched and eyes bulging, I began pounding the wall and shouting at my adoptive father. I was astonished at the level of fury that erupted from me.

A few minutes later, as I sank to the floor, exhausted, a girl called Cathy, a tiny blonde with rock-chick looks, came over from where she was sitting and put her arms around my neck.

'I was a victim of a paedophile ring too.'

All of a sudden she looked like a monster. I looked at Barry, who came over to me. 'This group have all been the victim of paedophiles,' he said.

I looked at him surprised. 'I don't belong *here*.' I felt hysterical and afraid.

'Why not?'

'There are no such things as paedophiles.'

'No?'

'No.'

'All these people are liars? Cathy is a liar?' His tone was cool, calm.

Cathy spoke up. 'That's why you went to that serial killer. He did what your father did to you. Mine sold me to a group. He was part of it. They do it for photos – money and to enjoy it. Paedophiles.'

Barry looked at me.

'No, those sort of things don't really happen. No. No.' I felt trapped.

'Ian Brady abused little children – took photos of them sexually before he killed and buried them where they could not be found,' Barry said.

'NO.'

'Come on. Why go to him?' Barry was patient, measured.

'I – I don't know.'

'Children who could not be found.' He shouted it. 'Children who could not be found.' He put his face into mine and whispered it harshly. '*Children who could not be found.*'

I screamed.

It seemed to me that the scream sounded like a small child's. One that I knew and yet had forgotten. I had even forgotten her death, when she was six years old and her father did terrible things to her in the night.

The scream echoed down a long corridor inside of my mind. In my mind's eye I could see a seven-year-old child. She walked towards me wearing the clothes that she always wore when she went with her Daddy to Ireland.

Barry led me by the hand into another room, where there was no one else. He picked up a small brown bear and wound a key in its back. Music, sweet and childlike, tinkled out, as he handed it to me.

'Would she like a bear like this? The little girl who has been dead.'

I looked into his eyes, shining with kindness, and I trusted. All of a sudden, I felt the child in me lurch forward and it was as if her heart started beating again. I could hear it – she lived. She began to live.

My recovery from this pivotal point wasn't easy, or straightforward. It was a case of two steps forward and one back – or sometimes two or three back – as I continued with the therapy, both in the group and individually with Barry, for the next two years.

In one group session Barry made us all lie face-down on the floor and shout goodbye to our fathers. I bobbed my head back up and said, 'I don't want to do this.' Barry came over, gently pushed my head back down and said, 'You know who you have to say goodbye to.' And I put my head on the floor.

The therapy brought up long, painful dreams and even more painful memories. But in time, I began to feel alive as I never had before. It was as though I had lived my life like a TV with the sound turned down, and now the volume was being turned back up and I could make sense of the programmes, because I had the sound as well as the pictures. I was getting my feelings back. Life without them had been a life not worth living. Numbness. Like watching life through a goldfish bowl. Barry, the therapist with the face like a hero from a Danielle Steele novel, had thawed me out of my lifelong ice box. He had brought me back to life and from now on, I would have a life.

While I was living through, and emerging from, this revelatory process, I moved in with Alex Martinez, a divorced man who became a great platonic friend of mine. I'd met him when he placed an ad in the local paper: 'Man with son and a puppy looking for someone to share his home. Please Apply.'

Alex lived in a large Spanish style villa, with its own swimming pool, in Westwood, an affluent suburb of LA. He shared it with his teenage son, Tony, and a fluffy white Samoyan called Puppy Child.

While I was there I made friends with a neighbour called Lucien Casselman, an actress whose father was a lawyer who had acted for the Beatles. Lucien drove me around LA in her burgundy Porsche and showed me a little of the nightlife – clubs like the Viper Room and restaurants like Chasens. We often stayed at the St James Club and chatted to Rod Stewart, the owner. Or we would drive out to Lucien's father's place in Palm Springs, shop for clothes in the expensive boutiques there – Lucien treating me – and then drive through the hot dry Mojave Desert to Las Vegas and stay at Caesar's Palace for the night.

As my life blossomed I began to feel normal. I felt I was coming alive under the hot Californian sun. Life began to feel like a blessing rather than the curse I had always found it to be. I even met a boy I liked, Andrew Weinberg. He was an actor who looked like Ray Liotta and had starred with Cybil Shepherd in a mini-series. He came from New York and had that glamorous accent, the same as Barry's. Of course, like all the girls in Primal I had a great big crush on the enigmatic Doctor Bernfeld.

Andrew and I took a rental car and drove across the border into Mexico. We spent three weeks exploring the architecture and eating in little roadside cafés. Mexico was stunning, lush green and mountainous. I loved it. It was in Mexico that Andrew bought me an antique gold diamond ring and got down on bended knee to give it to me. I said yes. I felt that I loved him and wanted to live in Los Angles forever. We planned to return Mexico to have the ceremony in a year's time.

The only drawback was that I had very little money left. Lucien had a trust fund and was always very generous, but I couldn't keep letting her pay for me. And before the therapy was halfway through I ran out of money. Completely.

I told Barry I would have to go back to England, get a job and forget Primal – but he said I couldn't. 'Once you've started on this therapy it's impossible to discontinue. There would be a constant upward seepage of pain and uncontrolled memory recall – without supervision you could end up committing suicide. You can't be alone Christine,' he said, matter of factly.

I knew he was right. There were times when I cried out, 'I can't stand this, I feel like I'm going insane.' I really felt I was. But Barry would say to me, 'No, Christine, you're going sane. If you like, I'll give you a painkiller to stop the pain.'

'No – I'll carry on.'

'Then take the pain,' he said through gritted teeth. 'There *is* no going back,' he said matter of factly. 'After inducing reality where you have blocked it, the symptoms like nightmares are probably going to get worse, as the reality of your life surfaces. You have deliberately involved yourself with an incredibly dark force and it will take time to recover.'

It was Barry who suggested that I do an interview with the press. I was still being hounded by reporters back in London, who wanted me to contact Brady or sell my story, but so far I had refused all their offers. When I hesitated Barry said, 'I know you can see that Ian Brady was abused and has acted it all out onto others. You feel pity. That is normal. However, because of his actions, he does not deserve pity. I want you to see that. I want you to stand with the children he murdered. I want you to use that powerful mind of yours to be a champion of their cause.'

After we'd talked I took the bus down to Malibu and the John Paul Getty Museum and went to the fine art section. It was where I went whenever I needed to think.

The Museum was situated in Malibu's Topanga bay, a beautiful landscape with high sandy cliffs and a bay criss-crossed by tiny blue and white sailboats with wind chimes attached to their sails. Their soft chiming harmonised with the gentle pulsing of the waves on the long flat beach.

I went and sat on the beach, and got soaked by the waves. I sat in soaked clothes for three hours, watching the large glossy tangerine of the sun slip behind the mountains. Then I paced the length of the surf's edge as it stretched into Santa Monica, towards the big wheel and bustling funfair at the end of the sunny pier.

I had written to Brady a couple of times while I was in LA, and he had written back. In my pocket was his most recent letter to me:

'I hope that this therapy will not make you hate me like everyone else. I was on suicide watch. Now I can take less of my medication because of you. You will not turn against me, will you? Become like them?'

I shouted out, 'I can run, I can and I must. If I don't run how can I tell everyone what it's like to be trapped in ice and darkness and how ugly and awful it is to lose your life and yet still have to walk the earth as a crippled child in invisible callipers? I must go. I must run for life and leave you alone in the darkness. You are dead. As soon as you took that first life. I don't want to live with the Devil in a dungeon – I don't belong there. You're dead, you're DEAD.'

I buried the letter in the sand and pounded the sand down on top of it with my fists.

'It's over,' I said aloud to the cold green sea. And I knew then that it finally was.

16

Love, New Life and Hope

I came back to England in late October broke, homeless and – though I didn't yet realise it – suffering from acute post traumatic stress disorder brought on by the primal therapy.

I missed Andrew terribly and slept with a photograph of him next to my bed. I rang him whenever I could, promising to return as soon as I could get some money together. He was broke too, and couldn't help me.

I missed LA, the sun and having a beach to go to every day. London was grey and miserable and as I couldn't get out of the habit of wearing shorts all the time I was almost permanently chilly.

On the days when I wasn't feeling too low, I contacted a few people. Linton had got married while I was away, and I was glad for him. We stayed friends, seeing one another from time to time. I also got in touch with my parents. I had left my car in their garage and I went round to collect it. As usual, my mother's attitude was sour, but I was no longer so troubled by her hostility; I found I didn't need her approval any longer, and that felt good.

Nonetheless, it was a very tough time and the fallout from my therapy in the States was far from over. After a few weeks

I found myself a therapist called Ron Dreyer. I arrived at his office one evening sobbing, with no one else to turn to. I was awash with old pain and finding it difficult to cope. Barry had been right; once my defences were down, the pain just kept on coming.

Janov, the creator of Primal Therapy had written a new book and in it he said: *Some patients can take two years to recover and may feel suicidal on a daily basis.* That was me, and I was terrified that I would never stop feeling bad.

Throughout the following year Ron, a Geordie, taught me how to live with the new me that was emerging. It was almost like getting to know a stranger.

I discovered things about myself as simple as liking the colour blue and loving yellow roses.

Out of the blue I was contacted by an unknown film maker who had read my story in the press and wanted to do a television documentary about my life. He gave me two thousand pounds for the option on my story, and I used it to pay three months' rent on a pretty penthouse flat in a lovely building called The Circle, in Shad Thames, close to the Tower of London.

In the end he couldn't get the funding for the documentary, and I was glad, and grateful that I didn't have to repay the money. By this time I was beginning to feel a little better and I began to have days that were clear and free of pain. These days felt so remarkable. The intensity of life was far deeper and richer than I had ever experienced before. I felt a strong connection to life, almost as if a new ego was emerging – one that was far more powerful than the last.

At last I felt ready to look for work. I put together a résumé of the stories I had filed over the years and sent it to the editor of the *News of the World*, Britain's most successful Sunday newspaper.

The news editor, a good-looking Ukrainian called Greg Miskiw rang and asked me to meet him in a pub called the Old Rose, a stone's throw from the paper's offices. We chatted and after twenty minutes he said to me, 'You're hired.'

I had a lovely place to live, and now a great job. Sadly my long-distance relationship with Andrew hadn't survived, but I felt that at last I had a chance to make a good life for myself and was determined to work as long and hard as I needed to in order to become a success.

I started work as a full-time reporter a few days later and worked seven days a week until till ten or eleven at night – making contacts, researching, investigating and working undercover. I felt I'd wasted the last few years and I knew I had to put my head down to catch up. I covered all kinds of stories, and made the front-page headline many times. People often asked how I could become a journalist after my life had been ruined by them. My reply was always that I tried to help others – to advise them that they didn't have to do a story, to tip off people in trouble. I tried to help the vulnerable and protect the not so vulnerable.

After two years Greg called me into his office and said, 'It's time for you to work with our top guy Mazher Mahmood. With the two of you working together I feel the sky's the limit.'

I had seen Mahzer about the office but had never met him. But I knew he was very attractive and highly intelligent. I grinned at Greg, 'Can we go on jobs where I play his wife!'

Mahzer, known as Maz, was famous for his 'fake sheikh' stings, in which he dressed as a sheikh and fooled famous people into spilling indiscretions about their business dealings, colleagues and families.

As well as frothy celeb stuff, he produced some hard-hitting news journalism, and the two of us worked together undercover on a number of serious investigative pieces. Together we put away three paedophiles and one child-molesting Catholic priest.

After six years on the paper, Greg sent me to Belfast in 1997 to investigate a claim that the Ulster Defence Association was bringing in guns from Eastern Bloc countries. I was interested in Irish politics and really excited about working over there. But when I arrived I wasn't sure where to start on the story. I was shown round the city by a knowledgeable local cabbie and what he told me fascinated me. The murals on the walls, the tribalism. He recommended some Martin Dillon books about the war between MI5, MI6 and the IRA and I bought them and read them in the Europa Hotel over a steak and salad lunch.

Eventually I got the full story on the gun-running from a police officer who was the father of an army guy I knew. That left me free for the rest of the weekend, so I took a bus down to Crossmaglen, a village in the heart of strongly Republican South Armagh, close to the border with the Republic of Ireland. I knew it was a bit of a no-go area, but there was a ceasefire between the British forces and the IRA (Irish Republican Army) at the time, so I felt safe, and I was curious to see the area.

I took a cab round South Armagh, from Dundalk, but when we got in the centre of Crossmaglen the cabbie jumped out and pulled me into the local office of Sinn Fein, the political wing of the IRA. He said I was asking suspicious questions.

Five IRA men then arrested me and took me to a safe house, where they questioned me and held me for a night. I was terrified, and wished I had never gone there. I hadn't expected something like this to happen.

At that time I had been doing some surveillance work on the side for CIEX Ltd – French for Company X.

The IRA men searched my bag and found pay cheques from CIEX.

They told me that they knew that the Company Director for Ciex Ltd was Michael Oatley.

Oatley was an ex-MI6 man and had been the man known as 'The Contact' who had liaised with the IRA for Margaret Thatcher. They were very unhappy that I was travelling around Crossmaglen with such credentials and, as they thought, passing myself off as a journalist and I realised that I was in very grave danger. I could have kicked myself for leaving the papers in my bag, but I really didn't expect a search, because of the ceasefire.

Suspecting me to be a Government operative seeking information on support for the then precarious Peace Process, they kept me prisoner for a night and two days, while they debated what to do with me. It was a nerve-wracking time, because I really didn't know what they might do with me. But in the long hours of waiting I got talking to the man who was guarding me and we became quite friendly, so I managed to capitalise on the situation by forming a strong and valuable contact. Eventually they decided to let me go and I went back to Belfast, relieved to have got off so lightly. Back in the hotel I had a long hot bath to wash off the smell and the sweat of the dusty dirty house where I had been held.

The captor I had made friends with had given me his number and told me to call him. I did, and he began to give me stories on the IRA. He wasn't betraying them, he was getting publicity for them, so they were happy about it. That contact introduced me to members of what was to become the Real IRA, a breakaway branch of the IRA formed that year, and I began to report on them too.

I wanted to do more Irish work, but Greg told me the paper wasn't very interested in Ireland, which was disappointing. Especially as by this time I was finding my London job very dull. I was running the investigation department on the paper, and earning a lot of money, but I wanted to do something that would make a difference, so I enrolled for a joint degree in philosophy and psychology at the University of North London and I loved student life.

Then, on August 16 1998, came Omagh. Twenty-eight people, nine of them children, were killed by a Real IRA bomb in the town of Omagh. I was in a strong position, having become the only journalist that the tightly-knit Real IRA trusted. I hoped that I could find out what had caused such a holocaust.

I took the decision to leave the paper and form my own agency, specialising in Irish affairs. It was a big step, but it felt right. It was an area of journalism I loved, and I knew that to stay successful I needed to specialise.

Soon afterwards the Real IRA set off bombs in front of the MI6 building and the BBC in White City and shot a rocket launcher into the front of the MI6 Headquarters from the River Thames. On both occasions I was despatched by the *Sunday Times* Ulster editor, Liam Clarke, to go to Dundalk to liaise with the Real IRA. This meant, among other things, staying in the pubs frequented by Real IRA members, till three or four in the morning. A lot of the Real IRA were hardline, dedicated Republicans who hated the English with a passion, so after a few drinks I could sometimes become a verbal punch bag. It was, in many ways, dangerous and difficult work. But now I did it as a skilled journalist, believing in myself. It was very different to the days when I took risks because I felt I was worthless.

I wrote a front page story, headlined '*We Get Inside The Real IRA*.' It was an unprecedented interview with the second in command of the Real IRA, done in a pub in Dundalk at three o'clock in the morning. The paper by-lined it with 'our girl investigates' and I loved the '*our girl*'. It was the first time since working with James as a spy that I felt part of a family.

After that the Real IRA stepped up their trust in me by giving me a warning to pass on to the authorities. I had to go to a phone box, where I was given directions to another and then another. Each time I was told I had ten minutes to find the next call box, then ring a certain number. When I rang I was told to go to another call box and given a new number to call. After six call boxes I was dripping with sweat. In the sixth a deep voice with a South Armagh accent said they had written to the British government to ask for better conditions for their prisoners, but the government was ignoring them. I had to pass on the warning, which was: 'We are going to bomb post boxes as you aren't listening.' I passed it on, but the conditions weren't met and the bombings went ahead.

After the phone-box episode one of my senior Irish contacts said, 'You've now been in the eye of the storm – how does it feel?' To be honest, it felt very unpleasant. The Real IRA weren't people to mess around with, and I didn't want to be caught between them and the British Government. I hoped there would be no more bomb warnings.

I went on to cover many more major Irish stories. When the Real IRA split into two separate factions it was I who announced it to the world on the front page of the *Sunday Times*. And after I was passed a message from Michael McKevitt, the husband of Bernadette Sands, who was sister of the hunger striker Bobby Sands, I was approached by the families of the Omagh victims and asked, 'Can you help us?' They needed publicity for their campaign for justice and I did several stories for them.

Soon after this I met a lovely looking blond man, ten years younger than me, called Paul Stevenson. He was a composer, songwriter and musician.

He was highly intelligent and knew what made me lighten up and laugh at life. He was fascinating to watch on stage; I loved the way he played and sang and held an audience captive. His music was so moving it used to make me cry. I was lonely living in my penthouse flat alone. Although my career success had brought with it designer clothes, a Lotus sports car and flashy holidays in the Bahamas, I had no one to share it with.

Paul was an outsider and something about his face and his liking for an intellectual way of studying music and literature reminded me of Jem. We dated for a year, and when the romance fizzled out we became best friends. He was from Northern Ireland and when he decided to go back home, after a few years in London, he persuaded me to come and live in Belfast. I decided I would – I loved Ireland and I was there often, covering stories. Why not base myself there full-time?

I arrived in Belfast in 2000, with Paul driving my Lotus and all my worldly goods following in a removal van. I lived in Ireland for the next three years and worked for the *Sunday*

Times on a freelance basis. Most weeks my by-line appeared on the front pages.

I started to work with the Ulster Defence Association (UDA) and got to know one of their leaders, a man named John White. He was suspected of being a major terrorist, known as Captain Black. He had been in the Maze serving a long sentence for double murder for the UDA. He began to trust me and when the UDA split with C-Company, I was taken to a safe house to meet him for an in-depth interview which appeared as a *Sunday Times* front-page exclusive one sunny morning in March 2002. The story was part of the paper's Focus in-depth Investigative series, and I was thrilled. The week's Focus piece was usually written by the editor, or a professor who was an expert in his or her field. It had been a dream of mine to achieve this and when it appeared I felt I had finally made it as a bona fide expert in terrorism.

I was well respected in Ireland, I loved my life there and I was doing something constructive. Then, one late April afternoon in 2002 I received a call from a man with a well-spoken Southern US accent, who said he wanted to hire me to carry out an investigation on his wife. He offered to fly me first class from Belfast to his offices in London so, curious, I agreed.

A limousine was at the airport in London to collect me. Bill Green turned out to be a very wealthy grey-haired American lawyer. His offices were in 55 Park Lane, one of London's most expensive areas, and he paid for me to stay at the Dorchester Hotel nearby.

He took me out to dinner at the Wolseley, but there was no mention of his wife. Instead he brought the conversation round to terrorism and gave me three books on Osama Bin Laden and his commanders and told me to read them. This was not long after 9/11 and he told me he was seeking compensation for the victims from the Arab banks in London, as they were allegedly funnelling funds for Al Qaeda.

I told him I couldn't help him as I hadn't made a study of Al Qaeda and it would take years. The next day he sent me back to Belfast, and a few days later I tried to contact him again, to check his credentials. The Park Lane offices he had hired had been cleared out. Clearly Bill Green was not simply the concerned American lawyer he claimed to be.

In 2003 I made a strong contact – a UVF (Ulster Volunteer Force) Commander who told me the Real IRA feared I was filling the UDA in on their secrets. He told me they had my flat under surveillance and my phone tapped and suspected me of being a British spy. Soon afterwards he told me my life was in danger and that I needed to leave Belfast. It was frustrating to have to leave, as I was doing some good work, and I was also writing a novel – a thriller about spying on the Real IRA. But by this time there was a more important – and very exciting – reason for going back to England: I was pregnant.

I bought a house in Surrey and settled down to wait for the birth. My beautiful son Arthur Charles was born on 13 December 2003. Paul held my hand as I pushed and sweated and cried my eyes out through twelve hours of labour, before doctors decided I needed an emergency caesarean. I was rushed into theatre and after a few minutes I heard a cry and then Arthur was put into Paul's arms. He wept and so did I. It felt like a miracle.

Arthur Charles became my sun and my moon and stars. He gave meaning to my life in a whole new way. I honestly think if I had known that this blond-haired, blue-eyed angel was waiting in the wings to be born, then I would never have had a lonely thought or one single unhappy moment.

When my son was a few months old I got a call from my old friend James Stratford-Barret. We'd lost touch during the time I was in Ireland, so I was delighted when he asked me to meet him for dinner. He chose Cliveden, the magnificent old house where the scandalous love affair between call-girl Christine Keeler and defence minister John Profumo began in the 1960s. I knew he still worked for MI6, and I wondered if it was business, or pleasure, that had made him contact me.

As soon as I walked in I spotted a tall, grey-haired figure sitting in front of the vast fireplace.

'James?'

He had aged. He had lines around his eyes and was grey-haired but he was still extremely good-looking.

We stood looking at each other and I felt full of emotion.

'Lovely. How are you? You've no idea how good it is to see you.'

He was his old, warm, charming self. He ordered the butler to bring us two icy White Russian cocktails and we chatted for a while about old times and my baby son.

Then James looked at me and said, 'Bill Green is CIA.'

'I know – I worked that out long ago.' I smiled at him. Had he brought me here to warn me, because he was scared for me, in case I had agreed to work for Bill Green and made myself an IRA target? I was touched, and a little thrilled at his concern for me.

I reached for his hand. 'I can look after myself, you know. It was Americans who cured me, but I can't repay them that way.'

He sounded excited. 'No one has got as close to a terrorist organisation as you have. You've done so well, lovely. But don't just feed it to the papers. OK, you're getting your name on front-page stories in the *Sunday Times* – but so what. Your stories are old chip paper within a few hours.' He sipped at his drink and looked deep into my eyes. 'Spy for us my lovely – not the CIA. You do realise it's Ireland they want you for, don't you – they flatter you it's the Middle East. You're not a master – my love – that's me.'

He sipped at his drink. 'I want you to spy on the Real IRA in the guise of looking for great stories and report it all back to me. We could meet up here weekly. I could rent us a room in this place. The Mountbatten suite is divine.' His eyes twinkled. 'Do you remember how it was for us? I was madly in love with you, you were madly in love with me.'

He sipped his drink and smiled at me, and I remembered that long-ago casual wave up to the window as I watched him go, my heart breaking.

'Yes, I remember how it was,' I said biting my lip.

He smiled again and looked into the fire. 'Let's put the past behind us and think of our future. You'd be so good at it. The Real IRA already trust you. Just burrow in further.'

While I knew it would still be possible for me to build bridges with the Real IRA, it would be long and dangerous work. And James knew that.

I felt sick and very hurt. At last I saw what I had never seen before. He had been everything to me once, but to him I was not important.

I stood up. 'James, before I got well . . .'

He interrupted. 'Ah yes, the mental health clinic in the States. We'll overlook that. You don't even need to speak about it.'

I took a breath and my voice trembled. 'Before I got well, I would have done whatever you asked. You expect me not to care about my own life. And you know what – before the clinic I wouldn't have. But now I see – I was blind and now I see. I'm free of you, James.'

I pulled my pashmina around my shoulders. 'Enjoy your dinner.'

'You're not going?' He smiled and I could see he was angry. 'I'm never going to let go of you, lovely.'

I looked at him and pain welled up in my chest. 'James. Why didn't you love me? Back then. Why didn't you take me away from the spy game – marry me?

He looked so uncomfortable. He fidgeted in his chair and looked grey and old. The fire burned in the huge grate and its high bright flames gave off an overpowering heat.

I remembered back then how young he had been. Just starting out on his life. He sipped at his cocktail and then spoke. 'You were like an ice princess in a tower. You wouldn't let me . . . I wanted to . . . I tried. I left you and I saw your face as I drove away. But how could I have ever reached you? I did my best – I came back and gave you a career and it served you well. I saved you. I came back and saved you. Did you forget that?'

I didn't know what to say. Perhaps he was right.

He went on. 'Will you help us now? Fight against these bombing bastards. You're using skills we taught you for the bloody press. It's not on. You owe us. You're the best Christine Hart. The best.'

'I've a child. They'd kill me.' I looked at him, he wasn't reacting. 'I said they'd kill me, James.'

I realised then that once you've lost someone's heart – you've lost it.

'Anything else?' I said, sadly. 'Goodnight, James.' And I turned and walked out of the door. There were tears in my eyes. James had been special and I had clung to him all my life as friend, mentor and father figure. But he was right about one thing; I had pushed away love. It had come to me, in various ways, throughout my life. But broken inside I had been unable to recognise it or let it in.

I climbed into the silver sports car my hard-earned money had paid for, and took the black soft-top down. The evening breeze was cool on my face as I sped through the dark countryside back towards Knightsbridge.

Feelings weren't always all they were cracked up to be. A lot of the time they were painful. But even painful feelings were better than a life that felt depressing, futile and empty. Primal therapy had given me a life and I was going to live it. Now my tears were of gratitude – for life, for my son, for my good health. I was still young. And I knew I would never ever be dependent on another person again. I had something far more safe and powerful that would never ever let me down or ever hurt me – I had myself.

Soon afterwards Paul and Arthur and I went off to the Ocean Club in the Bahamas for a fortnight of relaxation. I loved walking along the white sand and watching Arthur Charles on Paul's shoulders as they splashed around in the warm turquoise sea. One balmy hot day we ate tons of strawberry and chocolate ice cream in our beachfront villa and then, to burn off calories we rented two white Palomino horses and rode them slowly along the surf's edge – with Art nestled next to me in a sling. He adored the feel of horses under his tiny fists and to ride with him in such a place was heavenly. Every day watching my son was to see evidence of God. Art showed me joy in life with the lovelight in his eyes lighting my path.

I had the time of my life there. I felt God close by and the promise of a future filled with light and love and the opportunity to help others. I had my own family – I felt grounded and part of things at last. Thanks to primal therapy I was a good and loving mother. I felt so free and alive. Being a mother seemed like the most important thing I had ever done. I wished Arthur had been there all of my life. He was my raison d'être. My heart would skip a beat whenever my eyes touched upon him. I was smitten.

When we returned to London my mother phoned to say that my father was dying of cancer. She said he was in bed in the front room and screaming with pain. She told me he called out, 'I want to go home.' She had told him, 'You are home.' But he said, 'This has never been my home – I want to be with my mum back at the Fort.'

I didn't go to see him, but I went to his funeral, a few weeks later. At the wake afterwards I saw how little his life had amounted to; my mother eating sausage rolls and a few friends standing around.

It was a month before I cried. I hugged one of his checked shirts and sobbed into it and I said my goodbyes. I see-sawed between love and hate and knew that I always would for the man who had loved me and betrayed me with equal intensity.

After that I made an effort to visit my mother regularly. She was lonely, and I felt sorry for her. But when I asked her if she had read any of my articles, which I had sent her, she replied, 'Oh that rubbish. I threw that crap in the dustbin.'

Not long after that, my Aunt Cecilia died in a convent in Florence, aged seventy. I was heartbroken. Although I didn't have much contact with my mother, I rang her to ask whether they would bring Cecilia's body home. She said, 'No. Isn't it a shame.' I felt very sad to be missing her funeral, so I was devastated when, two weeks later, I discovered from a chance call to Nicky that Cecilia had been brought home, he'd been to her funeral, and I had not been told about it. I rang my mother, in tears, but she simply brushed it away, telling me that I couldn't have brought a child to the funeral, anyway. In the end, it wasn't the fact that I never said goodbye to my beloved Aunt Cecilia that upset me most, it was what my mother had done. She was seventy-six and yet, it seemed, she still hated me.

I was greatly helped in my understanding by one of the American nuns who had known Cecilia. Sister Mary Lou befriended me and she told me, 'Georgina is evil. All you can do with evil is pray for it – don't hate it back, don't try to understand it. You could waste your life doing that.'

I looked at myself in the mirror – I was forty years old. I had done exactly that.

A year or two later I decided to do something I had thought about for a long time. I would look for my birth parents.

I approached the rescue home and had a long discussion with a woman on reception, who said, horrifyingly casually, 'Oh, yes, lots of our children who were adopted were sexually abused.' She could have been talking about the weather.

I rang the woman in charge, who refused to help, and told me, 'You were probably the product of a one-night stand.'

Shocked and upset, I contacted the Catholic bishop who fronted the Adoption society, asking him to intervene. I got only a terse letter which said, 'I think you have been dealt with fairly.'

I decided to trace my birth mother myself. Days later, I had her phone number. Olivia's voice was tight and hard and rasping. The voice of a heavy smoker. When I first heard her, I went hot and cold with horror. I had imagined my mother to be like Joanna Lumley, well-spoken, warm and bright, not fag-ash Lil with a bad attitude. She was very cold towards me and kept saying, 'Why did you look for me? I was young. I've put it behind me. I gave you up to give you a good life. I was a good person.'

I told her that it hadn't worked out all that well.

She said, 'So is that why you've looked for me – for revenge? I made sure before I left you as a baby that you were going to be adopted by a really nice young couple that I met and they had a lovely little girl. I wouldn't have just left you in an orphanage. I knew you were going to a really good home. I did my duty by you.'

I could not take in her words. I knew for a fact she would not have been able to meet anyone interested in adopting me back then, let alone meet their child.

I told her I wished to find my father. She said coldly that he was a criminal. 'Why would you look for a lowlife?'

I said, 'I know that. I don't care. What did he do?'

It turned out that she regarded him as a criminal because he had made love to her when she was just fourteen. Even though they had dated for over a year, and he was only seventeen, she blamed it all on him.

I told her that because she'd told the authorities he was a criminal, I had been sent on a wild goose chase many years earlier.

She said, 'I made up a load of lies to those adoption people. So that he wouldn't be identified. To spare him prison.'

I was very angry. 'Didn't you think that the lies might one day be repeated to your child?'

She said she had only been fourteen, so what did I expect.

I asked her what time of day I was born at. She said, 'Did you think you were born on the sixteenth of November?'

I told her yes, that was my birthday.

'Oh no, it's not,' she said, gleefully. 'You were born on the fifteenth. They wrote it down wrong.' My head spun. It was clear that things were not going to work out between us. We tried a few more phone calls, but she still couldn't understand why I had come looking for her, and said that I was not like her other children. When she refused to let me meet my brother and sister I decided to end our contact. But she got in first, telling me, 'You're so unlike any of us – we aren't odd or unusual. I think you stole my daughter's details and she's still out there. You're not *my* daughter. You're just someone with a fixation about their father. My real daughter would just be interested in me. Goodbye.' And she hung up.

They were painful words to hear. I tried to ring her back, but she kept slamming the phone down. I felt I had been savaged and it was hard to come to terms with the fact that this woman was my real mother.

After that I became more determined to find my real father. Would he be the same as Olivia? Would finding him mean more rejection? She had told me that he had come to the hospital, said he was going to marry her and then just abandoned her. She said, 'Don't look for him, you'll get hurt. He wasn't interested in you then, and he won't be interested in you now.'

That terrified me, but I felt I had to look into his eyes, no matter what the pain, and find out for myself.

Eventually I made contact with his brother, who agreed to organise a meeting.

I met my father, Tom Hogan, for the very first time in a café next door to the Natural History Museum. It was a bank holiday Monday and it was raining heavily. Two men came through the door, bringing the cold wet of the outside into the steamy warmth of the café.

Both dressed in business suits, they were tall and dark and good-looking and they came straight over to me. One was Tom, my father, and the other was John, his brother, who had flown over from Tipperary especially to meet me. Tom was the more handsome of the two, with dark curly hair and brown eyes, while his brother had blue eyes.

I had brought Arthur, who was asleep in his basket. We sat and talked about the weather for a while. Then Tom brought out an old family album full of black and white photos of him aged seventeen, the age he had been when I was born.

He looked so handsome in the photos that he almost resembled a girl. And looking at the smiling young man I felt I had see this face before, staring back from the black and white photos of me when I was ten and eleven.

'It's yours,' he said, and his hands shook. 'All this is yours. It's so little – what can I give you to make up for the missing years?'

He started to cry and I felt embarrassed and a bit over-whelmed. His brother eased my tension by laughing and saying, 'What a thing, what a thing. When he came back from England he never told us he had a daughter.'

Tom said, 'I couldn't bear it. Couldn't bear it that I had lost you. You were my angel I knew was out there. I used to pray

to you – look for me – please never give up – keep looking –
keep searching – until you find me.'

'Olivia said you came to the hospital and proposed to her
and held me in your arms and said you'd look after us. Then
you never came back. She told me to not look for you.'

Tom leaned forward, tears in his eyes. 'I promise you, I
went back to that hospital over and over. Each time her
brothers and her father would not let me see you. They told
me I was a criminal and they'd get the police onto me. They
said, "This isn't your business, Paddy – get lost." I couldn't
believe it. I had never been in trouble with the police – but it
was because I was Irish that they didn't want her with me. All
the Irish were bad, they said.

'I went to her house over and over just to try and see you.
Her brothers threatened me at the door. I used to wait at the
corner of the street, hoping to see her push you in a pram up
the road. It was you I wanted – my darling little girl.'

I excused myself, slipped out of the back of the café and
rang Olivia for the very last time. 'I'm with Tom,' I said
excitedly, picturing my mother and father as young lovers
kept apart by an unfeeling family. 'He didn't abandon you,
after all. Isn't that great? He went back for you. There's no
need to be bitter. Oh, and he's so good-looking Olivia. He's
been crying.'

'Crying? What a creep. He's having you on. You must be
thick – how have you managed in the world for so long –
being so thick. I know he came back,' she rasped. 'Not many
men leave me. There was no way I was going to marry a
Paddy. It would have been beneath me. He was a criminal.
Date 'em, yes. We took the Paddies for a ride. They were all
over here mostly from country areas – green and yet with

money from building work – ten-a-penny Paddies. Now please don't ring me again. I have no interest in you.'

I let my mobile fall from my hands. She had known he cared, but she had simply wanted me gone. Written me off. I was his child and to her he had been beneath contempt – a dirty Paddy – so I had been too. I felt as if I had been mauled by something awful.

I went back into the café, shaken. John reached over and clasped my hand warmly. 'There's a photo of your grandfather above my mantelpiece – he's leaning forward reaching for a mayflower. When you come and stay at my house and meet my – your – family, it's yours.'

John seemed to have a humour that matched my own. Tom was more serious. He bred horses and loved to ride. I had an odd feeling whenever I looked at him – almost like falling in love. I had been warned by adoption counsellors that I might feel it. They said it was called genetic attraction and that most adoptees, meeting a long-lost parent, feel it. It felt like getting into a warm bath. Every time I looked at Tom, years and years of need welled up in me. I found it rather overwhelming.

'You know, not a day has gone by when I haven't thought of you,' he said. 'I knew there was something good out there. And you a well-known writer – sought after for your opinion, and with such a beautiful son. I cannot ever forgive that woman's family. They took my lovely baby daughter away from me and left you all alone in the world to fend for yourself. It's awful. It's just awful.'

He went on. 'At least I know from seeing what an elegant and fine woman you are, that you were brought up by a good family. Now that I know that I can forgive her and forgive her family and stop hating and feeling bitter – at last.'

I looked at his eyes, bright with tears. I didn't want to contradict him about my adoptive parents. What would life have been like if we had been together? If I had lived under that light of real love and pride in me that I could see shining out of his kind eyes? Would I have been a different woman? I could see a life – in my mind's eye – a life not wasted and filled with pain. University, medical school, a career I loved, a big house, a smiling husband and five children. But just as soon as it appeared, it went. I had my beautiful son. What right did I have to be anything but grateful to God?

The American therapy had awakened me from a lifetime of sleep. Inside me a fiery furnace, once snuffed out, had been re-lit and now burned powerfully. I was finally ready to take my rightful place in the world.

I started the drive home, feeling overwhelmed. Arthur was in the back of the car, sleeping. As I came to a fork in the road I suddenly swerved and drove off to the church I had known as a child.

Father Michael Fewell was the Parish priest now. He had grey hair and looked older but he was still a very good-looking man. I poured out the whole story.

I was surprised that I felt very angry at my father for not doing something – for letting me go – so easily.

The priest looked at me. 'He doesn't have to be your father you know. You don't have to accept him.'

I felt deflated. 'I feel like I have spent my whole life – wasted it really – in trying to understand evil – and I feel as if I've been chasing my tail. I don't feel – like I thought I would. Tom isn't my father – I mean he is – but not the father I dreamed of. I wanted Roger Moore – suave good looks and an Aston Martin, with a castle thrown in for good measure.' I felt like sobbing so I did and felt a lot better afterwards.

Then Father Michael spoke. 'Come with me a moment.' He smiled at me.

He led me into the church. It was odd to go there as I hadn't been for such a long time. Father Michael looked at the huge sculpture of Jesus on the cross. 'Would your Father in heaven be a strong man?' he asked, pointing at the sculpture.

'Yes – course He's strong, Father. Yes Jesus is strong.'

'And could you respect Him? Lean on Him maybe? Could He be the strong man that you run to when you feel weak, lost and afraid?'

'I have Father, but He doesn't seem real to me. He's not a man is he? Not a real live person.'

Father Michael told me to go over and feel the statue – so I did. Putting my fingers into the nails and touching his feet that had blood stains and holes in them. I realised then that He had once been a man. The torn flesh and spilt blood. Pain.

Father Michael was watching me intently. 'Jesus suffered. You've suffered. You and He are close because of it. He wants you as well.'

'How do you mean?'

'He wants you to know that he's your Father.'

'Oh.'

He left me there and I knelt and prayed for a while. As I did I remembered the dream I had had in New York where I had run to a place where it was warm and there was a Father for all of the ones who hadn't got a Father, or who had a bad father or had lost their Father.

As I knelt I felt that same warmth spread over me as I had felt in the dream. With my feelings thawing out, I could now connect with my spirituality. I had found what I had always been searching for: love. Safe, solid, never-rejecting, love.

Father Michael had returned and was standing watching me.

I got up and walked over to him. 'I've got to get home – this little angel will need his tea.' I smiled at him. The bitterness that I had held inside of me seemed to have lessened. As I left the church the sun was shining.

My son started to wake with the heat of it. I knelt down to his basket and whispered to my beautiful son.

'Darling – you and I have the most amazingly powerful Father. We share Him with everyone, yet He is profoundly and personally our own. I can't wait to teach you all about God.'

Acknowledgements

I would first and foremost like to thank my dear Friend Alex Martinez. We shared his beautiful villa in Los Angeles and he was the one who taught me to use a computer and insisted I write half a chapter a day before driving me to the beach in Santa Monica.

I love you Alex. Thank you for this book, without you it would not be.

I would also like to thank Nick Goodhue, my editor and Alex's best friend. Thank you to my other dear American friends – Lucien Casselman and Andrew Weinberg.

Back in London, I would like to thank the insightful Helen Coyle at Hodder for letting my writing breathe, Fenella Bates, Ciara Foley and Karen Geary in Publicity. The stress caused by writing the first part of this book was eased by my friend Terry Harkin. Your support and kindness saved the day, Terry.

I would also like to thank the peope who helped me in my career as a journalist, namely my long-time friend Greg Miskiw, editor of the *News of the World*, the charming and enigmatic *News of the World* news editor, Alex Marunchek and my co-worker Ian Edmonson; John Cassidy, the editor of the *Sunday Mirror* and Liam Clarke of *The Sunday Times* and Henry McDonald of the *Observer*. A special mention to my dear friend the journalist Martin O'Hagan of Ireland's *Sunday World* newspaper, who lost his life for telling the truth when he was machine-gunned down in the street in 2001. Marty, you taught me all about the streets of Belfast and its dangerous secrets. Rest in Peace.

Thank you to Edmund White of Able cabs who drove me around Belfast on that first day in the city. We shared your last roll up, you sent me off to Crossmaglen and the rest is history.

Thank you to the numerous therapists I have enjoyed over the years. My very first, Susannah Le Fere, is a highly talented hypnotherapist and she supported me through traumatic times. There is also the enormously funny and clever Glyn Powell of Hounslow and the gorgeous Mark Collins of the Priory.

A very special thank you to Dr Barry Bernfeld of the Primal Institute in Los Angeles. You dragged me out of the darkness with love and passion – and helped me to find my life. Words are not enough.

Thank you to Arthur Janov for his pioneering therapy and his book The Primal Scream. And to Judy Massaro, my talented and very kind co-therapist.

A tribute to the magnificent therapist Ronald Dreyer who nursed me back to health after America with love and patience and taught me that 'life lived as a victim is no life' and that 'your one and only problem is low self esteem.' I miss you.

To the patients at the Insitute, particularly Cathy Carlson and John; Tom Folland and Brett. And all the others who shared with me their joy and their pain. A special mention to

Floyd Wallace. You were my hero. I'm sorry, you know what for. And to Dave King – a special and kind man who showed me love. To Trevor Wakely – you still exist inside my heart and always will, my friend Robert "Barney" Barnett and his mother Claire Barnett.

I would like to acknowledge the writings of Whitley Streiber and Alex Collier with respect and to pledge my continuing support for The Disclosure Project. And to mention my English teacher Mrs Mannion who used to read out my stories to the whole class and tell me one day I would write something great. I haven't done it yet but hope in the next few books I'll get somewhere near it. I would like to thank anyone who has ever shown me kindness. Kindness is a trait often underestimated. At times it has sustained me.

Thank you to my darling friend and Daddy to Arthur, the talent composer and musician, Paul Stevenson, whom I love and who has shown me love and kindness beyond words. You didn't want me to call you my light, so I'm going to call you my candle in the darkness.

Thank you to my amazing four year-old son Arthur Charles who has made my life. And whose reaction to this book was to squeeze both of my cheeks tightly and say, 'I will be so proud of you when I see your book in the bookshop window Mummy.'

My love for you will exist throughout eternity. It will never die – never fade – nothing can knock down this house.

C. J. Hart